The Business Case
for e-business

IBM Press™

IBM®

The Business Case for e-business

Edited by Keith Rutledge, IBM

IBM Press

5650 El Camino Real, Suite 225

Carlsbad, CA 92008

www.ibmpress.net

The Business Case for e-business
Edited by Keith Rutledge, IBM

Published by IBM Press™
Program Director, IBM Centre for Advanced Studies: Gabriel Silberman
IBM Associate Publisher: Sheila Richardson
IBM Press Alliance Publisher: David Uptmor, IIR Publications, Inc.

For information on translations or book distribution outside the United States or to arrange
bulk-purchase discounts for sales promotions or premiums, please contact:

IBM Press
5650 El Camino Real, Suite 225
Carlsbad, CA
USA 92008
(760) 931-8615
www.ibmpress.net

First edition
First printing: October 2000

ISBN: 1-931182-00-0

To my wonderful family, who provide meaning and purpose in my life.

To my forebears, whom I am still learning to appreciate.

Finally, and again, to G.J. Dyer.

It is said the warrior's is the twofold Way of pen and sword and he should have a taste for both Ways. Even if a man has no natural ability he can be a warrior by sticking assiduously to both divisions of the Way.

—Miyamoto Musashi
A Book of Five Rings
(Translated by Victor Harris)

Acknowledgments

I would like to acknowledge the contributors to this book. The contributors in this book are all recognized authorities in the field of information technology and on AS/400e. I feel honored and humbled to be in such rare company.

I would also like to acknowledge the very substantial contribution of my manager, Jennifer Clarke, to this project. She has supported this project from the beginning. She has also been, since I've known her, the kind of corporate manager that everyone wants to work for. As the manager of the AS/400e Brand Technology team for the Americas, she has been a guiding force for AS/400e and has worked tirelessly in support of the product. The loyalty of AS/400e folks (customers, business partners, and IBM) is legendary and well deserved. Jennifer epitomizes that loyalty and represents what IBM can be at its best.

Finally, I would like to acknowledge the contributions of many of my team members on the AS/400e Brand Technology team. Though not all of them contributed writing to this book, they all contributed explanations and assistance when asked. I have never before worked on a team as effective, as knowledgeable, nor as hard working as the Americas' AS/400e brand team.

Contents

Introduction

E-business! Two bucks back for every buck you spend between now and the end of the year! Net companies with pitiful revenue and no hope of ever going profitable with a market cap that rivals General Electric. Twenty-three-year old, no-underwear wearing, coffee-swilling, multi-pierced, purple-haired millionaires! Has the entire business world lost its mind?

Not really, but it can sometimes seem that way. Between sensational news stories and hyperbolic advertisements, it can seem that e-business doesn't yield to rational analysis. How can a no-underwear wearing, coffee-swilling, multi-pierced, purple-haired person become a millionaire by twenty-three, anyway?

And, more to the point, exactly what is e-business? What does a businessperson really need to know about e-business? Does it really matter to a businessperson? How does one learn what one needs to know about e-business? Are there quick answers to these questions?

I think that you can approach e-business as you do most other subject areas. You learn most subject areas by starting with fundamental concepts, often at a fairly high level. (Gravity makes things fall.) Then you learn the details in the context of that high-level concept. (Things only fall from our Earth-bound perspective; actually, gravity just makes things move closer together.)

So it is with e-business. You can successfully learn the subject of e-business by starting with fundamental concepts at a high level and then filling in the details as required.

Sometimes the details, as with the preceding gravity example, are skewed by our vantage point. Due to our somewhat limiting context of being on Earth, we perceive the effects of gravity slightly differently than if we could observe the process from a disconnected vantage point. But the details work perfectly in the environment where we use them. And you don't always need the details. Frequently, just the fundamental concepts are required.

There are a great many examples in life where concentration on the "big picture" concepts and fundamental reality is more important than mastering the minute details. You don't have to be able to explain natural numbers to do grocery-store math. You don't have to be an accounting major to grasp the importance of keeping a check register for a checking account. You don't have to be a nutritionist to know that eating eight doughnuts for breakfast is not a good thing. Competent mechanics install new brakes on your car without having to understand coefficients of friction, heat transfer, and rotational inertia. Design engineers, who understand friction, heat, and inertia, take care of those tasks.

This book provides fundamental, high-level concepts and, importantly, maps those concepts to usable technology. A gap exists between technical literature and business literature on e-business. This book is intended to fill that gap.

Currently, there are many technical books covering, in very fine detail, how to do some particular e-business task like programming or putting up a Web site. Business literature on e-business is mostly at too high a level to be useful except as rabble-rousing material. It tends to be hyperbolic and vague at the same time. For example:

> Because 1000 percent of all new e-commerce transactions will occur over the Web, your business should just go home right now unless you, personally, can write an Enterprise JavaBean for your B2B strategy to innovate your ERP.

After reading the current so-called business level literature on e-business, I'm left wondering whether I should get a body piercing or an MBA. Maybe it's really the same. It's hard to tell.

In any case, this book provides practical, readable e-business information presented as fundamental concepts that are useful for decision making. The contributors to this book presume, as a base premise, that you have to make decisions about e-business technology. As business people who make daily decisions about e-business, the authors have a clear-eyed view of the rewards and the costs of e-business technology.

The first nine chapters of this book stay mostly at the concept level. After that, the focus moves to mapping the concepts to practical realities by explaining important e-business technologies in use today.

As you might expect, determining the limit line of the scope of a book such as this is not simple. You'll find that some of the chapters provide a great deal of detail. I encourage you, where practical, to sweat the details. For example, a firmly grounded concept of TCP/IP subnets (see chapter 12, on TCP/IP, by Chris Peters) is useful in making business decisions about locating expensive capital assets such as network servers.

This book is as detailed as needed for business decision-making and—I assure you—no more than that. With that said, you don't have to read the entire book to find it useful. Each chapter in this book can be read independently, allowing you to use it as a reference work. You might find that, as you read a chapter, it prompts you to explore another related chapter. But that's up to you.

When developing *The Business Case for e-business*, we spent a great deal of time thinking about—to borrow a phrase from Bob Seger, "what to leave in, what to leave out." What we left in is what we consider most important to your understanding and using e-business technology. Here, then, is a preview of what's in the book.

Chapter 1 develops and explains some of the most important economic factors driving the use of the Web for business. Many organizations are participating in a lemminglike free-fall competition to the Web, rather than following a pragmatically organized process that moves their business to the Web in a manner that fits their competitive market-space, business principles, and the world in which they live.

Understanding the overarching economic principles and the effect of the Web on the rest of the world is a key factor. Another key element is learning how to understand the effect of the rest of the world on the Web. Chapter 1 provides a real-world context for e-business and e-commerce. It also explains in economic terms why the Web is such a revolutionary phenomenon. There is a solid economic underpinning for the movement to the Web; it's just not often explained or understood. Knowing why you're moving to the Web can help you make the right decisions along the way.

In chapter 2, Jelan Heidelberg (AS/400 worldwide technical marketing consultant for IBM), makes a cogent case for a coherent, open e-business architecture. Jelan explains the IBM Application Framework for e-business.

Here's the unbelievable part for long-time IBM watchers. The IBM Application Framework for e-business has almost no IBM content. It's true. Instead, it's made up of open market (in some cases, open-source) standards. The point of the Framework is that open standards linked in a coherent fashion offer business benefits for everyone in e-business. Customers benefit because they can create better e-business applications faster at lower costs. Software and hardware vendors benefit because their potential pool of customers gets larger. It's a good thing.

Next, Nahid Jilovec (e-commerce partner at marchFIRST, Inc.) explains e-commerce. It's useful to draw a distinction between e-business and e-commerce. First, e-business is a business practice or transaction that is dependent upon Web information technology (especially the communications technologies of the Web). In contrast, e-commerce is a business transaction where money changes hands. Nahid covers business-to-consumer (B2C, in the ubiquitous slang) and business-to-business (B2B, in the vernacular) e-commerce. She explains the effects on consumers, on businesses, on distribution channels, and covers the important technologies in use.

In chapter 4, John Quarantello (worldwide e-business manager for AS/400e) explains Web application servers. Web application servers are important infrastructure technology for organizations that want to use their existing systems across the Web. John explains what Web serving is, why it is important, and draws distinctions between Web serving and Web-application serving. This chapter is required reading, in my humble opinion, for any organization that would like to reuse its existing information technology assets (software, data, and servers) on the Web for e-business or e-commerce.

I've noticed Web sources sometimes have an annoying habit of inappropriately claiming to invent things. One of those things is transactions. Transaction processing is an absolute business requirement. If you transfer a dollar from savings to checking, it isn't half as good to successfully get the dollar out of savings. This is an all-or-nothing transaction. If the money doesn't make it into checking, then the whole transaction has to be aborted. In chapter 5, Bob Tipton (partner and technology thought leader for marchFIRST) explains what a transaction is, why it's crucial, and what you need to know about ACID (hint, it's not a throwback to the '60s…at least not in the flower-child sense). This is must reading for anyone planning to do business transactions over the Web.

In chapter 6, Jennifer Bigus (advisory software engineer in the IBM AS/400 Custom Technology Center in Rochester, Minnesota) explains what a Web application is. This chapter takes the architectural approach of Application Framework (chapter 2) and shows how it's used in a well-designed Web application today. This behind-the-scenes view of Web applications reveals what consumers will never see, but will depend on every time they do business with you.

No discussion of e-business today would be complete without covering collaborative computing. Collaborative computing is computing that enables people to work together more productively. The key phrase is "work together." Collaborative computing enables working together in spite of geographic and time differences. In chapter 7, Jelan Heidelberg provides an explanation of how Domino, the premier collaborative computing product available today, solves many of the business problems of working together.

Chapter 8 provides a brief introduction to Web-payment technologies. How do you transfer money, from one party to another, knowing that the transaction is private and trustable? What is e-money? I answer those questions and explain why I think e-money is inevitable. It's very interesting to consider the evolution of money since the concept originated, to ponder the requirements we've insisted on for previous forms of money, and to ponder the implications for e-money.

Chapter 9 covers Java. I explain Java programming and program-deployment technology. I also spend some time on why portable software (software that runs without change on many computers) is an important business issue. And, I explain the effect of Java on business allocation of resources like capital assets and personnel. I believe that Java is a very important technology for Web software, and I explain why and how.

Various aspects of e-business and e-commerce depend on interoperability among many different software and hardware systems. In chapter 10, Mark Schreiter (senior software engineer for Kingland Systems Corporation) explains a messaging and queuing approach to interoperability. This is another one of those areas where you might hear Web folks claiming to have invented something. Actually, messaging and queuing have been important infrastructure topics in information technology for a long time. Mark approaches the subject from the point of view of the most popular messaging and queuing technology available: MQSeries from IBM. Mark explains the business problem that the MQSeries from IBM solves, what it is, how it works, and what you need to know to make decisions.

A key development in many other technological fields has been the rise of component-based manufacturing. From cars to oil pipelines to construction—where the end product is a complex assembly—businesses have found it necessary to build products out of components. Using standard components makes it faster, easier, and cheaper to produce a quality product. So far, programming has resisted the move to componentization by functioning as a cottage industry of craftspeople producing customized "one-off" products. This customized approach has been true even with very large programs.

With the SanFrancisco project, IBM has produced a standard set of Java business components to enable component-based assembly of software products. In chapter 11, Dr. Verlyn Johnson, senior software engineer for IBM SanFrancisco components, and Thomas Konakowitz, senior marketing consultant, explain component-based development and the approach taken by IBM.

Chapter 12 explains TCP/IP. TCP/IP is the label usually assigned to a group of networking technologies that underpin the Internet. Chris Peters (president of

Evergreen Interactive Systems, Inc.) decodes the acronyms, tells you what TCP/IP can do for you, and equips you to make business decisions about TCP/IP. While a fundamental understanding of e-business and e-commerce is often taken for granted, a small amount of time spent mastering this chapter will pay you big dividends. The technologies that Chris covers permeate every discussion of e-business and e-commerce. I encourage you to study this detailed chapter.

In chapter 13, Marian O'Shaughnessy (advisory programmer in the Custom Technology Center at IBM Rochester) explains two Web-programming language technologies that are pervasively used today. When discussing e-business, HTML (HyperText Markup Language) and JavaScript are fundamental terms and technology. To make business decisions about e-business and e-commerce requires knowledge of these technologies, where they apply, and when they should be used. With her explanations, Marian arms you with that knowledge.

Marian O'Shaughnessy also wrote chapter 14. JavaScript is a syntactical cousin of Java, but it's not Java. JavaScript is a "scripting" language that is used to add functionality to HTML pages. JavaScript can be used to add dynamism, to check entered text, to require the entry of specific information, or to add helpful text to HTML pages. JavaScript is a very useful tool when implementing e-business applications. It's a "just right" tool for many purposes. When full-bore programming (say in Java) is too much and HTML isn't quite enough, JavaScript often fits the bill. Marian explains it "just right."

Chapter 15 covers one of the most important developments in information technology since the relational database. Don Denoncourt (a senior technical editor for *Midrange Computing* magazine) explains the eXtensible Markup Language (XML for short). XML is so important because it can and is being used to provide access to information for any device from any server. That's "bold talk for a one-eyed fat man" but I believe that XML merits such hyperbole. On the Web, you can currently find everything from the complete works of Shakespeare to a mathematical markup language done using XML. XML is independent of any particular computer and information encoded using XML can be read and manipulated by any computer. It's an essential technological component of open business-computing systems. Don explains how and why in chapter 15.

You may have detected the faint stirrings of a trend towards universality, open standards, and independence from particular computer systems in e-business. Chapter 16 continues that trend with an explanation of the Unified Modeling Language (UML). UML is a universal, open, independent approach to modeling software systems under development.

As systems become larger, more complicated, and more distributed, it becomes more important to precisely define the behavior of the system ahead of time. I know that sounds like a platitude, but that is not how it has been done previously. Most software in use today is not modeled—at least in any useful way—ahead of time. Modeling, in the form of blueprints, schematics, computer simulations, and the like, is widely used in other industries.

You wouldn't build a house without blueprints. It wasn't always that way but, as folks recognized the value of thinking the house plan through ahead of time and as a notation (blueprints are the term for a symbolic construction notation representing a house on paper) developed, modeling became a pervasive and nearly universal practice. It's time for a similar movement in software. In chapter 16, Randy Ruhlow (staff software engineer for the Enterprise Systems Group at IBM Rochester, Minnesota) explains why.

Of course, security is essential. Rich Diedrich (senior technical staff member working in the IBM AS/400 Custom Technology Center) covers Web security in chapter 17. Rich covers security from the point of view of the client, the server, and transactional security. Taking a layered approach to security, he explains what's crucial when it comes to security and what to do about it. This chapter is required reading for every businessperson. Rich provides understandable explanations of security technologies that you won't find anywhere else.

In chapter 18, Dr. Joe Bigus (senior technical staff member at the IBM T.J. Watson Research Center) focuses on pervasive computing. Pervasive computing is the use of devices with sufficient computing power to do useful work in a non-traditional, pervasive, environment. For example, it might include using a Palm Pilot to access your company's computer systems, using a GPS in your car that's linked to a database of restaurants, using a cell phone to get stock quotes, and the use of a pager to send e-mail. One of the core issues about pervasive computing is its meaning. Joe explains that and covers the key points in chapter 18.

Finally, how do you manage all these technologies in the Web environment? In chapter 19, Nancy Roper (consulting IT specialist – AS/400 systems management) and Inder Singh (principal with the IT consulting and implementation practice at IBM Canada) explain how to do just that. If you want to make sure that your Web-facing systems are available when you need them to be and scalable to the levels that your business requires, then this chapter is for you.

Whew! That's a lot of ground to cover. But, even at this early point in the book, I hope you're convinced that you don't have to dye your hair or get a piercing (never mind the underwear thing) to understand and profit from e-business. E-business technology is actually fairly routine stuff; it's the employment of e-business technology for business profit that can be challenging, but rewarding. The rewards can be impressive ("two bucks back...."). That's what this book is really about; business profits from the successful employment of e-business technology.

Remember what I said earlier. You don't have to read the book in a particular sequence to find it useful, and you can certainly benefit from each chapter without necessarily reading every other chapter. Finally, I'm sure I speak for all the authors when I say that we hope you enjoy reading *The Business Case for e-business* as much as we enjoyed writing it.

KEITH RUTLEDGE, IBM

A firm will tend to expand until the costs of organising an extra transaction within the firm become equal to the costs of carrying out the same transaction by means of an exchange on the open market.

—Ronald H. Coase
The Nature of the Firm (1937)

1

Web Economics

KEITH RUTLEDGE

Understanding the effect of the World Wide Web on business requires asking a couple of fundamental questions and determining the answers in two different contexts: pre-Web and post-Web. Asking the questions in these two contexts exposes the effect of the Web on business. The questions are:

- Why does the firm exist?
- How are markets for goods and services made?

These questions have been the subject of much discussion and debate among economists and among business theorists since Ronald Coase's ground-breaking paper *The Nature of the Firm*, published in 1937. This paper, for which he later won a Nobel Prize, explained the formation of the firm as a result of differential transaction costs. Other reason's discussed in this chapter for the formation of firms (in this country, we tend to call a firm a business) are risk avoidance and re-

Editor's Introduction: The current structures and mechanisms of business will drastically change in the next few decades. What won't change is the fundamental nature of the transactions. Goods and services will still be exchanged and a medium of exchange will still be necessary. Understanding what mechanisms and techniques will change and what fundamental aspects of business will remain the same requires thinking outside the technology. It requires thinking about the nature of business itself and how business is affected by the world at large. In this chapter, I present some of the fundamental issues of business and the world and explain their effect on e-business.

–KR

quirement specificity. Theorists have advanced many other reasons for the formation of businesses, but space simply precludes discussing them in this chapter.

The Rise of e-business and E-Commerce

There are, as well, several societal and technical trends that bear on the preceding questions. These trends form a context for our discussion about the rise of e-business and e-commerce. These trends are:

- A relatively peaceful and prosperous world.

- Evolution of money into e-money (barter to exchange medium to fiat money to e-money).

- Perceived need for security.

- Ubiquitous devices with useful computing capability and adequate communications bandwidth.

- Mass customization of consumer products and increased digital content in consumer products.

- Rise of the information-based community such as a community of personnel who identify themselves as a group based on informational attributes (i.e., a chat group community or a Web community). These communities are not based on previous attributes like ethnicity, geographic location, or religion.

- Effective and efficient distribution networks.

Peace and Prosperity

A relatively peaceful and prosperous world is a prerequisite for e-commerce and e-business. This prerequisite has two basic aspects. First, e-business and e-commerce depends physically on a relatively peaceful world. In physical terms, the technology is very fragile. Physically fragile technologies depend on a physically stable world. War is the antithesis of a physically stable world.

Prosperity is a prerequisite because a hungry person doesn't surf the Web. It might seem obvious, but it requires leisure time and a certain minimum level of physical comfort to be an information consumer or creator. As people around the world achieve material comfort and wealth in excess of their basic needs and immediate requirements, they will become information consumers and creators. It's no accident that wealthy countries are the biggest users of the Internet.

Infrastructure at what many would consider the most basic level is a requirement for e-commerce and e-business. It is also a requirement that is not yet in place in many parts of the globe. According to an article in the August 1999 issue of *National Geographic*, half the people in the world have never used a telephone.

It's easy, sitting in a wealthy Western country, to suppose that everyone has access to Web technology and that it is important to all of us. That's not the case. In terms of importance, most people would place plumbing ahead of Web access. Nevertheless, throughout the world, more people don't have indoor plumbing than do have indoor plumbing.

Again, in terms of importance, most people would rank clean drinking water ahead of Web access. But there are many places today where clean drinking water, the most basic requirement of life, goes unfulfilled. Until those populations get indoor plumbing, clean drinking water, enough to eat, and the other basic necessities of life, the Web will not reach its full potential. By the way, this is true with some of the other modern technologies. Television does not reach everyone in the world. Air travel is available only to those who can afford it.

Evolution of Money

The new trading methods and the new markets (e-trades and e-markets) require a new form of money: e-money. It's not original that new markets require a new form of currency, but it's still a bit unsettling if you participate in the shift from one form of money to another. Money has taken many forms throughout history. Originally, of course, there was no money. Goods and services were bartered directly. Barter gave way to exchange mediums. Many exchange mediums have been used.

Precious metals—such as gold and silver that had direct, intrinsic value—have been favored since the earliest times for:

- Portability. It's easier to carry a bag of gold dust than a bushel of wheat.
- Durability. If you don't eat it, wheat eventually spoils and is worthless.
- Divisibility. You can measure out a small amount of gold.
- Anonymity. Gold needs no identification.

Gold and other valuables used for currencies were used to represent the underlying value of a good or service and to represent a portable medium that could be exchanged upon request into other goods or services. Paper and coin money is a fairly recent form of exchange currency. In the past, paper currency has sometimes been linked to an underlying exchange medium and has been at times convertible into that medium. In the United States, money was at one time backed by gold and could be converted on demand.

Fiat money is an exchange currency that is made legal by the decree or "fiat" of a ruling government. Fiat money has no intrinsic value and is made valuable because it is the only permitted medium of financial exchange. E-money will be a form of fiat money, but the fiat will eventually be that of the market. Initially, but probably not permanently, the "fiat" money of the Web will be denominated in some governmental currency like U.S. dollars.

E-money will have some characteristics that are different than most exchange currencies today, but in concept it will be quite similar. Since the earliest financial exchanges, all money has served as a proxy for the underlying value of goods and services. This is true to some extent even for the exchange mediums that have intrinsic value. The price of gold, silver, and other precious metals is influenced by economic factors that transcend the intrinsic value of the gold. Said another way, you can't eat gold. If food is scarce, the price of gold expressed in food will tend to fall (said more familiarly, the price of food expressed in gold will rise).

E-money will continue to be a proxy for the underlying value of goods and services and can be viewed, as all money can, as a storage medium for value that is convertible on demand. E-money will be much more universal than most modern currencies because there is less need to convert to local currencies when the whereabouts of a transaction is a virtual location.

E-money also will be a boon to multi-national transactions. If a U.S. firm is buying steel from a Chinese company in a spot market run by a Latvian market maker on the Web, who governs the transaction? The answer is that nobody really governs the transaction. One of the requirements for markets of this type (this has always been a requirement of a market) is a trustable currency. Whatever form e-money eventually takes will be trustable.

Surprisingly, one of the attributes of money that makes it trustworthy is anonymity. If a currency is linked to a particular individual or organization for its value, then the value of the currency is less trustworthy than if it depends only on the market and has no required linkages. Therefore, e-money will eventually be anonymous. This might take awhile as it is very appealing to governments to make money less anonymous. Eventually, though, the market requirement for privacy will win out, just as it has with every form of money so far.

Need for Security

It's the sharpest of ironies that this safest of times is regarded as unsafe by many members of our society. Statistically, it's provable that crime and danger of all types is down and safety of all types is up and continuing to rise. Nevertheless, we demand even safer streets, schools, cars, and homes. Home security systems are considered a necessity in any home above the most basic starter. Air bags for the driver, the front passenger, and the sides of an automobile are highly desirable features. The minimum age for everything from drinking to voting to driving to riding without an infant car seat creeps inexorably up. Car manufacturers mount successful advertising campaigns that stress safety to the exclusion of racy car features. Once it was enough to simply say, "sex sells." Now, safety sells whether there is a provable need for it or not.

This seemingly obsessive quest for safety will drive a lot of Internet consumer commerce in the future. In the context of this chapter, commerce includes some things that you might not first include in the category. Chat rooms are one way of purchasing, at a very nominal fee, conversations that are physically safe. Conversations in bars might have more experiential aspects, but they also are more physically dangerous. Internet pornography, a major source of Internet commerce, may be philosophically objectionable, but it provides a high degree of safety for the pornography consumer. Buying clothes from an online vendor is physically easier and safer than traveling to a mall, parking in a dimly lit parking deck, and traversing the perceived hazards of the night to return to your car. And don't even start about going downtown. That's where they film the television show *COPS*.

Of course, the Internet itself comes with hazards, but there's money to be made in thwarting those risks as well. Kidsafe ISP's, Internet filter software, and other service offerings make money from the quest for cybersafety. Of course, some firms also take it on themselves, as a public service no doubt, to point out the dangers of the Internet to the consuming public.

Handheld Computing

Handheld computing has been coming for a long time. Handheld devices with sufficient computing power to do real computing are now here. This is a revolution whose effect will be felt quickly. To completely understand the subject, it's necessary to do some comparisons to older technology and to explain the relationship between leading-edge personal computers, packaging, and price.

First, consider the comparison to older technology. In the early 1980s, you could buy an IBM PC with an Intel 8086 processor. The first IBM PC used an Intel 8-bit processor that ran at 4.77 MHZ (millions of cycles per second). These PCs had rudimentary displays that only displayed characters in one color (usually green, but you could buy after-market displays in amber or white for more money). They didn't really do graphics and they definitely didn't do color. These PCs had no hard drives and relied on either diskettes or cassette tapes for permanent storage of programs and data. Those options were very limited in the amount of data that could be stored permanently. The original PCs had 16 kilobytes (16,000 bytes) of main memory. You could, of course, add memory at a price.

These PCs seem very limited today and they were. But, they were sufficient to do useful business computing and therein is the promise of current handheld computing devices. Useful business computing is very much about the manipulation of numbers—numbers that represent money.

Today's handheld computing devices are much more powerful than the original IBM PC. For only a couple hundred dollars, you can purchase a "Visor" handheld computer from Handspring and get a computer that has a processor with multiple megabytes (millions of bytes) of memory. Permanent storage devices are available that store additional megabytes of programs or data. The screens, for now, display characters only in one color— just like the original IBM PCs.

If the original PCs could do useful business computing, so can today's handheld devices. The problem isn't their capabilities it's the way that we think of them.

There is a somewhat complex, but predictable relationship between leading-edge personal computers, packaging, and price. New personal computing technology, especially processor technology, is very expensive to develop. Because of that, it usually enters the personal computer marketplace at the upper end of the price spectrum. As the development costs are amortized, as new technology is developed, and—even more importantly—as competition arises for the successful technologies, the price falls. Eventually, the market price for a given technology sinks below the true manufacturing and distribution costs and the technology falls off the bottom end of the price structure. This is a very pronounced phenomenon in PC processors. A processor (such as the 80386) introduced a few years ago can enter the market as the performance leader, hold that position for a brief period, and then yield to another processor (the 80486). As the 80386 yields, it will briefly be the mid-price choice for processor, then become the processor of choice for discount PCs, and then disappear altogether.

As the processors (and other technologies) slide through the market window, they decrease in price, but not in capability. An Intel 80386 processor can do just as much today (assuming you can find a working one) as it could when first manufactured.

As processor prices decline, it becomes much more economically feasible to package these very powerful processors (from Intel and other vendors) into very inexpensive, powerful, and functional devices. Handheld devices today have the power of PCs of just a couple of technology generations ago. If you could do business computing a couple of PC generations ago, you now can do business computing on handheld devices.

A primary role for these handheld devices will be as a link to information and services that reside on large computers (sometimes called servers, as part of a client-server system). Handheld devices will access, manipulate, and return information from large enterprise computer systems. There are already examples of this in use today. When a package-delivery person asks you to sign on a portable plastic device, your signature is recorded and moved to the enterprise computer, where it will be stored for verification of arrival. This handheld computer is a special-purpose computer that interacts with the large enterprise computer system at the freight company.

As the handheld devices become more pervasive, and as the communications bandwidth available to the handheld device increases, the usage of them will become more commonplace. These devices can build a critical mass of users on the personal productivity applications resident in them. Then, that critical mass of users can add connectivity for enterprise computing. That should seem like a familiar scenario. It's basically the same growth path that personal computers followed in the 1980s.

First, PCs were used for personal productivity (word processing and especially spreadsheets), then they were connected into small groups by local area network technology, then they were used to replace mainframe computer terminals, and finally they grew up to function as servers themselves. While hand-held devices might not become servers, the rest of the growth path is already visible. It is a technological reality today to connect a handheld device to a large enterprise computer, such as an IBM AS/400e, and use it to request information and computing services from that large enterprise computer.

Mass Customization and Digital Content

Because many consumer products today cannot be differentiated on any traditional criteria, manufacturers are increasingly turning to digital content to customize and differentiate their products. Examples of this include automotive applications, musical instruments, "conventional" electronic devices, financial instruments, and toys. Cars now have passive digital security systems, global positioning systems, electronic monitoring of the automotive health of the drive train, and, of course, digital comfort electronics. Musical instruments have memory to record that riff you just created and electronic facilities to modify the basic musical characteristics of the instrument. Financial instruments can now exist almost wholly in cyberspace and some of the ultra-modern instruments depend on cybertrading for their very existence. And, of course, nearly everyone has heard of "Furby," the children's toy that appears to have life because of digital electronics.

As powerful processors become embedded in a wide range of consumer goods, it becomes more practical and more desirable to connect or embed goods and services into the Web. Then it becomes more practical to differentiate the product on the basis of the electronic content in the product.

It also becomes possible to customize the product more closely for each customer. Combined with this characteristic, I think e-retailing will lead to a dramatic change in product packaging. Today, much consumer packaging is designed to gain attention on a retailer's shelf. Without this "look at me" requirement, packaging becomes less important.

The point here is customer satisfaction. Customers are more satisfied as products fit their needs more specifically. Digital content used to personalize products can achieve that custom fit at an "off-the-rack" price.

Information-Based Communities

The rise of the information-based community is a crucial contextual development for e-business. In the past, communities have had easily identifiable boundaries. These boundaries could have been geographic (all the people who live in Greenville, South Carolina) or they might have been based on another attribute (all the military veterans who served in Vietnam).

Today, communities create themselves based on information. They usually have other attributes as well, but they will use information systems (i.e., chat groups, Web sites, news groups, and the like) to create, nurture, and maintain their communities. To a degree not seen before, these communities transcend conventional (especially regional) boundaries. And, to a degree not seen before, some of these communities are troublesome to societal institutions.

Examples range from German citizens who buys *Mein Kampf* over the Web (selling *Mein Kampf* is forbidden by law in Germany), to Chinese dissidents who spread information by the Web, to U.S. citizens who avoid some taxation by purchasing over the Web. The activities of these communities are unsettling to many.

For companies engaged in e-business (and for that matter business without the "e"), these communities are essential. For an example of what an information community can do, visit *http://www.untied.com*, where disgruntled passengers post complaints about United Airlines.

These communities can spread good news just as fast. Truth, lies, and rumors move at equal speed through the Web. It's vital that businesses of all kinds understand the information-based communities that exist and develop a strategy for dealing with them. This is really not very different than a press strategy. Most companies understand the need to deal professionally with the press and most companies do a decent job of that. The task is similar.

Distribution Networks

A little-understood requirement for e-business and especially e-commerce is the requirement for distribution networks that are effective and efficient at moving small items. As products become more and more specific to each customer, the unit of shipping decreases.

Instead of the case quantities or larger that we associate with shipping to retailers, unit shipping to a customer is generally one of a product. When you're shipping "one each" of a product, it's important that the cost of shipping be reasonable (or small) compared to the cost of the product. The value of the product relative to its physical size is the determining factor here. For example, it makes sense to ship PCs by premium shipping channels because the value of the product is high compared to the cubic space that it occupies. It's not so feasible to ship rice by premium networks because the value per cube is very low. Rice is best shipped in a boxcar through commodity shipping networks. It's also important that the temporal aspects of shipping not be an inhibitor to the consumer purchasing the product.

Consider a pharmaceutical company that locates their distribution warehouses close to the shipping hub of an overnight delivery company. The pharmaceutical company gains a big advantage when it comes to taking orders over the Web. Let's say you need to renew a prescription and it's 10:00 P.M. You forgot to go to the drugstore, but you have enough medicine to get through the night and part of the next day. You can go to the drugstore tomorrow or you can order it over the Web.

The pharmaceutical company with a warehouse co-located with the overnight shipping company has until 2:00 A.M. to get your package to the shipping hub for next-day delivery. By 10:00 the next morning, your prescription is at your house or your office with no more effort on your part. If that pharmaceutical company warehouse is located hundreds of miles from the overnight shipping company, then they can accept orders for next-day delivery only until the end of the business day (maybe 5:00 P.M. or 6:00 P.M.). In effect, they close early.

Companies with high-value goods (relative to the cubic measurements of the goods) tend to move their shipping and distribution operations to be near premium (overnight, next-day) shipping hubs. Real-estate values will shift, jobs will move, tax bases will change, road requirements will go up in places like Memphis, Tennessee and go down elsewhere. Over the long term of business operations, it's a big shift that at first didn't seem to be connected to e-business.

Why Does the Firm Exist?

This section explores the question, "Why does the firm exist?" in two contexts: pre-Web and post-Web. The reasons are the same, but the implementation and acceptance of the consequences of the implementations are very different. The question "why does the firm exist?" means why are business activities conducted inside a business rather than by individuals who make those business activities and their outputs part of an open market?

Most business activities can be conducted by an individual who can sell the activity as a service or the result of the activity as a product. Why do businesses form to incorporate the activities of groups of people and the products of those activities into a larger entity called the firm?

Risk Avoidance

One reason firms or businesses exist is risk avoidance by labor. A person who works for a firm surrenders the management of their time to the firm's management in return for assurances that management will compensate the employee for the time. It's up to management to take the risk of not being able to make use of the employee's time sufficiently to make a profit on the activities of the employee. In return for accepting the risk, management is entitled to the profit made by using the employee in business activities.

Risk avoidance for an employee covers several different areas, but two of the most important areas are lack of work and obsolescence of skills. Risk avoidance for lack of work delegates to the employer the requirement to manage cash and to pay employees during times when work is slow. Risk avoidance for obsolescence of skills delegates to the employer the responsibility to retrain employees when skills requirements change. Both of these responsibilities mean that the employer must plan for and reserve sufficient capital to absorb the associated costs.

Employee risk avoidance changes with the introduction of the Web. First, far greater visibility of work opportunities means that employees are more willing to take risky jobs and are less dependent upon employers for long-term security. Employees view risky jobs differently when they know that they can get another job quickly (they know because they saw the job listing last night on the Web).

This greater visibility is built on the communications functions of the Web, such as job Web sites (monster.com comes to mind), e-mail, and recruitment Web sites that most large businesses now maintain. With just a few minutes work on the Web, a person can determine available positions and they can compete for jobs with less physical effort than ever before. It literally takes seconds and has zero marginal cost to e-mail a resume in response to a job opening. It's very easy to customize an e-mailed resume to highlight skills appropriate to the job.

Specific Requirements

As a business can more precisely specify its requirements for employees, goods, and services, it becomes less likely to put in place long-term employees and capital to satisfy those requirements. The Web makes it easier to precisely specify requirements for employees, goods, and services by greater knowledge of market conditions, labor requirements, and available resources.

Examining another facet of the labor issue from the preceding risk-avoidance discussion, in the pre-Web world, businesses once "stockpiled" employees because they knew they would need employees in the future. In most businesses, employees would be used at a break-even level while being stockpiled. This stockpiling has been part of the contract between labor and management. In effect, a business says to its employees, "I'll carry you during the slow times and you permit me to profit from your labor during good times." Over a sufficiently long period of time, things balanced out.

In the post-Web world, employers have the same visibility into the labor market that employees do and can see the resources that are available at any given time. Businesses can also project more accurately what resources will be available in the future to meet their requirements. This leads to reduced stockpiling of employees. Said another way, businesses are less reluctant to cut employees if they know that replacement employees are readily available when needed.

The same logic applies to capital and expense goods. If a manufacturer can see through visibility into the market that the necessary resources are available to solve their specific requirements, then they are less likely to fill that requirement internally. In the pre-Web world, it was more difficult to locate and communicate with the market resources (other businesses, potential employees, and contract or short-term employees) that could satisfy specific requirements. Now, businesses in North America can locate and communicate with market resources in the Pacific Rim almost as easily as they do businesses in North America. It is worth noting that this does have a dependency on a peaceful world. War and violence are, to state the obvious, a significant impediment to commerce.

This also affects societal structures like towns. In the pre-Web world, the small retail businesses in a town or city served as end-of-the line stockpiles of goods and, to some extent, services. The small-town hardware store would stock a variety of hardware items in anticipation that someone would need them. And the store was the only practical source of those items. One attribute of being a good merchant in this case is the capability to forecast very accurately what items will be needed. Just as tangible goods were stockpiled, so were services. Local legal services, local accounting services, and many other kinds of services were stockpiled locally in the form of people.

The requirement for local stockpiling decreases in the post-Web world. Consumers of goods and services became more aware of the availability of goods and services specific to their requirements. Outside the local area, distribution networks improved and made it economically feasible to ship goods in small unit counts.

The preceding description is even more true for services. As services, like accounting and legal services, are delivered over the Web, the requirement for local stockpiling decreases. In this case, the Web attacks the very reason for existence of some businesses. Nolo Press (*http://www.nolopress.com*) delivers legal advice and legal help over the Web at rates that might put your local lawyer out of business. In several states, local lawyers have felt threatened enough by this to sue (so far, mostly unsuccessfully) Nolo Press.

If you can get exactly what you want from Amazon.com, and it's less expensive and it's easier, you are less likely to buy from your local bookstore, which has been stockpiling books in anticipation of your needs. If you can get good legal advice inexpensively over the Internet, then you probably won't spend the time and money on your local lawyer.

Businesses do exactly the same. As they become more assured of being able to find the good and services they need in the market, they are less likely to stockpile those goods and services (in the form of capital and employees) internally or locally. Over time, this means dispersion into smaller units of the assets currently contained in businesses (other, more specialized businesses and contract employees). The communications capability of the Web is a major contributor to this change.

Transaction Costs

Transaction costs are one of the fundamental economic drivers for moving to e-business. Every business process has transaction costs associated with it. Transaction costs include the cost of finding a good or service, learning about the product, bargaining to purchase the product, the costs of selecting among the alternatives, ensuring that the product is delivered as agreed, and enforcing the bargain. These costs apply to both buyers and sellers and are a fundamental economic reason for the formation of markets and firms.

The reduction or elimination of these costs by e-business technology in the post-Web world gives rise to new ways of doing business, new firms, new competition, and new opportunities. Understanding transaction costs and how they apply to your business helps you take advantage of the opportunities and avoid the risks.

Transaction costs are important because they predict the effect of e-business on your business. Transaction cost analysis can be applied to determine what competitive edge your company or your competitors can gain.

"Killer apps" are driving transaction costs down for nearly all products. Transaction costs are decreasing in the open market much faster than they are inside most firms. As transaction costs approach zero, so does the size of firms," says Larry Downes in his book *Unleashing the Killer App.* Downs calls this the Law of Diminishing Firms.

E-business and e-commerce significantly reduce, or in some cases eliminate, transaction costs associated with business processes. E-business does this, essentially, by replacing the content of a transaction cost with electronic content. Instead of searching for a product or service in person and expending the time, energy, and money associated with that search, the search is conducted electronically.

Consider the task of searching for a car. Searching for a car often means several trips to a car dealer, perhaps searching the newspaper for sales on cars, and compilation of information from several different sources and media. And, at the end, you frequently can't be sure that your search has been thorough. An electronic search engine on the Web today can return better information in far less time (a few minutes instead of many hours). In just a few minutes on the Web, a person can determine what cars are available, what the dealers' prices are, what a typical sales price is, and where the cars are located. There are even comparison sites to ensure that the price is the best available.

Transaction Costs Explained

There are six types of transaction costs.

- Search costs are buyers and sellers finding each other in the open market. In the preceding example, these are the time and costs of visiting the car dealers, of perusing the newspaper for car information, and of determining the sources of information.

- Information costs are the costs of learning or educating about a product. Buyers learn and sellers educate. For sellers (most firms), these are marketing and selling expenses. With the preceding car-purchase example, these are the costs of learning which cars have the characteristics that you are seeking.

- Bargaining costs are the costs of striking a bargain. These include negotiations, sales calls, sales contracts, and supporting activities for buyers and sellers.

- Decision costs, for buyers, are the cost of the actions necessary to select among offered alternatives. This could include testing, benchmarking, and evaluation of proposals. For sellers, decision costs are the costs of evaluating buyers and the offers from buyers. This includes market analysis, credit checks, profitability analysis, and the range of customer segmentation and selection activities.

- Policing costs are the costs of making sure the bargain is carried out as specified. This includes inspections of goods, testing of delivered products, reconciliation of invoices, verification of payments, and the other activities associated with verifying that activities comply with a business agreement.

- Enforcement costs are the costs of ensuring that deviations from the bargain are corrected. This includes AR dunning calls, negotiations on unsatisfactory product, and collections of penalties. Enforcement costs can include the cost of litigation when other remedies fail.

The risks of not understanding the transaction cost structure of business activities are:

Disintermediation: As transaction costs fall, middlemen (distributors, financers, and transporters) become less necessary or find that their roles dramatically changed. When a book is bought from an online bookseller, the beneficiaries are different than when a book is bought from a brick-and-mortar bookseller. The on-line transaction often benefits the U.S. Postal Service at the expense of parcel-shipping companies and freight-shipping companies that would previously have delivered the books in volume to the storefront.

Reduced Margins: E-business alternatives to traditional value chains drive margins down. Traditional value chains provide goods or services more cheaply or more expertly. E-business value chains, by reducing transaction costs, drive the margins much lower than traditional value chains. Where the value chain delivers an electronic product, the margin associated with delivery can be, and sometimes is, driven to zero. As traditional value chains lose the cost battle, they will be forced to differentiate their product on the basis of their expertise. Sometimes, as in the Nolo Press example, this will not be sufficient.

Loss of Customers: As buyers discover the benefits of e-business, they are less willing to do business with firms that can't do e-business. Transaction costs occur on both sides. This is the driver behind large retail firms requiring EDI from all their suppliers and behind the success of Internet consumer commerce. Large retail firms reduce their own transaction costs by doing business electronically. Their suppliers do as well. Internet consumers find that the open-market price bargaining benefits, availability of products, and reduction in search costs drive them away from traditional suppliers to e-merchants.

The benefits of understanding the effects of transaction costs and applying them to your business are:

New Markets: New markets can be opened without building traditional infrastructure. Customer reach is extended and mass customization by way of digital personalization means that each customer can receive a more specialized product that provides higher value for him or her.

Competitive Advantage: Digital personalization can be used to achieve customer loyalty. If your company can deliver exactly what a customer wants and no other firm can, you have an advantage. This personalization can be part of the delivered products (good or service) or it can be part of the relationship between your business and your customer.

Reduced Costs: Digitization means that some products can be delivered electronically at a near-zero cost of delivery. Cost reductions are achievable in many business processes while offering higher levels of service. Web self-help sites offer extremely high levels of customer satisfaction with very low staffing and operations costs.

How Are Markets for Goods and Services Made?

Markets are made by buyers and sellers who have sufficient need for the goods offered in the market, knowledge of the market, visibility of the goods, services, and participants, and access to the markets. At their cores, markets are simply the buying and selling of goods and services. Everything else is an inefficiency that is tolerated because it must be. Competitive forces are a relentless driver is to eliminate or reduce costs in order to gain an advantage in the market. These costs are primarily transaction costs as described previously.

Of course, the main components of a market are buyers and sellers. In order to make a market, you have to have a party with something to sell and a party who needs to buy. The next required component is visibility. Each party must be able to see the available goods and services in order to evaluate them for fitness, quality, and price. Competitiveness is an attribute of the combination of fitness, quality, and price.

Next, buyers and sellers must understand and agree to the market rules and mechanisms. Market rules exist to enforce government requirements like taxation, to enforce a perceived idea of fairness, or simply for the convenience of the participants. Market mechanisms control how transactions occur. In a stock market, transactions might occur verbally in a trading pit. In a conventional retail store, transactions occur at a register where a form of payment is presented in return for merchandise. In professional service environments, transactions (delivery of services) often occur separately from the billing and payment for the transaction. The point is that each market has specific rules and mechanisms, and the Web impacts these rules and mechanisms.

Finally, making a market requires access to the market. Access to markets has been a key economic driver of history for as long as we've had history. From the so-called Spice Road to the formation of modern cities, geographic history has been affected by the requirement for physical access to markets. Many a boundary dispute and territorial war of conquest has occurred in order to ensure access to markets.

Access to a market consists of the capability to buy and sell in the market. Perhaps you must drive the truck into town on Wednesday to sell the tomatoes. Perhaps you have to purchase a seat on the stock exchange to buy and sell stocks. In either case, a participant has to have access to the communications channels in the marketplace so that communications between buyers and sellers can occur. These channels range from direct (asking the farmer "how much are the tomatoes") to highly formalized and indirectly accessed (the specifically structured transactions conducted by floor traders on a stock exchange at the request of stock brokers). And, access to a market requires access to the currency of the market in sufficient sums to enable transactions.

Pre-Web Markets

The differences between pre-Web market and post-Web markets are as pronounced as the difference between society before and after television. Pre-Web markets often occur in a single geographic location. They originally sold goods that could not be produced by the buyers of the goods. They depend on all parties having physical access to the market. They rely on direct, real-time, communication between buyer and seller or a proxy for the buyer and seller (Stock Exchanges are highly formalized proxies). Therefore, pre-Web markets exist only at agreed upon times and at agreed upon places. In computer terminology, pre-Web markets are synchronous. That is the activities of the participants have to occur in time-based synchronization. This is a key difference for post-Web markets.

In these markets, identification of the buyer and seller is often taken for granted, but this is actually a key attribute of transactions. It's taken for granted because the mechanisms to verify identity have been in place for so long. A stock market may require all brokers to wear a badge. A business selling to a consumer might accept a credit card as sufficient identification or might require a driver's license to accept a check. Of course, in markets where cash is accepted, cash carries its own (usually) anonymous identity.

In pre-Web markets a buyer often has the ability to physically inspect the merchandise, at least where the merchandise has a physical form. Delivery may be taken immediately upon completion of the transaction. Pre-Web markets are oriented to physical or tangible products. In fact, the lack of a tangible good in the past has usually meant no need for a market.

Pre-Web markets are not well suited for the sale of information-based or digital products. Physical markets have as one of their premises that you're buying what you can see or hold. Information based on digital products contain much more (in the form of intellectual property) than can be seen. This is the fundamental reason that markets specializing in tangible or physical goods have little institutional respect for intellectual property. This is a primary reason why underdeveloped markets are rife with piracy of digital products like music CDs and software.

Finally, payment in pre-Web markets is usually in the local currency and there are limited options for paying in other currencies. Even when it appears that there are other options, like credit cards, usually the transaction is first denominated in the local currency and then converted at an externally determined exchange rate to another (the buyer's home) currency.

Post-Web Markets

In a post-Web market, all participants in the market are at the same cyberlocation. When you're bidding on an auction site or buying jeans from a clothing retailer or bidding on steel, the geographic location of your person is irrelevant. For all the purposes of the market, you are at the market.

Electronic access is required to a post-Web market. This is an important attribute, as it relies on communications infrastructure. As I've indicated, Web-capable communications infrastructure is not in place everywhere in the world. This lack of communications infrastructure is as important an issue as a lack of roads or plumbing when it comes to doing business.

Post-Web markets are "open" all the time and they are everywhere that electronic access is possible. Your customers can buy from you and you can buy from suppliers in the markets where you buy—anytime. This might require operational changes on the part of your firm. The idea that you're only going to do commerce between certain hours that are convenient in your time zone (say 9:00 A.M. to 5:00 P.M.) is rapidly disappearing.

A key characteristic of electronic markets will soon be that nearly anonymous access is possible. Privacy is a concern of consumers and until it is addressed to their satisfaction; they will vote with their money by staying away. Business-to-business privacy centers on transport security, and that requirement is mostly satisfied by current encryption technology. Consumer privacy centers on a different set of issues. Consumer privacy (the requirement for nearly anonymous access) centers on the question of who knows what they are doing or have done. Consumers want provable assurances that knowledge of their transaction can be limited to themselves and the merchant. Consumers also want provable assurance that their personal information won't be sold for reuse if they choose not to permit the sale of the information.

Currently, electronic markets provide only a limited capability to inspect the merchandise before purchase. Inspection is usually limited to an image displayed on the purchaser's screen. Because of this, most e-merchants have a liberal return policy.

Products purchased in an electronic market can be delivered at the time of the transaction only if they are digital or service products that lend themselves to electronic distribution (music, programs, telephone help, data files, etc.). A mutually agreeable distribution channel must deliver physical products. This can mean next-day shipping from an overnight company or it can mean rail cars loaded with sheet steel. This is one reason that electronic markets are strongest (right now) for goods with a high value per cube.

For example, personal computer companies manufacture a product that has a high value per cubic meter (thousands of dollars). Rice growers produce a product with a relatively low value per cubic meter (a few dollars). Obviously, the cost of premium shipping has less effect on the overall price of a PC sold over the Web than it would have on rice sold over the Web.

One key point is that access to shipping networks is crucial for markets that service consumers. A time-based advantage can be gained by locating the shipping warehouse near the distribution points of important shipping networks. Consider the hypothetical example of a pharmaceutical company that locates a warehouse in Memphis, Tennessee near an overnight company's air hub. They can take orders until very late at night over the Web for next day delivery because their cut-off time to have packages to the hub is the wee hours of the morning. A competing pharmaceutical company with a warehouse located on the East Coast might have a cut-off time for next day delivery of 6:00 P.M., thereby missing the vital evening shopping hours.

Electronic Markets Are "Good Enough"

It is an adage of technology that "good enough" wins. Good enough wins in technology because when a product crosses the threshold of minimum acceptable functionality, then consumers of that product start optimizing for other variables like price and quality. As those variables cross the threshold of accept-ability, other variables come into play. If all attributes are "good enough," then marketing takes over and tries to elevate other attributes (such as your status as a consumer of the product—the Rolex watch sale).

This concept is not limited to e-business or computer technology. For example, most people don't drive the most expensive or most powerful car that they can possibly afford. They drive a car that's good enough. Most people don't wear custom designer clothing. They wear "off-the-rack" designer clothing that's good enough. Most people don't have the most expensive telephone. They use a telephone that's good enough.

In this "good-enough" regard, e-markets are simply a continuance of the drive evidenced by markets to find the lowest-cost sales channel and distribution channel that is acceptable to consumers. People shop at Wal-Mart and Kmart because those retailers provide a distribution channel that is good enough when evaluated on the pragmatic requirements of buying mass-market consumer goods. That's also one reason Wal-Mart and Kmart compete so heavily on price. Because everything else (the products, the setting, the service level, etc.) is good enough, price is the differentiator.

E-markets are good enough for a lot of commerce and better than the current alternatives for some. The attributes that make e-markets good enough are ease of use and reach of access to markets for buyers and sellers. Ease means that it's easy enough today to access these markets using mainstream technology (the Internet, personal computers, and browsers). Reach means that the requisite technology is in the hands of a critical mass of consumers (whether those are individual consumers or businesses that consume the products).

Another attribute that makes e-markets good enough is that they provide a dramatic increase in the amount of information available to prospective consumers. This improves consumer confidence in getting a good deal. What's really happening here is that the visibility through the Web is enforcing the market price. If a consumer can quickly and easily find and then rank the alternatives (reducing their transaction search and selection costs) for a product, then each merchant is forced to ensure that their price is competitive.

Merchants should be able to sell at a competitive price in an e-market because the cost of selling is lower. The cost of electronically posting an image of the product along with some descriptive text is orders of magnitude lower than printing color catalogs and distributing them. It's also much easier to change or to correct mistakes. Therefore, the merchant side of search and selection transaction costs goes down as well.

A general state of prosperity contributes to making e-markets good enough. This is especially true for markets serving individual consumers. At least so far, most goods purchased over Web aren't crucial to sustaining life.

The potential does exist and is being exploited now for entrepreneurs to develop highly localized (intra-city) and efficient distribution networks for delivery of low cube-value goods such as groceries. Before these e-markets will thrive, these entrepreneurs have a number of significant problems to solve. Two of the most significant problems are inspection of goods and cost of delivery. Using groceries as the example, most consumers are accustomed to inspecting the bananas they buy. And, the cost of delivery of the order of groceries is a significant component of the total price of the order. Those are significant hurdles. I think that they will eventually be overcome—at least enough to create significant service markets for goods of those kinds—but it won't be easy.

Summary

Transaction costs, risk avoidance, and requirement specificity are aspects of why firms exist. Transaction costs are the fundamental costs associated with business processes. Risk avoidance is the propensity of workers to avoid the risk of unemployment and the tendency of businesses to stockpile resources when the price of resources is low. Requirement specificity means that, as businesses can more specifically determine their requirements for the factors of production (labor is one), they are more likely to purchase those requirements in an open market and less likely to maintain those factors inside the business.

Societal factors bear on the adoption of e-business technology by consumers and business. A peaceful and prosperous world is a requirement for widespread use of e-business technology. The evolution of money into e-money is inevitable, but will be neither simple nor easy. A perceived need for security will drive many e-commerce transactions. Information based communities are numerous and powerful.

Effective and efficient distribution networks are a requirement for e-business and e-commerce.

Ubiquitous computing technology will make it easier to customize many goods and services, leading to increased customer satisfaction with the "fitness" of the product and to lower manufacturing costs for the product.

Governments will struggle to understand, control, and tax the new e-business and e-commerce structures. Governments will, by these efforts, drive the efforts of entrepreneurs for security, privacy, and anonymity in e-business and e-commerce.

Physical markets will continue to exist as the primary market for some goods and services, but all markets for all goods and services will be affected by e-business and e-commerce. This effect will spread to other societal institutions in ways that are difficult to predict today, but that are sure to be significant.

References

[1] Anderson, Erin and David C. Schmittlein. Integration of the Sales Force, an Empirical Examination. *Rand Journal of Economics* 15, no. 3 (autumn 1984).

[2] Downes, Larry and Chunka Mui. 1998. *Unleashing the Killer App: digital strategies for market dominance*. Harvard Business School Press.

[3] Williamson, Oliver E. (editor) and Scott E. Masten. 1999. *The Economics of Transaction Costs*. MPG Books.

2

A Business Case for the Application Framework for e-business

JELAN HEIDELBERG

The Application Framework for e-business isn't a product or even a set of products. It's a structure or architecture. In fact, it's almost a philosophy and a belief system. Usually, when people hear the term *framework* in the context of computers, it makes their eyes glass over and their palms sweat. They're waiting for complicated diagrams and rules and regulations. Certainly, at its lowest levels, the Application Framework for e-business does have diagrams and detailed standards. Actually, it even has a snapshot diagram that serves as its logo (Figure 2.1). At a high level, the level that most business people care about, the Application Framework for e-business isn't about diagrams and blueprints. It's about e-business results, and it's actually quite simple and elegant and commonsensical.

Editor's Introduction: Information technology professionals live in a special case of a fantasy world, for it's surely a science fantasy to be able to instantaneously and easily move information around the world. This world, which is fantastically real, is created from the truth of scientific reasoning. Creating practical information systems that work in the real world means bridging from the ethereal truth and theory of science to the hardwired, practical world of cables, modems, disks, and displays. That bridge, in large part, consists of agreeing to do specific tasks the same, practical, standard way. After all, that's what standards are: just an agreement to do things in a practical, standard way. In this chapter, Jelan Heidelberg explains the IBM Application Framework for e-business, which is a complete and practical set of standards for e-business.

–KR

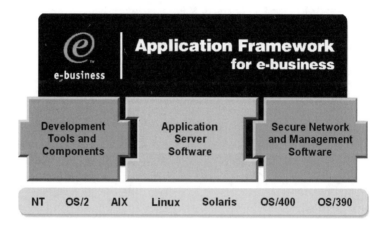

Figure 2.1: The Application Framework for e-business logo represents results.

The Application Framework for e-business provides a structure and architecture that technical people can use to turn reasonable business goals into reality. As you think about implementing e-business applications in your organization, you might have a common-sense wish list that looks something like this:

- We don't want to invest in all new computers. Maybe we'll buy a few new servers. But, we want to use what we have.

- We don't have the time or money to rewrite all of our software. We spent a lot of money writing (or buying) that software over the years. Why can't we just change it a little?

- Our Web site needs to be available all the time, and it needs to be secure.

- Our Web applications need to be easy to use. We can't afford to staff a help desk and have people all over the world calling us for help with our e-business applications.

- The world is changing so fast. We need to be able to respond.

Of course, the Application Framework for e-business isn't a magic wand that will make all these wishes come true instantly. But it is a blueprint for designing, building, and deploying e-business applications that meet these goals quickly, cost-effectively, with high quality, and with usability.

This chapter explores at a high level the major components of the Application Framework for e-business. By examining these components in several different ways, you can explore why they're important and why you, as a businessperson, should care. I want you to keep me honest here. Glance back at the wish list as you read. Make sure each item provides a "framework" for turning these wishes into reality.

Transforming Business with Spinning Logos

If you watch television at all (at least in the United States), you've probably seen the blue-bordered IBM e-business ads. One of my favorites is the interaction between a young techie—barely old enough to shave—and a middle-aged business manager. They're sitting together in front of a computer screen. The techie, clearly excited, is showing the business manager several special-effects options for making the company logo spin and dance on the Web site. The business manager sits back and ponders. Then he says something like this: "What if a customer could place an order on our Web site. The order could tie into our planning system, our order system, and our inventory—all automatically. Now *that* would change everything." To which the young techie replies, after a considerable pause, "I don't know how to do that…"

Initially, I enjoyed this commercial because (perhaps like you) I could relate strongly to the business manager. I understood that e-business was about fundamental business transformation (changing business processes and our business interactions). I knew that e-business was so much more than just building a jazzy-looking Web site with spinning logos.

But lately, as I've spent more and more time on the Web, as a consumer and as a "knowledge worker," my appreciation of that commercial has grown. The ad is still one of my favorites, but now I understand that it's a two-edged sword. While e-business is about changing business processes, but it's also very much about spinning logos—the symbol for a compelling user interface.

A Framework for Cooperation Instead of Consensus

For an organization to truly take advantage of the Web and become an e-business requires bringing together many diverse talents, interests, and components. You need young techies who can build exciting images on the Web.

You need seasoned business people who understand how "the business really works." You need legacy software that's been running your business for years and leading-edge software your people just dreamed up last week. You need a network with the latest and greatest Internet servers, but you also need the hardware that's been sitting in the back room running your business reliably for years.

This has the makings of one of those mega-projects that used to make IT managers salivate and line managers groan. Remember the total rewrite of the order-entry and invoicing system that took three years from design to deployment? The end-less meetings to get everyone to reach consensus and work in lockstep together?

An end-to-end e-business project—say creating a customer self-service application that ties to order processing and status, accounts receivable, contracts, and inven-tory—certainly has the same potential scope as those mega-projects of the past. Yet, business is moving in Web years (1 Web year = 3 months). The thought of a three-year project (12 Web years!) is laughable.

What's a business to do? One answer is to assemble e-business applications instead of building them. Combine components you already have—hardware and applica-tions—with new components that you buy or build. Assign teams of people to parts of the project. Let them work independently (and more efficiently). Adopt an ap-proach that requires cooperation where the components intersect instead of consen-sus on every aspect of the project.

The Application Framework for e-business is designed to provide a structure for this component approach to assembling e-business applications. Certainly an Ap-plication Framework alone isn't a guarantee of success. Just as a building needs an architect, a blueprint, and a construction manager, a successful e-business applica-tion needs the wisdom and ingenuity of project leaders and designers. But the ar-chitect doesn't start from scratch, designing plumbing and electrical systems from the ground up. Nor do the electrical contractor and the plumbing contractor work closely together. The contractors are each responsible for a component. They start with standard elements and customize them based on the blueprint and the vision of the architect. And they cooperate where their components intersect (say in sharing conduits). Similarly, the Application Framework for e-business provides a structure for component assembly and cooperation.

Delighting (or at Least Not Frustrating) the User

Whether you're creating a building or an e-business application, you want to do it efficiently and effectively, producing good quality at low cost. This chapter focuses on how the Application Framework for e-business can help you do that. But first, consider how you decide whether your e-business application project is successful.

Certainly one measure of a successful application is that it helps you achieve your business goals (e.g., increased revenue and profit, reduced expenses). The Application Framework really can't assist directly here. It won't help your people "think up" a good idea for an e-business application that will improve your business results. (Although the Application Framework will help them create and deploy it once they've thought of it).

But another important measure of a successful application is how the users feel about it. Actually, even if the application itself is a great idea, it might fail if the users hate it. Think about an unpopular application your company might have experienced in the past. Maybe response time was poor or the user interface was cumbersome—too many screens or codes. What was the result? Users complained. Morale suffered. Productivity went down. Eventually, your programmers probably made improvements until the users accepted the application.

Now, think about the users of your Internet application. They don't complain at the water cooler or call the Help Desk. They don't harass IT until they fix the user interface or response time. Internet users vote with a click of a mouse. If they're frustrated or bored, they simply try another Web site.

The Origin of a Bad User Interface

Bad user interfaces aren't deliberate. They aren't the result of application designers who are stupid or sadistic. They're a reflection of business processes that have evolved over many years and volumes of data stored in many different databases. Many of these processes are not intuitive or obvious to insiders, let alone to those outside your business. Navigating the data requires using a map and asking for directions. And we know that most people hate to ask for directions.

Just take a walk through the area of your business where Customer Service people sit on the phone all day answering customers' questions. Look at the work areas of your customer service reps. Are the walls of their work areas papered with notes on how to do things and where to find information? Does their computer screen have at least three windows open all the time, accessing different applications and databases?

Now, how do you translate all that knowledge and those "sticky notes" into an intuitive customer self-service application on the Web that any user can understand? (And remember you won't even have the opportunity to train this new Internet user.)

The Freedom to Build a Good User Interface

You probably won't build a good user interface by starting from scratch. Designing new procedures and new data structures that are easier and more intuitive is a luxury in time and money that few businesses can afford. I'm not against business-process reengineering. I'm just a realist. Instead, wouldn't it be nice if you could separate the user interface from the underlying complexity of the procedures and the data as much as possible? You could design a user interface that's easy and attractive and logical (the way you want people to perceive your business processes). Over time, you might streamline or reengineer some of the processes to match the vision that you created with that new user interface.

That's the beauty of the Application Framework for e-business. It provides a structure where what the user sees and does is separated and isolated from the complexity underneath. It's far better for the user. And it's also better for the application creators. Some people are good at designing and building user interfaces. Others are great at creating the logic to reflect your business processes. Make them subcontractors (like our electrical and plumbing subcontractors mentioned previously) responsible for components that cooperate but don't have to work in lockstep.

Figure 2.2 shows an end-to-end structure, starting with the client (a user with a browser) and ending with the "legacy systems" that house your data and run your core business applications (such as order entry, accounts receivable, and inventory). In the middle is the application server with "active business rules" that links the two ends.

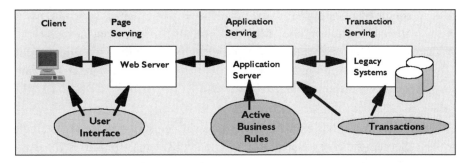

Figure 2.2: The architecture of the Application Framework for e-business has end-to-end structure.

Before describing these architectural roles in the Framework, the following example will put some flesh on this notion of separating what the user experiences from the business processes and data "under the covers."

A "High-Flying" User Interface Example

I've spent quite a bit of time on airplanes in the past few years, traveling to conferences around the world to talk to customers and Business Partners about Domino and e-business on the IBM AS/400. I've also spent time on the Web site of my favorite airline, booking reservations and gathering information. During that time, the user experience on this Web site has evolved several times, always for the better. They've discovered how to make things faster and more accessible, especially for the frequent visitor who "knows the ropes" of the Web site. The Web site provides four main functions:

- Reservations (schedules, fares, and actual bookings).
- Flight status (actual departure and estimated arrival).
- Frequent flyer account information.
- Promotions.

I don't know anything about the underlying architecture of their computer systems, but I'm willing to bet that each of these four functions is a completely different application system, probably each running on completely different hardware.

When I call my favorite airline, a different group services each of these areas. I select a different response number on the voice response unit. Perhaps the same people aren't even trained or authorized to do all these functions. Yet, from a single page on my browser, I can access all of them easily. And my access is more than just selecting one of the four options from a graphical menu. From the front page of this Web site, I have "quick entry" for booking a flight or checking flight status. In other words, from a single page, I have the potential of data entry into at least two different "legacy" systems.

Refer again to Figure 2.2. It shows a single user interface and a single Application Server (the glue). But it shows "Legacy Systems" (plural) at the end of the chain. Now think about customer service in your organization. Ask your customer service reps how many applications they access. They'll list them for you. Do you begin to see the beauty of an Application Framework that separates the user interface from what's underneath?

The Price of Admission Is Minimal

Consider your e-business user again (the client in Figure 2.1). What equipment (hardware and software) does the user need to enter your Web site and use your e-business application? Very little, if you're using the Application Framework for e-business. Because the Framework is based on a thin-client model, your application runs on your servers and not on the client. The client (meaning the user's PC or other workstation device) needs minimal software such as a browser like Netscape or Internet Explorer. The browser accepts requests and input from the user and presents responses (Web pages) from the server. The server does the work.

The thin-client model is great for users. Access to e-business applications is basically independent of the hardware and software that they have. Users might have the latest, greatest 700 MHz PC, a "vintage" 486, or even a PDA device (like a PalmPilot or a smart cellular phone). The responsiveness of the application might vary a little, based on the device type and capability. But functionally, all users can get what they need, regardless of what client device they have. Thus, for the user, the price of admission is minimal.

No Setup Required

The thin-client model benefits your business even more than it benefits your users. One reason why the much touted "client server computing" wave was really more of a ripple than a tidal wave stemmed from deployment issues. To put it simply, keeping the right level of software (operating system software, drivers, application software, etc.) on each client workstation was incredibly labor intensive, time consuming, expensive, and a general pain-in-the-neck. That's the huge downside of the "fat client" model of providing services to users.

When you adopt the thin-client model, you basically need to worry only about your servers. Because the requirements (the price of admission) that you impose on the user are minimal, you don't need to worry about maintaining those clients. What you're requiring of them is generally available to everyone (like the latest level of a browser that's downloadable free on the Web) and generally understood by almost every PC user.

You are completely in control of the e-business application software because it's on your servers. You know users are running the current level (there's only one), so you don't have to worry about maintaining or supporting multiple versions. Because you're developing to a thin-client model that has a very low dependency on the specific client environment (PC operating system, PC versus Network Computer, versus PDA), you can enhance your e-business applications whenever the need arises. The impact on users is positive (easier user interface, more functionality) without the downside of requiring them to make changes to the applications on their desktops.

No Mirrors and Magic Here

The thin-client model sounds so good it almost seems like magic. But it's not. Actually, the thin-client model and the entire Application Framework for e-business are built on rigorous, detailed industry standards of arcane alphabet soup you hear about: HTML, XML, SSL, MIME, etc.

Perhaps you've heard the VCR analogy at some point in your career. It's often accompanied by gnashing of teeth associated with the price tag for converting a much-desired piece of software to run in your environment. It goes something like this: "Why can't computers be like VCRs? With a VCR, it doesn't matter where you buy the videotape. It doesn't matter what filmmaker produced the movie. You buy or rent a video. You pop it in your

VCR. It runs and you see this great movie. Shouldn't programs be like videotapes?"

I spent many years of my career patiently explaining why computers are more complicated than VCRs and programs are more complicated than videotapes. (Even though secretly I always believed that it was a very valid question and complaint.) Now, with the emergence of a very robust set of industry standards and with Java and the Web application server environment, we're getting much closer to the VCR world.

Your users' client device—in the thin-client model—is like a VCR. If the client conforms to a set of industry standards (like the browser's capability to interpret HTML and run Java applets), then the client will be able to "play the videotape" (run the e-business application) that you provide on your Web site. That's assuming of course that you're building applications that conform to these same industry standards. Following the Application Framework for e-business is a good way to ensure that you conform.

The Answers Are in Your Software

I've touched on the value of your legacy applications already. Explore this a little more deeply. Legacy applications are crucial to your business, and they are a key benefit of the Application Framework for e-business. The application software that's running your business today probably contains more about your business—its policies and procedures—than is known by any person in your business. Perhaps if you locked 10 different people from 10 different departments in a room for a month, they could recreate all the knowledge that's in your software. But it would be a stretch. And why would you want to do that? You spent lots of time, effort, and money encoding your business knowledge into your software. Shouldn't your e-business applications take advantage of that knowledge instead of reinventing it?

Think about providing order entry from the Web as an obvious example. How do you price orders? Do you have promotional prices for some items? Volume discounts? Do you charge shipping and handling? How do you choose a shipper or promise a delivery date? Which warehouse will you ship from? Your software most likely holds the answers to all these questions already.

If You Could Just Make the Connection...

Figure 2.3 shows the components of the Application Framework, with a slightly different twist than Figure 2.2.

In Figure 2.3, you see your users (the thin clients) using the services of Web application servers. Web Application Servers combine content (the Web pages that the user sees) with external services, which is another name for the knowledge and the data in your current software (your "legacy" systems).

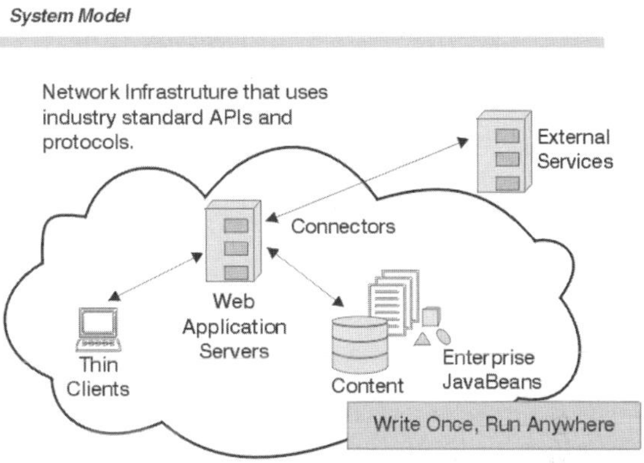

Figure 2.3: The system model of the Application Framework for e-business is simple and elegant.

Even if you have a completely redesigned *user interface* for entering orders through the Web (which is housed in the content part of your new Web application), you can still make use of the *logic* you've already built for pricing, shipping, etc. The Web application server uses something called a *connector* (a standard way for two applications to talk to each other) to communicate with external services (your current legacy systems). The connector asks your legacy systems for data and for procedural help ("calculate the shipping and handling charges for this order").

Earlier, I mentioned that the Application Framework for e-business is simple, elegant, and commonsensical. You should now begin to see why it makes sense. You should be able to separate what the Web user sees from the complexity required to access your data and conform to your business processes. That's the philosophy of the thin-client model.

And you should be able to use all that data and knowledge you have in your legacy systems by treating them as "external services" resources and advisors from which your e-business applications can benefit.

As discussed, industry standards are an important element of this elegant solution. So is the Web application server: the hub and glue that ties all the elements together.

The Middleman Provides Essential Services

Many different industries have the concept of a middleman as an individual or an organization that brings two diverse parties together and facilitates transactions between them. The middleman might provide services between a manufacturer and a consumer, or between a buyer and a supplier. Often, the middleman bridges the gap between different ways of doing business and different terms and conditions.

The Web application server shown in Figures 2.2 and 2.3 is a type of middleware whose function is analogous to that of a middleman in business. The Web application server facilitates the interaction between the client, the facilities of the server, and the external services that the legacy system provides.

Different Conversation Styles

One important gap that Web application server bridges is the "conversational difference" between traditional transaction-oriented business applications and the Web.

Think about one of your core business applications such as order entry. The individual entering the order (perhaps a customer service rep) begins by entering a customer number or searching for the customer by name. The application then retrieves information about the customer, such as the name, address, open contracts, available credit limit, and so on. The customer service rep verifies that information and then proceeds to enter each of the items the customer wants to order. Each item is checked for availability and price. Finally, the customer service rep asks the system to total the order and submit it for shipping.

This order entry application is like a conversation: a give and take of information. It depends on sequential interaction between the customer service rep and the application, which in computer terms is called a *session*. It's an efficient way to build an interactive application because each new screen (like the detailed item screen) doesn't have to reestablish knowledge that was requested from an earlier screen. It remembers what you (the user) just told it.

Now contrast this with surfing the Web. You sit at your browser and request a Web site by typing a URL such as *http://www.ibm.com*. The Web server sends you the Web page (URL) that you requested. You read it, find another link that seems interesting, and click on it. Your response (clicking on a link) goes back to the Web server, which sends you the new Web page you requested.

The interaction of Web surfing really isn't interaction at all. It's random and doesn't really depend on maintaining any kind of conversation between the user and the Web server. The Web server doesn't need to know what Web page you're looking at now in order to correctly respond to your request (a clicked link) for a new Web page. Basically, you seem like a new user every time you talk to the Web server. That's a bit of an exaggeration, but not by much.

Using Technology in Unintended Ways

We all know that some of the world's best invention stories (like the story of Velcro or Post-It notes) revolve around accidents. The inventor sets out to invent one thing and ended up with something completely unplanned and unintended. The Web and e-business are a lot like those accidental inventions. The World Wide Web and the browser came about as a simpler way for the uninitiated to surf the Web and chase the hypertext links between documents. They weren't designed or intended to mimic the interactive, conversational interfaces that we have in transactional business systems today.

Yet, the whole premise of e-business is to use the Web for much more than publishing and linking Web pages. In other words, e-business is about conducting business transactions on the Web—with the basic tools that the Web provides. It's about an easily accessible public network (the Internet) and readily available, easy-to-use software (the browser). Somehow, through the miracle of programming, we need to transform the random, single-click interactions between browsers and Web servers into "conversations" with the characteristics we expect from robust business transactions, such as audit capability, recoverability, and security.

Enter the Web application server (WAS). A WAS provides a set of services to make the interaction between a browser and a Web application look more like the transactional conversations traditional business applications expect. The

WAS "remembers" who the user is from one click of the mouse to the next. It ensures the integrity of the transaction (that it completes or gets nullified) in case of network disruptions or a user who decides to wander off to a different Web site in the middle of a transaction.

True, many clever programmers have developed methods for creating transactional Web applications without using a Web application server. But, in general, these methods aren't very portable from one application to another. And they aren't the best use of an application programmer's time. Wouldn't you rather have your programmers use a set of standard services to solve technical problems and focus their attention, instead, on solving your unique business problems?

Chapter 4 of this book is devoted to exploring the many services that a Web application server provides. For our purpose here, suffice it to say that a WAS is a fundamental component of the Application Framework for e-business. A WAS provides linkage between your user interface and legacy applications so that you can build and maintain them separately. It provides a variety of technical programming services so your programmers can focus on solving business problems. (These services are provided through the Enterprise JavaBeans shown in Figure 2.3.) A WAS makes your applications portable (able to run on more than one kind of server) because it isolates your applications from the specific details of the underlying hardware and software.

Expect Interruptions

Let's revisit the difference between a conversation or session in a transactional system environment and a surfer on the Web. An important role of the WAS is to make the interaction between browser and Web application more session-like, where the screens appear in sequence and the application remembers what the user did last. However, even with these facilities, it's probably not reasonable to expect e-business users to honor a specific sequence that you've designed into your application. Think about how many windows you have active on your PC at a time. Think about your Generation X offspring or coworker talking on the phone, surfing the Web, doing homework, and playing video games—all at the same time. Most of us just don't have the desire or the luxury to operate sequentially any more.

E-business application design needs to accommodate interruptions and multiple, unexpected paths through a set of screens. And the ideal programming vehicle for life in this hectic, non-sequential fast lane is object-oriented programming and Java. In simple terms, with object-oriented programming, you treat business entities (like a line item in a customer order) as something that is capable of standing on its own with its own rules and behaviors. Each part of a customer order is a component. When the user indicates that the order is finished, your application assembles the components and does the final calculations.

Why is this important? It makes it easier for your applications and your programmers to deal with users who are completely clueless about your business processes. Continuing with our order-entry example, think about adding items to an order after you've already totaled it once, or deleting items, or changing the shipping address. Your current application might require that you do these things at a certain point. Perhaps, doing things out of sequence causes an "application uproar." (Have you ever stood at a cash register and watched the clerk void and redo your entire order because of a forgotten discount or promotion?) But really, there's no true business logic behind requiring someone to specify the promotion at the beginning of the order. It's just that your sequentially designed application required it.

The more you can divide your e-business applications into separate, logical components that can operate independently the better you can accommodate users who have their own ideas about the correct sequence for creating an order. And, as mentioned earlier, these components you build need only cooperate, not work in lockstep. Therefore, you can divvy them up to different designers and programmers to get the job done more quickly.

Object-oriented programming (and Java, the premier object-oriented programming language) go hand-in-hand with the Web application server. The various services that the WAS provides are all built into standard objects that your business objects can use. You're now in a position to assemble an application from components provided by the WAS, business components that you build, and perhaps business components that you buy. The WAS provides an environment for this final assembly to take place, on the fly, as each user takes his or her own individual path through your e-business application.

The Workbench and Tools Are a Personal Choice

By now, you have a sense of some programming decisions that are "dictated" by the Application Framework for e-business:

- Separate the user interface from the business logic.
- Use a component assembly approach.
- Use object-oriented programming.
- Use a Web application server.

Does this mean you've put your programmers in a box and stifled their creativity? Absolutely not.

Think about my building construction analogy again. Most construction workers choose at least some of their own tools. They have their favorite hammers, screwdrivers, and drills. They're free to choose as long as their tools conform to the standards of the project (such as metric versus inches and pounds).

Similarly, a variety of tools exist for building the components of an e-business application. A variety of programmer workbenches exist for assembling the components into full-blown applications. Figure 2.4 (a repeat of Figure 2.1) shows the position of development tools in the Framework.

Notice that Figure 2.4 does not mention specific tools and components. Many different tools and workbenches fall under the umbrella of the Application Framework for e-business. From a business perspective, what matters is that your technical people choose tools that conform to the Framework standards.

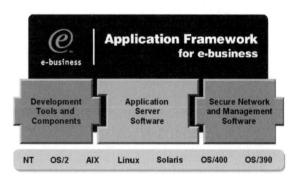

Figure 2.4: Note the position of development tools in the Application Framework for e-business logo.

Nor do they necessarily need to all use the same tools, any more than construction workers need to use the same type of hammer. Your designers and programmers can use the tools and workbenches that they prefer to build a set of highly individual, creative components, as long as the components conform to certain standards and mesh together.

Hardware and Software Can Cooperate, Too

I've emphasized using a component assembly technique, where the participants in your e-business project work independently but cooperate. This philosophy doesn't stop with the people who participate in your e-business project. It also applies to your hardware, operating system software, and application software. The Application Framework for e-business name for this cooperation between diverse hardware and software platforms is called *interoperability*. It protects your investment in the hardware and software that you already have. It makes it easier to adapt to the mergers and acquisitions that are a way of life in today's business world.

The application development approach previously discussed—building object-oriented Java components that conform to industry standards—is one important aspect of interoperability.

With a Web application server as the glue in the middle, the Framework approach lets you leverage the applications and hardware that you have along with the new applications and user interfaces that you're building or buying. But application development is just one piece of the puzzle.

The other important aspect of interoperability is the part of the Framework illustration (Figure 2.4) that depicts secure network and management software. Under the Application Framework for e-business umbrella, your technical staff will find tools to help them manage a network of different hardware. Your network might range from the dependable, robust hardware you have running your core business applications today to the hot new servers used to run your Web site. Actually, these might be all one server or several different servers. Your server deployment decisions shouldn't be dictated by the limitations of a particular operating system or application design architecture. The whole point of the Framework is to provide an adaptable, consistent architecture without enforcing conformity to a single hardware or software choice.

Along the same vein, the Framework encompasses software and tools to ensure that your Web site itself is secure and that your Web transactions preserve the security of your core business systems and data. The security element of the Framework ties to the thin-client model by using industry standard security capabilities—including SSL (secure sockets layer) for encryption to protect the privacy of transmitted information and x.509 digital certificates to authenticate users. You can ensure security without forcing additional hardware and software requirements on your users.

Of course, an important goal of network and management software is high availability (an appropriate topic for an entire chapter). Tools and software focused on high availability are an important part of the Application Framework for e-business. Remember, from the user's perspective, any error is perceived as an availability problem. Most people involved with computers will tell you that the majority of "availability" problems are actually software problems—not hardware failures.

Quality and availability of e-business application software is an important by-product of the Framework approach to developing applications. When you design a component around a specific business object performing specific well-defined behaviors, it's logical to assume that the component will be simpler and less error-prone than a complex application performing many functions. In software, the goal isn't necessarily "fewer moving parts." Instead, it is simpler moving parts that are easier to test and debug. The segregation of function and the object-oriented approach to building components conform to that goal.

Sign Me Up!

Now that you appreciate the value that the Application Framework for e-business can deliver for your business, you're ready to rush down to your IT department and tell them to buy it, right? Wrong. Remember that the Framework isn't a "thing" that you can buy in a box (or even six boxes) from your local computer superstore or a Web site. The Framework is structure, architecture, an approach.

Certainly, there are products—a variety of products meeting a variety of specific needs— that fall within the Framework. Selecting the right products under the Framework umbrella should probably be left to the judgment of your technical designers, programmers, Webmasters, etc.

As a business manager, you should be more concerned with whether your technical people have adopted the Framework approach and philosophy. Therefore, your e-business applications will be portable, maintainable, scaleable, and extendible—all those great attributes. So do you ask your staff, "Are we using the

Application Framework for e-business?" Probably not. They might just say "of course" or they might look at you like you're from Mars. Instead, try asking some of the following questions.

"Are we using a thin-client approach for our e-business applications?" If you get a vague or glassy-eyed response to that question, try asking:

- What software do customers have to download if they want to use our e-business applications?

- What level of browser do we require?

- Will our application work with all the popular desktop operating systems (Windows 95/98, Windows NT, UNIX, Macintosh, Linux)?

If you get a long list or a lot of "ifs" (e.g. "if they have this hardware, they need this software..."), that might be an indication that you've got trouble. You're probably requiring your users to have "fat clients." The price of admission to your Web site might be too high.

"What Web application server are we using?" You should get an answer such as WebSphere, Domino, Bluestone, or Weblogic. If you get an answer you don't recognize, a good follow-up question is, "That's a Java application server, right?" If you get "we're not using Java," it's trouble again. (Refer to the sections on Java in this book.) By the way, it's okay if your staff lists more than one application server. Remember, interoperability is an important part of the Framework. But don't let them snow you by confusing a Web server (e.g., IBM HTTP Server or Apache) with a Web application server. You need both. The Web application server is the glue between your user interface and your legacy business systems (see Figure 2.2).

"Are we developing components that we can use more than once?" You might get some hemming and hawing here. It takes a while for organizations to truly adopt object-oriented programming and start to see the benefits of reusable components. But, you should get a sense that they're focused on components and reuse. It should be an important long-term strategy and goal of the IT organization. To be able to adapt quickly and extend your applications, you need a component approach. You need to be assembling applications rather than building them from the ground up.

"Are we trying to make our applications and our skills portable?" To probe a little deeper here, you might ask how many different types of servers you have with how many different operating systems. Having more than one server or system isn't a bad thing. It's reality. Then ask:

- Are we trying to develop applications that will run on more than one server with little or no change?

- Do most of our programmers work on more than one server?

The answers should be "yes." Or at least you should hear, "that's our goal."

"Do we have people whose main job is designing our user interface on the Web?" You're looking for a couple pieces of information here. First of all, you want to know that at least one person is really focused on the user experience. That's crucial to the success of your Web site. Second, this is an indication that your designers have adopted an approach that lets them separate the user interface from the underlying business systems and data. Remember how important that is.

The purpose of these questions isn't to second-guess the detailed technical decisions your staff makes. You shouldn't second-guess your staff any more than you would second-guess the detailed decisions your electrical contractor makes about suppliers and materials. By asking questions about the Application Framework for e-business, you're focusing on whether your e-business projects are structured well for quick, cost-effective development and deployment and for adaptability and extendibility in the future.

A Not-So-Wishful Wish List

Let's look back at the initial wish list and see how it matches up with the elements of the Application Framework for e-business.

We don't want to invest in all new computers. Maybe we'll buy a few new servers. But, we want to use what we have. The Application Framework for e-business is an architecture that spans multiple hardware and software platforms.

It's built on cross-platform industry standards that many vendors have implemented. It includes both application development tools and management tools that are designed for interoperability (the term for multiple computers working together invisibly to provide application services to the user).

We don't have the time or money to rewrite all of our software. We spent a lot of money writing (or buying) that software over the years. Why can't we just change it a little? The Framework architecture depicted in Figure 2.3 shows a definite role for the software that you have today. All the data and the business knowledge that's encoded in your current (legacy) systems become external services to the new front-end e-business applications that you build or buy. Your current applications are like seasoned business advisors working hand-in-hand with your leading-edge Web designers. The Web application server is the intermediary (middleware) that enables your legacy systems and your user interface to communicate and work together.

Our Web site needs to be available all the time, and it needs to be secure. This chapter briefly touches on the availability and security software and tools that are part of the Application Framework. Subsequent chapters explore both of these areas in more detail. Beyond tools and software, availability and security are by-products of good application design. I've explored component assembly and separation of roles at length. Both are important for availability and security.

Our Web applications need to be easy to use. We can't afford to staff a help desk and have people all over the world calling us for help with our e-business applications. A goal of the Framework is to separate the user interface from the underlying business processes and data organization. This gives you the capability to invest in designing a user interface that's both attractive and usable without having to rewrite your back-end applications. A good user interface is half the battle in avoiding high support costs for your application.

The thin-client model minimizes the requirements that you place on the user and on the Help Desk. You don't require a lot of specific hardware or software on the user's desktop. You don't need to worry about which version of your application the user has. There's only one version: the server version. This "no-setup required" philosophy is the other half of the support-cost battle.

The world is changing so fast. We need to be able to respond. By now you have a picture in your mind of a responsive Framework that will let you adapt quickly and economically. Here are just a few "change examples" as your final food for thought:

- Will your architecture embrace the growth of new client types—smart phones, Internet appliances, etc.?

- Will your architecture let you easily create a new "Web face" for your applications as you receive feedback from your users?

- Is your architecture flexible enough if your organization merges with a different organization that has different applications and different hardware and software platforms?

The Application Framework for e-business is indeed about transforming businesses with spinning logos—today and into the future.

There is no conflict of interests among men, neither in business nor in trade…if they omit the irrational from their view of the possible and destruction from their view of the practical.

—Ayn Rand
John Galt in *Atlas Shrugged* (1957)

3

E-Commerce

NAHID JILOVEC

Electronic commerce, also referred to as EC or e-commerce, is the application of technologies to automate business transactions. E-commerce is a crucial piece of the e-business puzzle. A number of years ago, when the term *electronic commerce* became popular, people thought it was a new name for electronic data interchange (EDI). Soon, due to the popularity and proliferation of the Internet, many began to think of e-commerce as buying and selling products on the Internet. Today, the most generally accepted definition of EC is transacting business online.

E-commerce is at the core of every business, whether it sells to other businesses or directly to consumers. EC is not solely about EDI or the Internet or any other technology. It's a comprehensive business strategy that must be embraced by executives in a company. Technology is the enabler of e-commerce. Historically, innovative technology implementations have produced large gains only when the organization has changed to support them.

Editor's Introduction: Trade has long been a peaceful means for people to reconcile their conflicting interests and requirements. E-commerce has great potential to create and sustain economic prosperity around the world, reducing conflict through peaceful trade. E-markets are already stitching together international trading communities around primal commodities like steel. In this chapter, Nahid Jilovec explains e-commerce. Understanding e-commerce market models—such as business-to-consumer, business-to-business, and e-markets—is important as your firm creates its strategy to take its place in the global electronic markets of today.

—KR

Today, companies must be open to new ideas and to take calculated risks. They must be willing to invest in new technologies that can enable the business strategy. Businesses also need to remember that e-commerce requires close working relationships and, in many cases, partnershipswith other businesses or trading partners. Trading partners today include not just suppliers and customers, but also business partners—such as those who sell complementary products and services—as well as competitors.

Many competitors in different industries have already banded together to maintain or regain their competitive positioning, given the agility and proliferation of dot-coms. For example, the Big Three automotive companies (Ford, GM, and Chrysler) collaborated to form the ANX (Automotive Network Exchange) to facilitate the processing of transactions (EDI, e-mail, CAD/CAM drawings, etc.) between them and their suppliers. Recently, the three banded together again to form an online e-market aimed at selling parts.

Allowing customers to conduct business with you electronically means giving them access to key, and sometimes sensitive, information (such as your inventory levels). But this creates a new level of intimacy with customers, suppliers, and trading partners while breaking down organizational silos and geographic barriers. Today's e-commerce requires compressed business cycles that organizations can achieve through more efficient and better-managed business processes.

E-Commerce Applications

E-commerce applications offer business application functionality, interfaces to enterprise applications, transactional capabilities, and communications components. Companies have to decide which approach to e-commerce best suits their needs as well as those of their trading community. This is a business strategy decision and, as such, should be made by the CEO rather than the IT department.

Business to Consumer

Even though business-to-consumer (B2C) e-commerce that allows consumers to shop at virtual stores and electronic malls has become more popular recently, most online stores aren't profitable. For instance, Amazon.com (Figure 3.1), which has 75 percent of online book sales, has yet to post profits. Yet, all eyes are on dot-com companies. Traditional brick-and-mortar businesses view virtual stores both as a threat and a challenge to their existence. This is because their dot-com equivalents are much more agile, less bureaucratic, and more likely to obtain infusion of venture capital funds without having to post profits.

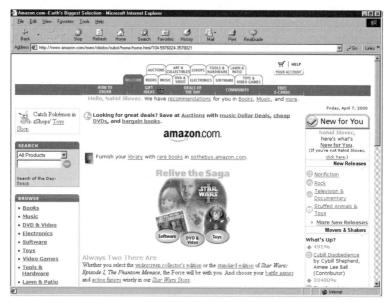

Figure 3.1: Amazon.com's home Web page is a leader in business-to-consumer e-commerce.

Business-to-consumer e-commerce takes full advantage of easy and inexpensive Internet access. An electronic storefront is available to consumers anywhere in the world through a standard Web browser and Internet access. After signing on, consumers can browse, get information, in some cases sample the merchandise (such as listen to excerpts from a CD), and make secure purchases. Although virtual stores are becoming more popular each day, some issues stand in the way of universal acceptance.

People tend to abandon Web sites if they take too long to open. Even if you implement the most efficient and speediest servers, routers, and software systems, factors beyond your control can still slow responsiveness. An example is the bandwidth of your ISP or the consumer's ISP.

Another factor that inhibits acceptance and use of consumer Web sites is human nature. It generally takes people a while to adapt to technological (or any other) changes. Consumers are used to going to physical stores and touching, feeling, trying on things, and talking to a real person in the store. Although many people are comfortable with, and in fact prefer, online shopping, most prefer traditional stores that also provide social and entertainment opportunities.

The primary reason consumers are hesitant to buy products over the Web is the perceived lack of security. Although customers readily give telephone salespeople or store clerks credit cards when they purchase something on the phone or in person, most consumers feel uneasy about submitting the same information over a Web site. And for good reason.

Some sites claim your credit card data is secure when, actually, it is simply e-mailed across the Internet before it reaches a secure server destination. This makes the data extremely vulnerable during transport. According to Visa International, 50 percent of its credit card disputes and fraud result from Internet transactions. In contrast, those Internet transactions account for just 2 percent of Visa's business. Even so, Internet transactions are still more secure than traditional credit-card uses. However, most consumers don't think so. And perception is reality.

Business to Business

Analysts estimate that business-to-business (B2B) transactions will be the biggest e-commerce growth area over the next few years. According to Forrester Research, B2B e-commerce has accounted for almost 80 percent of total dollars spent on Internet-based transactions in 1999. Actually, a large portion of the growth is expected to occur in the manufacturing industry as companies use e-commerce to automate their supply chains and offer Web-based transaction processing to their smaller trading partners as an alternative to EDI. These companies, as well as those in other industries, are expected to expand their e-commerce systems and extend them to trading partners in an effort to reduce cycle times and the cost of doing business.

Business-to-business e-commerce uses many tools, including EDI, bar coding, and imaging. Companies leverage their investments in these technologies by integrating them for more efficient access to data and stronger relationships with trading partners. In many cases, companies are making new investments in Internet-based tools to take advantage of the newer, more effective, and more open systems.

B2B can be parsed into two distinct areas: sell-side and buy-side.

Sell-Side Applications: Sell-side applications, often at the forefront of e-commerce investments, are efforts to better serve customers. Companies that use call centers to respond to customer inquiries or take telephone orders are reorganizing them to support online sales and inquiries. In these environments, Voice Over IP-based systems integrate the customer telephone calls with Web-based applications. Therefore, customers can browse the catalog while talking to a customer-service representative.

Software applications help support online catalogs, which are updated dynamically with a customer's catalog items and contract prices. Business customers can browse a catalog and make purchases and payments online in much the same way consumers do. They can place purchases in a ubiquitous shopping cart and make payments using a wider variety of options, including procurements cards, smart cards, and e-checks.

The Web does not replace traditional sales channels for sell-side applications. Rather, the Web offers additional, extended sales and marketing channels. The Boise Cascade Office Products Web site (Figure 3.2) is just another option for customers to browse their custom catalogs and pricing or make purchases. Boise's other ordering offers include telephone-based, fax-based, and EDI.

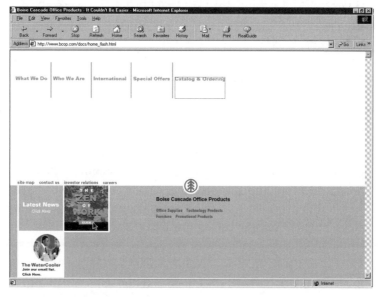

Figure 3.2: The home Web page for Boise Cascade Office Products provides consumer access to online catalogs.

Many believe that Web-based storefronts entice customers to buy when they usually would not. For example, a sell-side vendor can broaden its reach to small-business customers. Previously, those customers might have found it difficult to buy from the vendor due to any number of reasons. In the case of Boise Cascade, its small customers who did not have EDI systems did not have an automated (or accurate) means to order from Boise. The Web-based systems made it easy and inexpensive for every customer to make purchases, regardless of size or technological capability.

Sell-side applications can reach businesses as well as consumers, allowing companies to leverage their investment in e-commerce software and hardware systems. With this scenario, many companies go from selling through distributors and retailers to selling directly to consumers (bypassing the traditional sales channels). But sell-side applications must include the complete set of tools—such as catalogs, shopping baskets, product configurators, and custom pricing—needed to manage the entire sales cycle. In addition, they must include robust fulfillment applications to manage and track orders, process various types of payment, ship and track shipments (sometimes through external links to third-party shippers such as FedEx or UPS), and manage post-sales activity.

Buy-Side Applications: Buy-side applications are used primarily to help manage a company's supply chain. Also referred to as *e-procurement*, these applications provide the means to acquire one's own goods and services from suppliers using e-commerce channels such as Web sites, extranets, or e-markets. Here, the best opportunity for e-commerce application has been in procuring of maintenance, repair, and operating supplies.

By automating the requisition approval process, buy-side applications offer a tremendous opportunity for productivity gains. But even more significantly, they provide buyers with online, real-time access to supplier catalogs, pricing, and inventory information. This data is vital because it helps buyers make quick, informed buying decisions. Some companies elect to host and maintain their own catalogs and others opt to use a third-party vendor.

For a buy-side e-commerce application to be successful, it must have the capability to ensure that catalogs are accurate and that data captured from the Web is fully integrated with back-end legacy or ERP systems. It also must enable large companies to procure goods efficiently and cost effectively.

The use of B2B applications is limited and sometimes experimental. Challenges include adherence to open-buying security standards as well as platform compatibility and independence. While some B2B packages offer low-end applications for the NT platform at low costs, others offer well-built and functionally rich applications for UNIX platforms that can be cost prohibitive for many to consider.

Perhaps the most notable B2B application is the very popular and profitable Cisco Systems Web site. The king of routers and switches has taken the e-commerce world by storm, making 80 percent of its sales online. According to the Organization for Economic Cooperation, processing orders through e-commerce can reduce order-processing time by 50 to 90 percent. According to Giga Information Group, Internet-based order management applications can cut the cost of processing orders from $8 to $25 per order down to 3 cents to $1.

But Cisco is part of the minority. Most companies that invest in online stores for their business customers don't expect a quick return on investment. They establish online stores for a variety of other reasons (such as protecting their market space and attracting new customers). Whatever the reasons, B2B e-commerce is more likely to produce positive, long-term results when adopted as a business or investment strategy.

E-Markets

Electronic markets or e-malls are composed of suppliers that agree to sell their products together on a site on the Web. Unlike traditional Web sites, companies don't manage e-markets, which often are built around a specific industry or across industries. You can readily find e-markets on AOL, Prodigy, MSN, and many other sites. Companies participate in e-markets for three reasons:

- To reach new customers.
- To lower the cost of sales.
- In reaction to competitive participation.

The biggest benefit of e-markets is not only that they can reach tens of millions of customers and prospects, but that they allow market segmentation. Buyers receive more knowledge about the goods and services that they buy. But with insufficient data and methods to measure added revenues, some companies are taking a "wait and see" approach to e-malls.

E-markets are popular in the online business-to-consumer world. Travelocity.com (Figure 3.3), which has captured about 13 percent of the online travel business, is a form of an e-market. Travelocity is industry-focused in that it offers the best prices for travel, including airfare, hotels and rental cars.

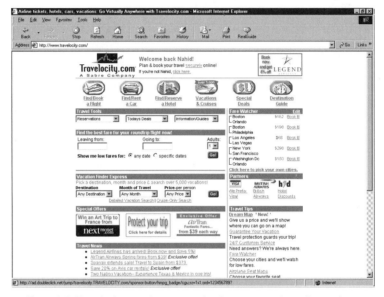

Figure 3.3: Travelocity.com is an example of a consumer-based e-market.

After the consumer enters the desired date and location of travel, along with any preferences, the site brings up a variety of options. Participating airlines such as United, American, and Delta openly display their schedules and prices, giving the consumer an opportunity to select the lowest priced, most convenient option. Other e-malls allow customers to go to specific shops to purchase a desired item. AOL offers e-malls that allow you to choose a product first and then takes you to stores that offer that product.

E-markets also are becoming popular in the business-to-business world these days. Most are industry specific and have large volumes of online sales. The giant Metalsite.net boasts very successful sales of excess prime steel and secondary material. Major steel manufacturers participate in the mall, putting up their inventory for sale to anyone who has access. Customers have 24-hour access to a large array of competitively priced steel products. There are currently 18 companies selling materials on the site. Sellers pay a fee of 1 to 2 percent of the sale price, depending on volume. Purchase requests are collected and evaluated to determine which interested buyer has won the business. The successful buyer is then notified electronically. Companies ponder whether they should participate in e-markets or stay away from them. The Forrester Group predicts that the number of B2B e-markets will grow more than 75 fold in the next two years. E-markets can benefit a company by increasing market exposure and awareness, but they also can put a seller in precarious positions regarding pricing. E-markets tend to provide buyers with a price transparency that puts sellers on the spot to defend their pricing.

The trends in the B2B e-markets include consolidation and addition of other value-added services. When the customers makes a buying decision in an e-market, they also can coordinate distribution and logistics and arrange credit and payment. By assisting in settling disputes, managing transactions, and ensuring quality, the e-market can play other roles besides just being the portal.

Auction Sites

Auction sites are similar to e-markets in that both bring together a wide variety of buyers and sellers on the Internet. Most of us are familiar with business-to-consumer auction sites such as eBay and Ubid. Another site allows home sellers to put the sale of their home out to bid. At homegain.com, consumers can anonymously post their property information. Real estate professionals then have the opportunity to send proposals regarding the seller's listing. The seller can compare qualifications and proposals from a number of qualified, professional, local agents before choosing one.

Although popular, auction sites are cause for concern for some businesses. The auction sites will require much more openness regarding prices, forcing them into more of a commodities-based pricing approach. Companies that participate in auction sites potentially minimize the effectiveness of their brand and identity, and customers might lose sight of the true value-added benefits sellers offer.

Many businesses look to auction sites to get rid of excess or obsolete inventory. On e-Steel (Figure 3.4), a site launched in September 1999, buyers submit an inquiry or quote request to prompt negotiations with sellers. The winning seller is charged a fee of up to 1 percent. Anderson Consulting estimates that half of the world's steel sales will one day take place on the Internet.

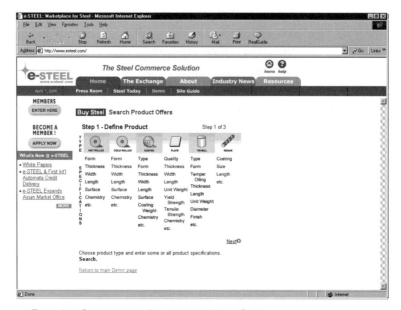

Figure 3.4: One example of an auction site is e-Steel.

Extranets

A few years ago, companies rushed to build intranets to give their employees efficient access to important business information. Soon they realized the benefits— including reduced internal administrative costs and faster access to information— of providing such access to trading partners. Estimates suggest that more than half of large companies will soon give trading partners access to their intranets to facilitate electronic transactions. Once made accessible to trading partners, an intranet becomes an extranet. Extranets take advantage of existing investments in Web and Internet technologies. Further, companies that use EDI, e-mail, or FTP software to exchange business data can continue to do so by channeling them through the secured extranet.

An advantage of an extranet is that it is based on standard Web technologies. Therefore, companies can leverage existing investments in Internet infrastructure, servers, e-mail clients, and Web browsers.

Because extranets are often built to accommodate the needs of a community of interest or commerce, access is generally restricted to collaborating parties. Extranets are designed to allow more rapid and joint product development by giving the manufacturer, designer, and customer immediate access to any-thing—such as engineering drawings, project and budget reports, or test re-sults—relating to product development.

Another key advantage of an extranet is that it can facilitate data and knowl-edge sharing. Knowledge is non-transaction-based communications and infor-mation (in other words, facts and opinions). Traditionally, companies have captured and studied data, while knowledge has remained in people's minds. But in today's highly competitive market, knowledge can make data more meaningful and provide a competitive edge. Integrating EDI with collaborative tools such as Domino extends a company's reach into data (using EDI) and knowledge (using Domino) on an extranet.

A notable example of an extranet is the ANX. ANX, as described at the begin-ning of this chapter, provides an Internet-based platform to allow suppliers to safely and quickly use the same connections and protocols. Although the origi-nal equipment manufacturers (OEMs) have rolled out EDI processing to their first-tier and some second-tier suppliers, the rest of their trading community is at odds with the expensive and extensive investments required to communicate electronically. ANX allows the automakers to extend their enterprise to all sup-pliers, large or small. The extranet has eliminated the need for disparate, pro-gram-by-program connections and provided a generic, robust network infrastructure that supports the entire trading community.

E-Billing and Payment

Companies expect to be paid once their customers receive the goods they've purchased. While many companies still send invoices and receive checks through the mail, electronic billing and payment have emerged to accommo-date Web-based transactions.

With paper checks, companies cannot be certain of payment because the bank doesn't confirm deposits immediately. But with EDI, companies can obtain confirmation within a day or even minutes of a payment. Using electronic funds transfer, companies actually can be notified of the payment date and amount ahead of time. With advance notice, they can manage cash flow with more certainty.

Financial EDI transactions generally travel safe and secure paths via value-added networks (VANs) or private lines. Today's challenge is transmitting the same information using the Internet. Furthermore, due to the openness of the Internet, companies are receiving payments from unknown or one-time customers, adding to the risk of actually getting paid. These new concerns present challenges to billing-payment systems.

Banks prefer electronic payments because cash and checks are very expensive and time consuming to process. E-commerce applications allow bank customers to access their accounts online in real time, relieving bank personnel of some duties. Further, customers are becoming more open to using newer payment methods. These new methods improve accuracy and make it faster and less expensive for banks to process payments. Banks allow two types of payment systems in e-commerce environments: real-time payment token (smart cards, debit cards, or digital cash) and postpaid payment tokens (credit cards, procurement cards, or electronic checks).

Smart Cards

Smart cards are credit-card-sized computers. They resemble credit cards and have a built-in microprocessing chip that allows systems not only to read data from them, but to also write back on them interactively. In addition to monetary value, smart cards store customer-specific information. One benefit of smart cards is that they leverage existing investments in similar technology. Companies that have invested in credit/debit card and ATM technologies can integrate smart cards inexpensively. To allow for secure fund exchanges across the Internet, smart cards can be programmed in high-level languages to hold and protect users' digital identities.

Debit Cards

In e-commerce, debit cards function the same way as they do in the retail world. Instead of scanning the card at the grocery store, the user enters information on the seller's Web site to transfer cash instantaneously.

Digital Cash

Digital cash, or e-cash, is the equivalent of paper cash online. Shoppers purchase digital cash by opening an account at a digital bank, where accounts are held, and act as the central clearinghouse of the exchanged funds. Digital cash can be purchased using paper money, by transferring funds from other accounts, using a cashier's check, or using bank-authorized credit. Because banks haven't agreed on a standard type or means of exchanging digital cash, digital cash users must use a single bank.

The shopper goes online, makes a purchase, and uses special software to generate payment information. Just like paper money, serial numbers assigned to each digital "coin" are matched with bank records to prevent double spending. The bank must digitally sign the message to confirm receipt and acknowledge payment. Digital signatures nearly eliminate the possibility of fraud. The monies can be transferred instantly.

Credit Cards

Most consumer e-commerce transactions use credit-card-based systems for the payment process. Credit-card information is received and processed by online retailers using three approaches: unencrypted, encrypted, and third party.

Unencrypted information is the least expensive but also the least secure option. The data is vulnerable to hacking. Although consumers are fairly well protected (their liability is capped at $50), merchants and banks have a lot to lose. Encryption expenses include software and setup. Nevertheless, this is a much more desirable option for trading credit-card data across the Internet. Today, in most cases, credit-card information is encrypted, offering security and reliability for consumers and merchants.

Another option uses a third-party provider to allow customers to set up an account. A customer profile can be secured with an existing credit card or a company's existing line of credit. By making a purchase online, buyers authorize the third party to access their account and receive payment. The third party, prior to releasing payment to the seller, sends a notification and request for approval to the buyer. If the buyer agrees, the debit/credit transaction takes place. The advantage of this approach is that it is relatively inexpensive (around $10 for the merchant and $2 for the buyer), and ongoing transaction costs are very reasonable. An example of a third-party vendor is e-wallet.

Procurement Cards

The procurement card is a corporate purchasing card that allows companies to consolidate payments for inexpensive but frequent purchases. A financial institution issues the card following an agreement between the buying and selling companies. When users want to make a purchase, they give their procurement-card number to the seller. The seller's computer systems connect to a third-party administrator who validates the user and the authority to make the purchase. No purchase orders or invoices are generated for these transactions. The financial institution creates monthly electronic statements detailing each transaction for the buyer and seller.

A key benefit of procurement cards is eliminating the need for purchase orders and invoices, two transactions that are paper- and labor-intensive. Because the cards are used for small purchases, purchase orders are unnecessary. The supplier does not need to generate invoices for each purchase because payment is authorized upon approval of the monthly statement. The result is significantly lower administrative costs. Procurement cards are generally used for the purchase of things such as office supplies or small repair and maintenance transactions.

Electronic Checks

Electronic checks, or e-checks, allow users to pay later. They are modeled after paper checks, but the transaction occurs online and the signatures are electronic. E-checks use digital certificates to authenticate payers and their bank. Whereas digital cash is designed for consumer-based transactions, e-checks are designed for corporate transactions. Using e-checks, companies can make payments and also attach the remittance detail through an EDI transaction. E-checks are easy to integrate with other EDI-based payment systems.

Similar to digital cash, e-checks require users to register with a third-party financial institution, which may require some credit-card or bank-account information for backing. Once the account is established, the buyer can send an e-check to the seller using e-mail. Once the seller deposits the e-checks, bank-to-bank transfers occur. E-checks can be set up internally to function like procurement cards by allowing employees to pay for small purchases such as office products or product repairs.

E-Commerce Technologies

Although often not recognized as such, e-commerce has been around for the last 30 years. In the 1970s, when automotive companies faced a highly competitive world market, they began electronically exchanging key business documents with major suppliers. This method of doing business later evolved into what is known as EDI. Companies in numerous industries, such as transportation, manufacturing, and distribution, implemented bar-coding systems to facilitate faster retrieval and better tracking of goods and shipments. Banks began making electronic monetary transactions, known today as electronic funds transfer (EFT). Prior to the '70s, electronic transactions using credit and debit cards became an alternative to paper money and checks.

However, e-commerce did not receive much publicity until the Internet became a household term. Internet and Web technologies have revolutionized the way business is conducted. Organizations make electronic business transactions using tried-and-true technologies. New technologies are born and old ones are reinvented to improve the efficiency and accuracy of making and selling products. Old, proprietary EDI systems have given way to open standards. Private, company-to-company connections have been replaced with public, standard Internet gateways. E-commerce is comprised of multiple technologies that automate and streamline business processes among buyers, sellers, and trading partners. In addition to EDI and bar coding, popular e-commerce technologies include electronic document management and telephony.

Electronic Data Interchange (EDI)

EDI is the computer-to-computer exchange of standard business documents. In its early days, EDI was proprietary, as large companies would define the format of standard documents and allow only key suppliers to participate. EDI has evolved into a robust application that can carry many business transactions across private or public telephone networks. Today's EDI systems are open to any trading partner that is willing and able to participate.

EDI is based on standards that define the format and content of standard business documents, such as purchase orders and invoices, that allow computers to readily accept, read, and interpret data. In order to translate a business document into a standard EDI format, companies must use translation software (a so-called translator) that prepares EDI documents and places them in a queue.

At predetermined times, the batched EDI mail is forwarded to the recipient using a variety of delivery vehicles.

EDI mail can be sent directly to the receiving company's computer by dialing directly into its network. It also can be sent using a value-added network that acts as a third-party clearinghouse and post office for EDI documents. Once EDI documents arrive at a VAN, they are placed in the recipient's mailbox. Recipients can dial into the VAN and pick up delivered mail. In addition, EDI documents can be sent by way of the Internet. Figure 3.5 shows a typical model of how EDI works.

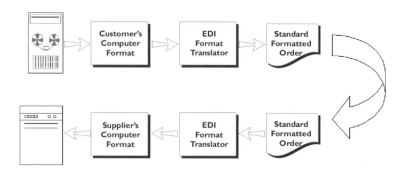

Figure 3.5: The EDI translation process is typical for how the model works.

Many companies have found EDI to be time consuming, labor intensive, and expensive. Besides the initial investment, EDI systems require ongoing enhancements to comply with new standards and new business partners. Small- and medium-sized companies often find EDI cumbersome because it requires skilled technology resources. New advances in EDI include integration with XML (eXtensible Markup Language), a data format for structured document interchange on the Web. Although still in development, XML integration promises to offer users more user-friendly, inexpensive, and intelligent EDI processing.

Bar Coding and RF Technologies

Bar coding and radio frequency (RF) technologies automatically capture and use product-specific data. To provide notice of an incoming shipment, bar-code information is sent by EDI to the customer. Armed with this information, the customer can better plan and prepare for receiving inventory. Upon arrival, the product's bar code label is scanned. Automatically, inventory levels are adjusted, open purchase orders are relieved, and even the payment process can be initiated.

Bar codes also are commonly used on name badges at conferences (making them easy to scan if you stop at an exhibit table), on insurance forms to allow faster processing, and for product tracking during shipment (FedEx and UPS are great examples).

Electronic Document Management (Imaging)

Electronic document management (EDM) is creating, storing, and retrieving electronic versions of paper documents. Many companies use EDM to capture and store official records of business transactions. Using EDM, companies integrate imaged information with other EC technologies. For example, some companies send customers promotional e-mails. Included in the e-mail might be an image or sample of the item (imagine getting one or two chapters of a book or sample songs from a new CD). The latest EDM technologies allow companies to receive orders by fax in addition to other means.

Telephony

Used daily in homes and businesses, *telephony* is the integration of voice with data. One example is checking credit-card balances or bank-account history using the telephone. Because call centers use telephony successfully for business-to-consumer transactions, it's no surprise that the technology has been extended to business-to-business transactions.

Call centers leverage the Web as yet another way to reach customers. Web-based telephony applications allow customers to press a CALL ME button if they are lost or have questions. When customers push the button, they automatically are connected to a customer service representative. A new Web-based application using Voice over IP technology allows customers to click a LIVE CONTACT button and talk to a customer-service representative through their desktop computer (and a telephone line, of course) while browsing through Web pages.

Web-Based Transactions

It is important to mention Web-based transactions when e-commerce technologies are discussed. Web transactions use various software components that allow the creation and exchange of business documents. Anytime a business transaction is generated using a Web site and travels across the Internet, it is a Web-based transaction. Such a transaction could take the form of EDI.

Web transactions take on a variety of formats and standards. ERP or application packages often generate proprietary file formats. In some cases, the transaction is based on the XML standards. Many financial transactions use SET (Secure Electronic Transaction) standards. Because there is no universally accepted standard for the exchange of Web transactions, they can take on any form. Therefore, Web-based transactions must be integrated with applications using middleware and custom-developed software.

The Business Value of E-Commerce

The benefits of e-commerce fall into five major categories:

- Reduced cost of doing business.
- Enhanced operational efficiency.
- Increased revenue stream.
- Increased customer satisfaction.
- Competitive positioning.

Reduced Cost of Doing Business

Businesses exchange numerous documents to buy and sell goods and services. The exchange of such documents (specifically, transactions and messages) can be a time-consuming and paper-intensive process that increases the overall cost of the goods and services. By using e-commerce to automate transactions, both supplier and customer can save significantly.

Streamlined Processes: E-commerce automates and streamlines business transaction processing and produces more accurate information, allowing companies to better coordinate their operations and sales, production, and distribution decisions. The result is lower overall costs.

Lower Prices: With automated tools, e-commerce allows companies to reduce warehousing costs, increase inventory turns, and reduce labor and administrative time. By reducing expenses, they maintain lower prices.

Lower Costs: With electronic exchange of business documents, preprinted forms, envelopes, and postage can be eliminated. With a reduction of data entry and other manual processing, staff can be freed to do other value-added work. Expenses associated with the processing of business transactions, therefore, can be reduced. In a recent report in *Businessweek*, it was noted that it costs banks only a penny to process an Internet-based transaction. Comparable costs are $1.07 for a teller and 27 cents for an ATM.

Inventory: E-commerce inherently requires just-in-time processing environments. Therefore, companies that need supplies no longer have to carry large safety stocks, and inventory costs are reduced. Inventory levels are aligned with order lead time, demand, and seasonal or environmental changes. Because purchase orders reach the supplier within minutes, e-commerce reduces lead time. Order data is received accurately, assuring correct stock requirements. Also, inventory adjustments for items affected by seasonal or environmental changes can be made quickly. Because you can place an order quickly, the supplier can make the goods to order. With less stock needed, warehousing costs are significantly reduced. According to the Organization for Economic Cooperation, $250 billion to $350 billion in reduced inventory costs could be realized as e-commerce facilitates just-in-time inventory systems. This would cut current U.S. inventories by 20 to 25 percent.

Shipping: With more advance knowledge of shipments to customers, companies can better plan their shipments. Smaller shipments can be consolidated and more closely coordinated with company-owned or third-party transporters, making for more efficient shipments. By consolidating shipments, improving routing, and finding cost-effective transport alternatives, companies can lower shipping-related expenses.

Enhanced Operational Efficiency

Accuracy: Because it is computer-generated, e-commerce data is received exactly and accurately. As a result, you should have fewer product returns, lost orders, backorders, and credit/debit memos. Companies can trust that when a customer's order arrives, it will be accurate, complete, and timely. Those features will help the company fill orders quickly.

Better Information: New types of information are available to customers and suppliers. Access to real-time inventory levels allows buyers to make wiser purchasing decisions. Customers can get the most competitive prices by searching for the same item on multiple Web sites. The capability to access sales and usage information makes it possible to adjust buying decisions based on factors such as climate changes and fashion trends.

Improved Cash Flow: Online payment options allow vendors to receive payments in real time rather than days or months later. In most cases, companies use e-commerce technologies such as EDI and EFT to automate the payment process and improve cash flow. Electronically transmitting the customer's payment remittance detail to a supplier allows for quick reconciliation with their accounts receivable system. Advance knowledge of incoming funds also improves cash management and cash flow.

Increased Revenue Stream

New Market to Channel Products: E-commerce potentially can increase revenues by offering a new way to market existing products. In addition to traditional sales channels, companies can sell products and services using the Internet. E-commerce also gives companies the opportunity to sell new products. For example, in addition to buying CDs from the local music retailer, you might be able to download your favorite songs from a Web site (for a fee) and burn your own CD at home. E-commerce offers suppliers the opportunity to better serve their customers through new service delivery channels. For instance, customers can check account balances on the Web.

Increased Sales. Because e-commerce allows suppliers to respond quickly to customer demand, many companies can increase sales to existing customers. For example, some retailers that transmit point-of-sale information to their suppliers increase sales because suppliers can replenish shelves with the right product at the right time. Out-of-stock situations can be avoided. It's a truism that if the right products are available at the right time, customers will buy them.

New Customers: The Web and e-commerce technologies increase exposure to customers and prospects. E-commerce allows start-ups and small companies to compete with large organizations. Attracting new customers, they extend their reach into markets and geographic areas previously beyond their access. In addition, some companies gain additional exposure and sales by participating in online e-markets and auction sites.

Enhanced Marketing: Although traditional marketing approaches using print, television, and radio are still effective tools, the Internet offers e-commerce sellers a tremendous new opportunity to do one-on-one marketing. Efforts include opt-in e-mails where periodic promotions are sent to the buyer. For example, major airlines e-mail their weekly e-fare special or other personalized ad campaigns. According to the Yankee Group, Internet marketing is estimated to be 60 to 65 percent cheaper than traditional direct-mail marketing.

Increased Customer Satisfaction

In creating an opportunity to better serve customers, electronic commerce technologies provide quicker access to the information customers want. Because data is more accurate, customers get the products they ordered. They can shop when it's convenient for them and compare multiple sites to make the best possible buying decision. This all leads to increased customer satisfaction. Furthermore, a benefit of using Web-based, customer-service functions is that it can save anywhere from 10 to 50 percent of costs associated customer service.

Quality Assurance: E-commerce technologies aid the production and delivery processes. With e-commerce, a retailer can capture daily sales and return information and send it directly to corporate headquarters and the supplier to analyze trends and identify possible quality problems. Using bar coding, retailers can capture and analyze data about a product throughout its manufacturing life cycle, isolating any problem areas.

Responsiveness: Due to the reliability and timeliness of the information exchanged with e-commerce, suppliers are quicker to respond to customer orders. With order information available from a customer within minutes, the supplier can react quickly. Many companies transmit point-of-sale or usage information to their vendors to facilitate automatic stock reordering and avoid order-processing lead time. Access to a customer's point-of-sale or usage information helps the supplier quickly adjust to changes in the marketplace.

Meeting Customer Needs: Many companies use e-commerce to meet rising customer demands. The e-commerce system can anticipate frequently asked questions or offer product fix-it-yourself instructions. With e-commerce, companies can go to great lengths to meet customer needs such as custom ordering online and online billing. Dell encourages customers to place a custom order for a PC. GM and Ford are looking to offer customers the same sort of capability by having custom-ordered cars ready in two to three days!

Enhanced Partnership: E-commerce requires buyers and sellers to redefine business partnerships because the business functions of one company depend heavily on those of another. As a result, key people communicate better and share improved results. E-commerce requires trust, coordination, and cooperation in order to bring companies together into true collaboration.

Competitive Positioning

Competitive Advantage: Some companies get on board with e-commerce because their competitors do. Without e-commerce accessibility, long-term customers potentially turn to the competition. Others implement e-commerce to gain a competitive advantage over a competitor. In an e-commerce world, customers and suppliers can exchange key business information quickly to engineer, manufacture, purchase, and sell products more efficiently. These capabilities improve a company's internal procedures and external relations.

Summary

No matter the size of your company, jumping into e-commerce is no easy task. Technologies are still evolving and tools are still immature. Many buyers and sellers are not completely comfortable sharing their data, let alone managing their common business processes jointly. Consumers and business customers are not quick to change their behavioral patterns to suit suppliers' timelines.

E-commerce requires collaboration between trading partners and members of a trade community. Such collaboration must benefit everyone in the linked chain. E-commerce should be viewed and adopted as a long-term business strategy rather than a technology investment. The benefits of e-commerce will accrue as more trading partners feel comfortable using it to automate business procedures and transaction management. Over time, customers become comfortable with giving their stable suppliers access to relevant information about their needs. Such interaction will allow for better, proactive decision making.

Recent published reports indicate that perhaps we shouldn't foolishly rush to conduct our business electronically. Only a small fraction of good and services are sold through Web-based storefronts. But consider the astronomical growth possibilities of such sales. Whether the year is 2002 or 2005, whether goods sold over the Internet are $200 million or $100 billion, one thing is for sure: the face of commerce has changed forever. Consumers and business customers have access to data that allows them to make more informed buying decisions.

A successful special operation defies conventional wisdom by using a small force to defeat a much larger or well-entrenched opponent. Simply stated, relative superiority is a condition that exists when an attacking force, generally smaller, gains a decisive advantage over a larger or well-defended enemy.

—William H. McRaven
Spec Ops (1995)

4

Web Application Servers

JOHN QUARANTELLO

When you were in high school you probably were a member of some kind of a group or clique sharing common goals and ideas. Maybe it was the group that was into sports, cheerleading, or the band. Whatever the group, you became part of it because it enhanced your personal identity. Plus, you enjoyed being with other kids with similar interests. I'm sure that you recall individuals who were not part of any club or group but were considered quiet, smart outsiders. These kids were often loners and didn't seem to have a lot of friends. They were the geeks. The friends they hung with were also geeks. And they spent most of their time with their noses in books. The popular kids kept to themselves and never talked to the geeks unless it was to make fun of them.

How the times have changed. The sports stars and cheerleaders have grown up to be managers of small, medium, and large businesses. But their future success and perhaps even

Editor's Introduction: We are at a point of disruption in business. Today, a small, highly trained and motivated business can use special Internet tactics and technology to gain relative superiority over much larger and well-defended business competitors. Competing in this fast-moving, highly technical business space requires becoming more nimble and more technologically savvy. One required area of savvy is with Web application servers. Web application servers are the standard for linking existing enterprise software onto the Web. Web application servers are an important step beyond having a Web site. John Quarantello explains what Web application servers are, why they are important, and what you should do as a result.

–KR

survival of their companies now depend on the geeks. The geeks have been spending their time learning about computers, programming languages, and Web technology.

As the Internet has become more and more popular, the clubs, cliques, and groups of the past have been replaced with e-clubs and e-groups on the Internet. Today, businesses must be a part of the biggest club of them all, the Web, in order to thrive and survive. And, businesses need the help of the geeks in order to have a successful future. Image that. The big-shot football star and the prom queen's success are directly related to the skill level and the talent of the geeks developing and supporting applications on the Web. Welcome to the world of the Web.

This chapter reviews the exciting world of the Web and Web serving. I briefly discuss what Web serving is all about and spend a fair amount of time discussing the newest Web crazes—such as Java, Web serving, and Web application servers—businesses are embracing. I explain the differences between a Web server and a Web application server. I also discuss why Web application servers are becoming popular and why they are poised to become the predominate way businesses will be taking their transaction-based applications to the Web. If your company has a group of geeks who have already successfully Web-enabled your business, congratulations. Pay them well so you don't lose them. If you don't have Web geeks, go to your competitor and pay them better than their current employer. Yes, steal them from your competitor. The cost of not having enough geeks might kill your company.

Getting on the Web

A couple years ago, it was enough for a business to just have a presence on the Web. Your company was "leading-edge" if it had a home page that served as a basic electronic storefront. Your site could be comprised of basic, static Web pages that announced that you were in business. The documents on your site allowed prospects and customers to browse your products and see the prices and delivery options for your offerings.

While initially this was a leading-edge approach, today this meager presence is "trailing-edge." Having only a Web presence today could be a recipe for financial disaster. If your business on the Web is comprised of "brochure-ware" but your competitors are selling products on the Web, your company is at a distinct competitive disadvantage.

You only need to consider what Amazon.com, e-Toys, eBay, DLJdirect, and countless other companies are doing to realize that businesses not generating revenue on the Web are on their way out of business. Some e-businesses have gotten their geeks to extend their traditional businesses to the world of e-business and e-commerce. The shopping carts their customers are using aren't steel devices that wobble down the aisle. Their shopping carts are electronic devices that say hello to their customers when visited, make suggestions on purchase options (based on previous transactions), provide discounts on products, and offer delivery options. These shopping carts are generating revenue, attracting new customers, and satisfying the wants and needs of existing customers. The geeks who support Web-based applications generating these kinds of results have proven to be pretty valuable.

First things first. Your business must get on the Web. Believe it or not, lots of companies don't even have static Web pages available. Shame on them. They must have spent all of their IT budgets on that pesky Y2K thing or updating their accounting program with a new discounting formula. It is estimated that over 50 percent of businesses currently have a Web presence. In contrast, the 50 percent that don't are determining when, not if, they will extend their businesses to the Web.

Once a company has set up a basic Web site, the next thing they need to do is to deploy a site capable of supporting applications that will allow customers to order products and services from the company site. This is no small feat. In order to go from a static Web site to a dynamic site that allows revenue to be generated is a major leap in capability and complexity.

When companies conduct business on the Web, many important considerations—such as interoperability with existing accounting practices, the security of transactions, and the reliability of the Web site—come into play. These Web-based applications must be able to seamlessly tie into existing applications (order entry, inventory, A/R, etc.). This means integrating the Web site with their relational databases that hold customer and inventory information. It also means companies must set up procedures that allow customers to safely and confidently transact business on the company Web site.

When automated teller machines were first introduced, many people would never consider using them to withdraw money from the bank because they just didn't trust these new fangled devices. Over time, the fears went away and now everyone uses ATMs. This is the same thing going on today with Web-based purchases.

Perhaps 18 months ago, it would have been difficult to determine which of your friends had purchased products on the Web. Today, I bet you have purchased books from Amazon.com or have bought stocks from an online broker. If you haven't made a purchase over the Internet, I bet you know someone who has. The fear about buying or selling products on the Web is going away quickly. That is the reason the Web is exploding with business-to-consumer and business-to-business transactions.

One of the main reasons the fear of doing business on the Web has dramatically decreased is because there is a security protocol available for the Web that makes transactions safe. This protocol is called Secure Sockets Layer and it allows safe communications between a browser and a server. SSL encrypts the messages to prevent eavesdropping, tampering, or forgery. When building your shopping cart applications, make sure that SSL technology is used when setting up your company's Web site.

Return on Investment

One of the main objectives of a business is to make money. That's the only way to ensure that a business will continue to thrive and survive. There are costs associated with Web-enabling businesses. It's not acceptable to spend money Web-enabling applications without considering the costs and potential return on investments.

In a recent McKenna Group study (Figure 4.1), they found that companies were most successful with Web-based applications when they spent $200,000 or more on their projects. This included the costs associated with hardware, software, and services. It didn't include the costs of personnel (geeks). McKenna also concluded that there was a definite correlation between the size of the Web investment and the application return on investment. In other words, the larger the investment, the greater the probability of a larger return on investment. Interestingly, the applications which provided the lowest return on investment (ROI) are the most popular Web-based applications today (e-mail, workflow, product configurators). The applications with the best ROI were those—such as an electronic catalog, transaction processing, and legacy integration—that were most likely to generate revenue.

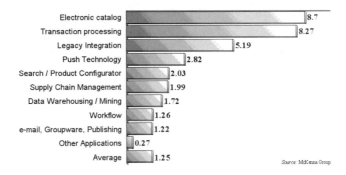

Figure 4.1: A recent McKenna Group study found that companies were most successful with Web-based applications when they spent $200,000 or more on their projects.

Setting up a Web Server

Step one in setting up a company Web site is to set up a Web server or HTTP server. The HTTP server provides the basic infrastructure (plumbing) required for hosting a Web site. In its most basic form, a Web site serves up static Web pages. Static Web pages are electronic pages that allow you to publish "brochure-ware" about your company and products.

Static pages don't mean that the information on your Web site doesn't change. On the contrary, your prices may change frequently, products may be added or dropped, and your terms and conditions may be modified frequently. However, static Web pages don't change when customers access your Web site. Static pages don't recognize who the customer is when accessing the site. Therefore, static pages don't say hello and static pages don't allow customers to order products and services. While static pages are okay, they aren't great.

The role of the HTTP server is to receive requests from browsers for specific Web pages (URLs), locate the page, and return the page back to the browser. The basic sequence of steps followed by an HTTP server is shown in Figure

4.2. There are lots and lots of HTTP servers on the market today. Some are vendor specific like IBM's HTTP Server for AS/400, Microsoft Internet Information Server, Netscape Enterprise Server, and BusinessLink/400. Some are not vendor specific and are known as *freeware*. Apache is an example of a leading freeware Web server.

Each HTTP server has specific features and functions. Some are better than others in the area of security, management capabilities, performance, scalability, and reliability. Companies extending their business to the Web typically favor the Web servers that provide the best reliability, security, and the capability to integrate the Web server into their existing business information using its relational databases. Because of the requirement for reliable and secure Web servers, many companies favor HTTP servers that have been built by the vendor, such as IBM or Microsoft, who provided them with their operating system. They figure that these vendors spent a lot of time and money developing the operating systems and relational databases and, therefore, they probably built a very good Web server and provide excellent integration.

Web Server or HTTP Server

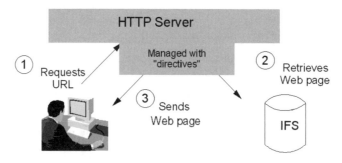

Figure 4.2: The HTTP server operation has a basic sequence.

The next step beyond static Web pages is the capability to begin interacting with customers through forms. This is similar to the way customers initially set up business accounts the old way. In order to sell anything to a customer, basic information has to be collected. The company name, address, telephone numbers, credit information, etc., has to be collected the first time a customer comes into the shop. The same thing is true for Web-based transactions. Companies can automatically set up Web accounts for their existing customers or they can force their customers to enroll themselves over the Web. Obviously, it's a lot better for companies to enable their customers to easily transact business on the Web. By tying existing customer information from the relational database to the Web, customers only need to identify themselves by customer number to set up their account the first time they visit the Web site.

For new customers, existing information does not yet exist and the enrollment process will be longer and more complex. However, this is a one-time event. Once the complete form is initially filled out, the customer record is stored in the database for future reference. On subsequent visits, all this information is easily accessible and available.

The Role of Java on the Web

Java has a very important role in the Web-enablement of a business. Java is the almost magical language that geeks have fallen in love with. The promise of Java is the capability to "write once, run anywhere." In other words, a company can develop an application once on a specific kind of system (NT for example) and port this same application to other server environments such as AS/400 or UNIX. Pretty powerful stuff. In the past, you had to have an NT geek developing applications for Intel servers and separate AS/400 geeks developing applications for OS/400. Separate development teams duplicating efforts for disparate server environments. Pretty expensive stuff.

While Java has lots of capabilities and functions, business people only need to understand the "big picture." The geeks, well—they will understand it all. From a business perspective, Java does three main things:

- Java provides a graphical user interface (GUI) to the user. Most everyone who works with computers prefers a GUI to a text-based interface. Java does this great.

- Java is "network-enabled." It's the first programming language built specifically for the Web (Internet, intranet, or extranet).

- Java applications are portable.

These three attributes are the keys to the success of Java. Today, there are more Java geeks than there are C++ geeks. More than 2 million of them. Many Java programmers started off as C++ programmers. However, a C++ program is typically developed and deployed for a specific kind of computer environment. A C++ program is not portable from one type of computer to another different type of computer. Java features this portability attribute and provides a more stable and reliable environment compared to C++ because of better memory management (garbage collection) and the elimination of software pointers.

As long as the environment supports Java, applications can be developed and deployed for different architectures by the same geeks. Because the Web interacts with lots of different clients and servers, it's crucial that Java be a part of the Web application. Java was initially used to create dynamic Web sites.

Instead of a boring-looking Web site that just served up static brochures, pictures, and text, Java applets jazzed up the sites. A Java applet is a little piece of Java code that is downloaded from a server to a browser the first time a Web page is accessed by the user. This type of Java code was initially used to liven up a boring Web site. The Java applet might be a bouncing head, a moving stock ticker, a football scoreboard, or a file that can play music.

Java applets are a great way to provide a much more interesting and entertaining Web site. The more interesting a Web site is, the more likely a customer will come back. This is "goodness" from a business perspective. Unfortunately, applets also are limited from a business perspective. Applets have to be downloaded and this takes time and requires a fast Web connection. If the applet is quite big, the time it takes for the Web page to be viewed by a customer can be very long and frustrating. Instead of encouraging customers to come back, the applet might drive customers away. The geeks needed to figure out a way to provide the benefits of Java applets without the pain of poor performance. And they did with Java components called servlets and JavaServer Pages (JSPs).

Servlets are also small pieces of Java software, but they run on the computer server. In contrast, applets run on computer clients. Servlets provide the same type of dynamic Web capability as applets, but servlets don't have to be downloaded to client browsers. Instead, they reside on a server and only send and receive HTML to attached browser clients. No more long downloads and no more bandwidth problems.

Java servlets also provide additional function not possible with applets. One of the most important functions of a servlet is the capability to easily communicate from a Web server to a relational database. This allows Web applications to access files containing business information such as customer records, inventory information, and pricing. In the past, CGI programs provided this capability for Web servers. However, CGI programs are slower than servlets and they are not portable. Java servlets provide the best of applets and the best of CGI programs.

JavaServer Pages (or JSPs) are another server-based way to help deploy Web-based transactions. JSPs are HTML files that include Java extensions to provide dynamic content and increased functionality. JSPs are automatically compiled into servlets before they are used on a Web server. HTML programmers may prefer to build JSPs versus servlets because of their HTML programming background.

Finally, Enterprise JavaBeans (EJBs) are the big brother to servlets and JSPs. EJBs are server-side Java components that are designed for distributed environments. They can be more functional compared with servlets and JSPs, and they provide improvements in the areas of security, naming and directory services, and persistent storage.

Web Application Servers

Up to now, I've discussed setting up an HTTP Web server, adding forms capability to the site, sprucing up the site with applets, servlets, JavaServer Pages, and EJBs. However, it's important to know that not every HTTP server supports all of this capability. HTTP servers provide the first step in the commercialization of a Web site. Web application servers provide the crucial second step.

Web application server technology is relatively new and Web application servers are sometimes referenced as Java application servers because of the requirement for a Java Virtual Machine capability in order to support servlets, JavaServer Pages, and Enterprise JavaBeans. Figure 4.3 defines Web application servers. A Web application server is a middle tier (either a logical middle tier or a physical middle tier) computer where applications run in a specialized application execution environment. On AS/400e, this middle tier can be logical. Using most other servers, this middle tier must be a separate physical computer.

A Web application server has an HTTP server as a prerequisite. Every Web application server has an HTTP server as its base environment. It then uses the HTTP server as its base infrastructure to serve up Web pages. It then extends the Web server by providing an environment to build and deploy business logic in the form of servlets, JSPs, and EJBs. Think of the HTTP server as the infrastructure of the Web application server.

On top of the HTTP server, business logic is created in the form of Java components (servlets/JSPs/EJBs). The geeks in your business don't need to worry about the plumbing. The HTTP server handles this. The geeks spend their time building business logic in Java so that your Web application server can start to support applications requiring transactional support. These are the kinds of applications that allow customers to buy your products and services on your Web site. These also are the applications that allow you to expand your business, increase revenue, attract new customers, and improve customer service.

What Is an Application Server?

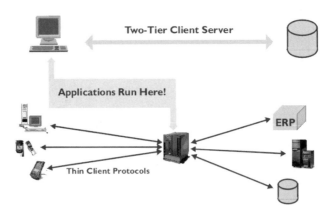

Figure 4.3: The definition of an application server includes a middle tier.

In order to appreciate the value of Web application servers, it's appropriate to briefly discuss why this programming model has so much more value than the previous "hot technology" model of client/server computing. Prior to the Web, consultants proclaimed that all businesses needed to adopt client/server technology or they would go out of business. However, client/server failed and failed miserably. It failed for a couple of basic reasons. In a client/server application, the focus of the application was on the client. Some or all of the business logic was performed on the client PC. The server part of the client/server application was the passive part and only served as a data repository. The client was where the action was. The client accessed the server only when data was needed.

While this architecture did a great deal to promote modern graphical user interfaces (GUIs), client/server technology failed because of cost, complexity, and bandwidth limitations. Most of the client/server programs were run on a "fat" PC client. These PCs had to be incredibly powerful and loaded with tons of disk, memory, software, and networking capabilities. As applications changed, programmers had to update all the programs on all the PCs. Tens or hundreds or thousands of programs on tons of PCs!

As applications became more functional, faster and more powerful PCs were required. Therefore, expensive upgrades had to be made to PCs and, in many cases, new PCs were purchased. In order to use the new PCs, geeks had to install new software, hardware and new client-based applications—over and over again. And what about the reliability of PCs? Everyone knows what the "blue screen of death" means. Client/server technology was certainly cool for its time, but it just didn't make business sense due to complexity and costs.

Why is the architecture (Figure 4.4) of the Web application server so much better than client/server? I'm glad you asked. Web application servers do support a "thin client" approach to application development. All that is required is a browser on the client. The client can be a PC, a Network Station, a server, or a pervasive computing device like a PalmPilot, a cell phone, or a personal digital assistant. There isn't a requirement for the fastest PC technology available on Earth. Even old PCs (remember 486s) can serve as adequate clients. This makes it much more affordable for companies to equip their work force with network-enabled clients to access their Web-based applications.

Instead of the applications running on the client, the application runs—where it belongs and where it runs the best—on the server. In this approach, applications are developed for the server and (if developed in Java) are portable across AS/400, NT, UNIX, and S/390 servers. Instead of buying expensive PC technology for every employee, companies buy fast, reliable servers and allow in-expensive clients to access them with a browser. In addition, when applications are changed, the programs are changed once on the server by the geeks. The applications on the clients don't have to be changed at all. That's a good deal.

Web Application Servers: Two-Tier, Three-Tier, or N-Tier?

The server-side functions of a Web application server can reside on one server or multiple servers. As shown in Figure 4.4, the server-side functions are the Web server, the application server, and the legacy or enterprise systems. This is referenced as n-tier architecture. The first tier is the client and, as mentioned previously, only requires a browser-enabled client. The back-end is where the relational database resides so it's typically an IBM, Sun, or HP server.

What Is a Web Application Server?

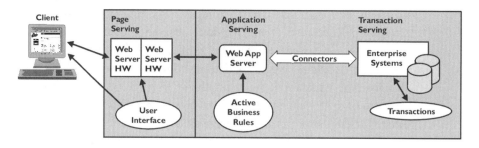

Figure 4.4: The server-side functions of a Web application server are the Web server, the application server, and the legacy or enterprise systems.

The middle tier of the Web application server can run on the same server as the back-end server or it can be a stand-alone server sitting between the thin client and the back-end server. From a logical perspective, this is a three-tier environment with a client, a middle-tier server, and a back-end server. From a physical perspective, it can be a two-tier environment with a thin client and a server, which performs the functions of the middle-tier and back-end tier. Or, physically, it can be a three-tier environment with a client, a middle server, and a back-end server. Actually, the architecture of a Web application server can physically be more than three tiers (n-tier) because the middle tier could be multiple middle-tier servers performing multiple stand-alone tasks such as security, firewall capability, as well as business-logic computing.

Determining if the Web application server topology should be two-tier, three-tier, or n-tier is an important decision. This decision will dictate how applications are built and maintained. The overall benefit of having multiple physical tiers is flexibility. Developers with specific skills in the area of security or naming, for example, can focus their efforts on a stand-alone server dedicated to perform this function. However, when you add a multiple middle-tier server to the mix, complexity is increased and the result can be a reduction in "up-time" or an increase in the time it takes to develop and deploy your Web application server. AS/400 customers building Web application servers often use the two-tier approach with the AS/400 serving as the Web server, the Web application server, as well as the database server.

Summary of the Services
Provided by Web Application Servers

The following points summarize the services provided by most Web application servers. Some Web application servers do more or less than this list, but this summary will provide you with a good overview of the most important services:

- **Web Transactions:** The capability to run a transaction on a server and to allow the transaction to be completely reversed if something unforeseen occurs. This requires the Web application server to effectively communicate to the servers database. Should a transaction not be completed, the entire transaction can be reversed.

- **Security:** A Web application server typically implements security to enable Web transactions to occur safely. Digital certificates and SSL communications are implemented often and some server operating systems also come into play to help with secure transactions.

- **Database Pooling:** In order to optimize performance, database pooling manages the connections to a server database.

- **Load balancing:** If one computer is busy, load balancing finds another computer to handle the request. The computers providing load balancing don't even have to be the same.

- **Fail-Over Support:** If a computer suddenly fails, fail-over support allows an application to be completed on another server. In some cases, the application starts over again on the new computer and in other cases, the application is simply moved and completes on the new system.

- **Event Manager:** If something happens which is expected to happen, the event management service knows about it. In addition, if a program needs to know about a specific event, the program will monitor the event manager.

- **State Manager:** The Web application server monitors the state of transactions.

- **Naming Services:** This is a standard way for a server to name objects so that they can be identified and accessed in the future. Because Web application servers have to handle and locate thousands and thousands of objects, it's crucial that the naming service knows what to look for.

- **Component Model:** Provides a consistent way to create and use software components such as servlets, JSPs and Enterprise JavaBeans.

- **ORB:** An object request broker is important technology. Web application servers use ORB to provide interoperability among servers in a network.

ORBs and CORBA

CORBA is an acronym for common object request broker architecture and it is an important Web-based architecture that allows application programs and data to interoperate between different types of computers. Because Web-based applications involve client-to-server and server-to-server communications, it's important to rely on standards that allow the machines to talk to one another. A system designed to be CORBA-compliant makes interoperability a key feature. Because the CORBA standard is documented, programmers learn and follow this standard to ensure that their programs will work together.

The heart of CORBA is the object request broker (ORB). An ORB is a piece of software that acts like a traffic cop, allowing programs to connect with multiple servers and to interoperate together. Instead of requiring programmers to define the path a program has to take in a multiserver environment, the ORB provides the routing transparent to the program. The ORB isn't concerned about the most direct route in all cases, but it is concerned about finding the most effective and efficient way for programs to interoperate across the Web.

IBM's Application Framework for e-business and Web Application Servers

The whole idea of a Web application server depends upon the success of standards. If computers don't use the same languages and protocols, then it is impossible to communicate together. Because of this requirement, IBM has developed the Application Framework for e-business (Figure 4.5). You'll hear IBMers discuss this as "The Framework." The Framework should be very important to customers because it represents the inter-relationships of hardware, software, and protocols to allow applications to provide communication among disparate computer architectures. It's important to note that the Framework is built on open, industry standards rather than IBM proprietary standards.

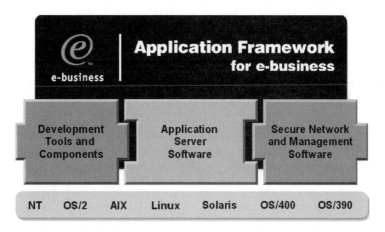

Figure 4.5: IBM's Application Framework for e-business means open software.

Application servers have their own category in the Framework. As shown in Figure 4.5, Application and Integration Server Software is the central category of the Framework. While IBM has multiple application servers used by customers (including Domino, WebSphere, and CICS), WebSphere is the application server that customers will use most often when transactional applications are extended to the Web.

Note that the Application Framework for e-business includes multiple computer servers from IBM and other vendors, too. Its three main horizontal layers include Development Tools and Components, Application and Integration Server Software, and Secure Network and Management Software. To review more about IBM's blueprint for building and deploying Web-based applications, see chapter 6.

Vendor-Specific Web Application Servers

Today, there are over 30 vendors—including IBM, Netscape, Sun, Oracle, Bluestone, BEA, Silverstream, and Novera—providing Web application servers. My objective is not to review all of the vendor-specific offerings in this chapter. However, you should be aware that multiple Web-application server offerings do exist and you need to determine which ones you will evaluate before committing to one vendor. The next section reviews IBM's WebSphere family of products be-cause IBM happens to be my employer, and I happen to make my living marketing WebSphere. Mama didn't raise no stupid kid!

While some of the Web application servers stress "bleeding-edge" function, others stress flexibility by allowing you to "plug-in" you favorite IDE, ORB, system-management tool. Other Web application servers stress a rapid development environment that includes application development tools in addition to the base Web applica-tion server. These are known as rapid application development (RAD) environments. Which approach should you consider and what vendor has the best stuff?

My advice is to evaluate two or three products to determine which ones provide the best capabilities. You also need to seriously evaluate two important considerations beyond features and function. These two considerations are the vendor's financial strength and references. Financial strength means "will this vendor be in business in three to five years?" While this favors the bigger companies, it's a fact that many of the vendors currently offering Web application servers will either be bought out by a bigger company or they may not be strong enough financially to compete with the big boys over a prolonged period of time. Because your Web site will probably never go away, make sure that you don't need to change your application server software a couple times in the next five years.

One of the biggest critical success factors is demonstrating a strong track record. That means successful customer references. Take the time to get a list of references from the vendors who make your final cut. Contact them and let them tell you the good, the bad, and the ugly parts of their experiences. For example, the Web project finally did get up and running but it was a little painful because this technology is so new. Find out how the pain was addressed by the vendor. Did the customer have to bail out the vendor or did the vendor truly provide "added value." Did the Web application server vendor provide good support and service or did they just point the finger at the database vendor, the operating system vendor, or perhaps even your employees.

Because Web application servers are often used for shopping-cart Web applications, reliability is very important. Make sure to ask the references how stable their Web environments were and, when they go down, how quick and effective is the vendor to respond to problems. Once your customers start to rely on your Web site to do business, you better make sure that the site is up, working, and performs well. Otherwise, your customers will go somewhere else.

IBM's WebSphere Family of Products

WebSphere is a family of products that includes application development tools (WebSphere Studio), Web application server middleware (WebSphere application server), and tools to manage and optimize the performance of WebSphere Application Server (Performance Pak). Because Web application servers use Java to develop and deploy applications, sometimes you'll hear them being referenced as Java application servers. Same thing.

WebSphere Studio

Starting with WebSphere Studio, let's take a closer look at the major parts of WebSphere family. WebSphere Studio is a collection of development tools that are used to develop the components necessary to produce a typical Web site. WebSphere Studio includes IBM's VisualAge for Java, Professional Edition, NetObjects Fusion, NetObjects Bean Builder, NetObjects Script Builder, and the WebSphere Studio Workbench and wizards. A whole bunch of good stuff exists in WebSphere Studio that enhances the productivity of your Web geeks.

IBM's VisualAge for Java is an Integrated Development Environment (IDE) that is used to create Java components and applications. VisualAge for Java is a repository-based tool that allows developers to incrementally compile Java course code and also includes a powerful version-control feature that helps developers manage the progress of an application being built. It includes a visual programming environment to help to assist in the development and deployment of Java components and graphical applications. It also provides strong support to access and leverage back-end relational databases using servlets, JSPs, and Enterprise JavaBeans.

NetObjects Fusion is a tool that—using a template-based approach to programming—assists in the creation of entire Web sites. The sample templates included capture a particular look and feel with facilities to add different Web site components such as text, graphics, and plug-ins to each page as it is created.

NetObjects Script Builder is an IDE for developing scripting required for Web pages. It includes support for the scripting technologies used in Web servers from IBM, Microsoft, Netscape, and Sun. The IDE supports syntax checking and highlighting for scripting languages and includes an integrated debugger.

The WebSphere Studio Workbench is an electronic workbench that groups together all of the files that make up a Web site under development. Each file, or group of files, can be edited with any of the Websphere Studio development tools. In addition, new tools can be added and integrated into the workbench. Wizards also are provided to allow the easy creation of Java servlets.

Developing, Building, and Assembling Web Applications

Developing and deploying Web-based applications is very different from traditional programming roles and responsibilities. The traditional way to build and deploy applications typically involved multiple individuals with either business skill or programming skills. Application design specialists were needed who were well versed in the flow of business applications and their objective was to map out the business logic of applications. These were the business guys.

In addition, there were geeks who knew how to code and debug programs. These programmers knew little about business rules or business processes, but could write programs quickly as long as they were allowed to play video games on their breaks. These two types of application developers, the business-smart employees and the code-quick geeks, were the ones who programmed applications for the traditional host-based applications in the past.

On the Web, things are different when it comes to programming roles and responsibilities. While individuals with business logic skill are still required to architect applications, the geeks who program the Web have different talents and skills. For example, in order to develop and deploy a successful Web application, companies may require a geek who specializes in the Web-user interface. This person specializes is how the application appears to the user.

Another difference with Web application developers is that geeks will assemble applications versus building applications from scratch. Because Java components are reusable, programmers are able to "borrow" pieces of software previously used with other applications. Traditional programming skills are still required for business logic, application design, and systems management. However, the world of Web-based programmers is very different from traditional programming perspective because much of the success of a Web site is based on the way applications "look" in addition to the function provided by the site.

IBM WebSphere Application Server

Under the category of Web Application Servers for IBM, there are three editions of WebSphere Application Server. There is the base edition called the Standard Edition. A more advanced edition is appropriately named the Advanced Edition. Finally, there is the Enterprise Edition for S/390 requirements. Each edition of WebSphere is based on the prior edition. For example, the Advanced Edition includes all the capabilities of the Standard Edition and adds support for CORBA and Enterprise JavaBeans. The Enterprise Edition expands upon the Advanced Edition of WebSphere and is based on IBM's TXSeries and Component Broker product families, which are based on legacy S/390 environments.

WebSphere Application Server—Standard Edition

WebSphere Application Server (Standard Edition) is used to build active Web sites and Web applications using hypertext markup language (HTML), Java Servlets, and JavaServer Pages. It allows application developers to build these Java software components on top of the Web server being used (HTTP server).

Typically, WebSphere Standard Edition supports the creation of a basic Web site. Developers implement extended HTML content to create applications.

Developers build and test the Web site with the appropriate Web tools and then publish the site. Applications can be a rich mixture of static and dynamic content that includes graphics, audio, and persistent content from relational databases. WebSphere isolates programmers as much as possible from requiring any knowledge about relational database programming or administration.

Websphere Standard Edition supports several Web applications programming models, including static pages, HTML pages containing text, HTML tags, hypertext links, embedded pictures, and sounds. It also supports JavaScript, applets, and JavaServer Pages.

WebSphere Application Server Standard Edition provides a runtime for deployed Servlets and JSPs. It is multithreaded and implements basic thread management and scheduling policies for managing the dispatch of incoming requests. It also provides a database connection manager that improves interaction between Web applications and relational databases.

WebSphere Standard Edition also supports server administration. The tools included in WebSphere Standard Edition provide a single-site solution for integrating the basic management of applications and their data with the overall management of the Web site. The System Management tools provide support for user and group management, authorization management, Web application deployment, and server operations.

WebSphere Application Server—Advanced Edition

The Advanced Edition is a step up from the Standard Edition of WebSphere. The Advanced Edition of Websphere includes all the function and capabilities of the Standard Edition. Additionally, it supports the Enterprise JavaBeans specification from Sun Microsystems.

EJB support allows your application to include sophisticated business components that run on the server. These components may include business logic with sophisticated, automatic, distributed transactions, and complex persistence to a relational database. Enterprise JavaBeans is an industry-standard Java specification for building applications that run on the server. Essentially, EJB is a set of "application infrastructure" containers that provide common application requirements, such as transaction processing, security, session management, and object persistence. EJB is built on the CORBA standard that provides a common method for an application to request a remote object (e.g., an object on another computer). Using CORBA to access remote objects is similar to using remote a procedure call (RPC) to communicate with remote programs.

Enterprise JavaBeans makes it easier and more productive to develop and manage business-critical Java applications. The EJB standard is relatively new. IBM's overall Web strategy includes support for this unifying programming model. With EJB, Web developers can start with a common set of building blocks for their dynamic Web applications. They can focus on creating unique connections between their Web pages and the business data on the server. EJBs are distinguished from JavaBeans by their quality of service. EJBs manage their own persistence, are fully transactional, and have built-in security.

WebSphere Advanced Edition provides intelligent "containers" for EJBs. Because WebSphere Advanced Edition manages theses containers, developers need not concern themselves with the distributed object "plumbing" issues that can consume more than 70 percent of a large-scale, application-development project.

Websphere Application Server—Enterprise Edition

WebSphere Application Server Enterprise Edition combines WebSphere Application Server Advanced Edition with IBM's TXSeries and Component Broker. TXSeries and Component Broker are oriented towards large enterprises with existing CORBA, CICS, Encina, and DCE programming investments. TXSeries and Component Broker also offer an alternative for enterprises with a large base of C or C++ code.

WebSphere Performance Pack

The WebSphere Performance Pack increases Web server availability, scalability, and performance to allow companies deploying Web sites to confidently support mission-critical applications for their high-volume, transactional Web sites.

Performance Pack integrates three software components that work together to increase the availability of content in Web environments. Performance Pack helps to handle peak loads efficiently, securely, and with 24/7 availability.

Performance Pack includes IBM Web Traffic Express, a Web caching and proxy server that provides optimized performance and enhanced proxy solutions. It also includes IBM SecureWay Network Dispatcher, a load-balancing solution for balancing requests among multiple HTTP servers. Also included is IBM's AFS Enterprise File Systems, a scalable file management system that allows customers to efficiently manage and replicate files in local or distributed-server environments.

XML and WebSphere Application Server

Extensible Markup Language (XML) is a new language that has recently surfaced with much promise. XML is important because it's a platform-independent means for separating data content from its presentation, giving many different programs easier access to that content. The XML language is supported on all WebSphere editions.

The way to think about XML is to compare XMLs key attribute of portability to Java. As discussed earlier, Java is the mystical language that provides application portability using bytecodes. Therefore, application developers can write an application on one type of computer and easily migrate it to other computers. XML does something similar but it focuses on data portability.

XMLs provide a means of describing the structure of information and interfaces to format and access information from multiple sources. For example, companies might have data stored in multiple locations and in different file structures that include relational databases, flat file systems, embedded databases, and more. XML allows applications to be built seamlessly by combining the data from some or all of these sources.

XML is a key technology that works in a complementary manner with Java and WebSphere. Actually, it is one of the main ways pervasive computing devices such as PDAs, cell phones, and PalmPilots will communicate to servers in the future. Just imagine that you are at the seventh game of the World Series and your pager beeps you to let you know that your computer just ran out of paper. It could happen.

As shown in Figure 4.6, the WebSphere family has three main phases: build, run, and manage. You'll recognize the products in the boxes as the products discussed in prior sections.

WebSphere Product Family

			Enterprise Edition	
			• Composed Business Components	
		Advanced Edition	• Transaction application environment	
WebSphere Studio		• Clustering and scaling	• CICS	
• Workbench	Standard Edition	• Enterprise Java Server (EJS)	• Encina	
• Wizards			• Clustering and scaling	Tivoli
• Content Authoring	• Database Connection Manager	• Database Connection Manager	• EJS/EJB	
• Site Development			• Database Connection Manager	
• Content Management	• Java Servlet Runtime and services	• Java Servlet Runtime and services	• Java Servlet Runtime and services	
VisualAge				
• Application Programming		WebSphere Performance Pack		
• Component Development	• Caching • Load Balancing		• Filtering • Distributed Files	
• Team Development		HTTP Server		
	NT AIX	Solaris OS/400	S/390	
Build		**Run**		**Manage**

Figure 4.6: *The WebSphere product provides functionality from application development (build) to deployment (run) to performance and load balancing (manage).*

WebSphere Success Stories

I've including three success stories in this section to demonstrated how companies are successfully using Websphere with AS/400. The companies profiled include Oriental Trading Company, HMV Media Group, and Welsh's Foods, Inc.

Oriental Trading Company

The Oriental Trading Company started as a family-run business with eight employees in 1932, and it has grown to over 3,700 employees and annual sales in excess of $300 million. Oriental Trading Company is an industry leader in the sale of value-priced toys, novelty gifts, crafts material, and home décor.

Oriental Trading didn't think the majority of its target audience—parents and young children—was even on the Web, let alone buying online. When the company's informational Web site began receiving up to 700 catalog requests daily, that perception quickly changed and OTC accelerated its e-business initiative.

To build brand awareness on the Web for its catalogs, OTC created four distinct e-business sites using IBM AS/400s and WebSphere (Standard Edition). Once the sites went live, any doubts about the viability of e-business in this market were dispelled. In just one month, online sales equaled 3 percent of the company's total sales. More than 5,500 shoppers visit the sites each day, with 9 percent making purchases before leaving. Contrary to expectations, the average value of online orders has exceeded that of mail orders from the print catalog, averaging 10 percent higher than print.

Although it is too soon to calculate precisely, OTC believes the returns from its investment in e-business will be substantial due to reduced telemarketing and mailing costs, and incremental online business.

HMV Media Group

The HMV Media Group is the largest music specialist retailer in the world and the UK's largest book-specialist retailer. With sales of $2 billion worldwide and 9,500 employees, HMV Media Group has 484 stores, of which 278 are HMV music stores and 206 are bookstores (mainly Waterstones).

With the dramatic rise of Internet sales of books and music, the main business challenge for HMV Media Group was to integrate e-commerce with its physical stores, to the benefit of both parts of the business. To achieve a truly effective Internet presence, HMV Media Group needed to have a secure, robust, and scalable solution that they could also roll out worldwide.

HMV chose the AS/400 and WebSphere (Standard Edition) as the easiest and most cost-effective implementation of their e-business solution. In addition, HMV believed that the AS/400 had a long-term future, a very scalable solution, and a high level of security and availability.

The combination of Java and WebSphere technology has enabled the rapid development of a very functional and flexible Web application for HMV Media Group, which will scale to many thousands of users.

Welch's Foods, Inc.

In 1869, Welch's Foods was founded in Massachusetts and is a well-established firm by any standards. Long an American household name well known for its juices, jams, and jelly products, Welch's is also a company known for embracing technology to make its business more effective. Welch's has kept loyal customers over the years by providing consistently high-quality products.

Beginning in 1996, the company began to look at ways to use the Internet to improve its business. By 1999, Welch's had rolled out three major new AS/400 applications. The Web-based applications use Java and IBM's WebSphere Application Server (Standard Edition).

As the Welch's IT staff first sought ways to get the Marketing Development Fund process under control, it first looked at outside service offerings, but eventually rejected them because they required Welch's brokers and retailers to invest in equipment and IT skills. They needed a system "universally" available to all participants (even for sales people working out of their homes).

Welch's decided to develop a system in-house and use the Internet and browser-based PCs to connect. This led to the development of an AS/400-based Java solution where Welch's brokers, retailers, sales staffs, and customer service reps all see the same data regarding promotional events and the associated payments. This improved promotion management system will yield between 10 to 20 percent savings, and return their investment in six months.

Welch's went through extensive education of its programming staff to create the skill base for the new application set. Today, five programmers are fully skilled at object-oriented programming methodologies and Java coding. This has resulted in a bonus of two other Java-based applications rolled out in 1999. Welch's employees can now access human resource files and receive full-time, self-service for most personnel and benefit-related matters. A new forecasting and reporting system provides sales people and brokers with their forecasting data over the Internet and helps them monitor the actual shipments in real time.

When Welch's first prepared its prototype for the Marketing Development Fund application, IBM's WebSphere Application Server was not available. Therefore, the IT group wrote its own AS/400 server engine. In 1998, Welch's was one of the first beta customers of IBM's AS/400 model 720e. That system was dedicated to the new Web-based application. When WebSphere became available in 1998, Welch's restructured the application to take advantage of the servlet APIs and monitoring functions.

Working with IBM all along, the addition of WebSphere to the application went very well. Mr. Deepak Mohapatra, Operations Manager of Welch's Foods, summarizes his company's IBM experience in the project. "We had direct access to the Java and WebSphere development teams. This was very helpful in giving us the skills we needed to write and deploy this very successful AS/400 Java application."

Summary

The case stories from Oriental Trading, HMV Media Group, and Welch's Food's, Inc. demonstrate that companies can go beyond the science of Web serving and Web application serving and start to reap the major benefits promised from e-business and e-commerce solutions. These companies were successful at extending their current business applications to the Web and enhancing their capability to generate revenue, attract new customers, and to increase customer satisfaction. They all must have pretty smart geeks working for them.

This is only the beginning. Hundreds and hundreds of companies have successfully deployed transaction-based applications to the Web and thousands more are determining when (not if) they will do so in the future. A large percentage of them will make plans to develop and deploy similar e-commerce applications using Web application servers in the 2000-to-2002 time frame. Good thing, too. If they don't act quickly, they just might not be in business. The geeks working for them will certainly be gainfully employed in this exciting time frame, even if it's with their competitors. Pretty smart geeks, huh?

*Integrity without knowledge is weak and useless, and knowledge
without integrity is dangerous and dreadful.*

Samuel Johnson
The History of Rasselas, ch. 41 (1759)

Text found at
http://andromeda.rutgers.edu/~jlynch/texts/rasselas.html#41

5

IT's New ACID Test:
e-business Transaction Integrity

ROBERT S. TIPTON

Say the terms *e-business transaction integrity* and someone invariably says, "Isn't that an oxymoron?" No, e-business and transaction aren't the questionable words; it's that bothersome *integrity* word. Okay, maybe I'm showing my age (yes, the hairline is receding a little, and what's there is graying up nicely), but this is one time that I'm happy to be a member of the old school.

When I was just a DP pup (yes, data processing was the favored term then), I had a boss/mentor who drilled some basics into me. Two things have remained after all these years:

- Keep the transaction detail. *Always* keep the detail. If you have the detail, you can recreate anything. Any report, any document, any piece of information can be recreated as long as you have the detail.

Editor's Introduction: Web operators have discovered, somewhat to their surprise, that complete efforts are what counts when it comes to business matters. Getting it right, completely right, is an immutable requirement. Failure rates of any size are not tolerated when it comes to the money part of the transaction. It's not half as good just to get the money out of savings; if it doesn't get deposited into checking, then the whole transaction must be reversed. In this chapter, Bob Tipton covers the fundamentals of information technology transactions. From an IT point of view, transactions are rigorously defined and must be rigorously sustained. Bob explains why it's important to the Web world as well as to the accountants.

–KR

- Expect the system to fail during a transaction or during a batch process. *Always* plan for it, and take steps in your application design to recover from it.

Thank you, Ross Nelson, for those sage words of advice, lo those many years ago. Certainly, rule number one remains vital today. Nevertheless, I believe rule number two is even more crucial in the e-business world in which we are living.

Further complicating life in the IT department in the "better-get-in-fast-or-you'll-be-amazoned" world of e-business, the perception is that getting in first is better than getting in right. Companies are running like lemmings after the Holy Grail of garnering market share as quickly as possible. Their poor IT departments have the daunting and unrewarding task of dealing with crumbling IT architectures. Certainly, waiting to get into the digital economy could prove costly or fatal to many businesses, but we shouldn't throw "IT meat and potatoes" caution to the wind as we deploy these new e-business applications.

Now, there's a strange metaphor: IT meat and potatoes. What on Earth does that mean? First, I'll admit that I've crossed the line between business issues and IT issues. In other words, in order to understand the major issues related to e-business transactional integrity, a business person must understand some basics IT issues. Therefore, in order to understand my metaphor, you'll need a basic level of understanding in the lingo of IT.

In the old days (say, the early to mid-1990s), business executives actually could be effective in their jobs without having to know much about IT. However, with the advent of e-business, where technology plays such an integral and vital role in future business opportunities, few non-IT-savvy business executives will last in their current jobs.

As a result, I'm convinced one of the most profound changes e-business is bringing to the economy relates to the need for non-IT executives to dig in and understand the business-oriented implications of technology decisions. That's where this chapter comes in. It's my goal to help you understand the issues surrounding transactional integrity in the world of e-business (without causing you to sprout propeller beanies in the process).

In the context of information technology, what is a transaction and what factors lead to its integrity? As we've known since the dawn of the age of CRT-based terminals like VT-100s, 3270s, and 5250s, online applications are prone to failures at a much higher rate than the card-based systems preceding them. (Okay, what does CRT stand for? Cathode Ray Tube–aren't you sorry you asked?). After all, once we introduced real people into the world of transaction processing, we created the potential for human failure into our systems. Instead of being able to rely upon highly trained and accurate keypunch operators, we had A/P clerks and billing clerks actually interacting with the computer. Blasphemy!

Now compared with client/server, CRT-based systems seemed childlike. Instead of having a "safe" and predictable technology environment (one with captive terminals and a data-center-bound mainframe), client/server taught us all about the perils of running a single business transaction across multiple technology platforms. This mix included PCs (potentially running different operating systems) and a plethora of server platforms—each with its own specific technology issues.

With client/server, many more variables came into play when PCs and servers and databases and middleware (software that strives to link the complex world of PCs to the equally complex world of servers and databases) are working together to bring sense to transactional integrity. In reality, client/server was application anarchy. I pity the poor IT department struggling (or continuing to struggle, as often the case remains) to make client/server implementations work. It's no wonder that the IT industry regards nearly every client/server installation as being been more time-consuming and expensive than originally planned.

Enter the World Wide Web, the Internet, and e-business. Yes, we've done good things from a technology viewpoint related to simplifying much of the technology-related mishmash we forced upon ourselves with client/server. However, we're just starting to understand the business-related complexities in an e-business transaction. Instead of worrying about which version of what PC is running which operating system, and what database supports which version of what middleware on which server, we basically struggle only with browsers and Web servers from the Web-facing side of the e-business transaction.

However (and here's where we need to start hearing some church music), integrating Web-facing applications with back-end systems is neither easy nor inexpensive. In business-to-business e-business transactions (as in supply chain management), we now are at the mercy of an entire group of other companies and their capability to ensure integrity in their entire group of IT implementations. Ooh—just the thought of it is enough to make even the most hardened IT professional grimace.

Why? Because we're no longer directly in control of our IT solutions. We have to rely on others.

Figure 5.1 depicts the new e-business relationship among trading partners. At the top, you can see things that translate into business value:

- Strategies
- Process
- Knowledge
- Applications

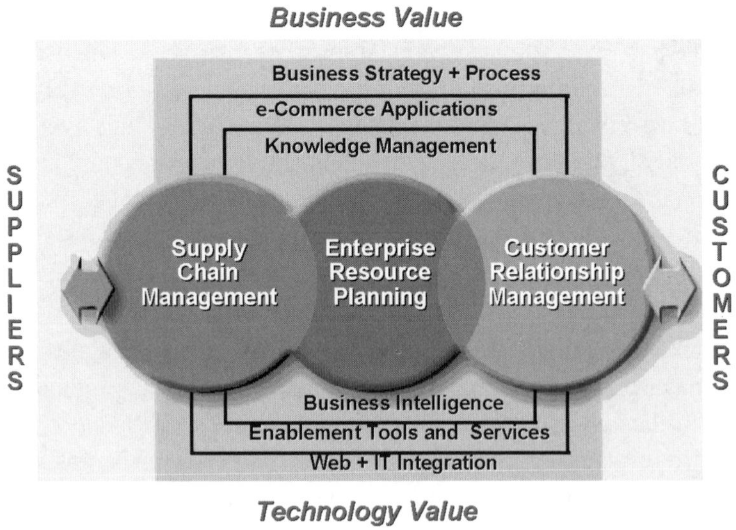

Business Value

Business Strategy + Process

e-Commerce Applications

Knowledge Management

SUPPLIERS

Supply Chain Management

Enterprise Resource Planning

Customer Relationship Management

CUSTOMERS

Business Intelligence

Enablement Tools and Services

Web + IT Integration

Technology Value

Figure 5.1: An example of e-business trading partner relationships includes strategies, process, knowledge, and applications.

Even the most technological-neophyte business professional understands the need for strong business planning, excellence in process execution, the power of putting knowledge into action (many times this is what really separates you from your competition), and the need for strong information systems applications to drive everything. However, just as crucial in the world of e-business is the need for excellence in the underlying technology infrastructure.

As shown in Figure 5.1, the categories above the business value heading are where strength in e-business transactional integrity is found. As you see the integration and overlap among supply chain management (SCM), enterprise resource planning (ERP), and customer relationship management (CRM) systems, I hope you gain somewhat of an understanding of why transactional integrity in e-business is important. Clearly, without this integrity, the foundation of e-business is compromised.

IT Transactions

Before discussing some strategies to assist you in having a snowball's chance of delivering 100 percent integrity in your e-business transactions, I suppose I ought to jump (once again) off the diving board into the pool of IT terminology and definitions.

To define a transaction, from an IT viewpoint, I'll use a time-tested approach called the ACID test that I learned about some 20 years ago. Sometimes a blast from the past shows just how smart some of our predecessors were.

ACID testing in transaction systems is exactly what Ross taught me related to ensuring transaction integrity. I'm not sure they even teach ACID now in IT courses (I hope so). For those new to the field that haven't heard about ACID and for those of us old-school types who learned about it years ago and may have forgotten about it, here's a refresher. ACID is an acronym for atomicity; consistency; isolation, and durability. Stick with me on this. It will make lots of sense in just a minute.

Atomicity

Atomicity describes the notion that all operations happening as part of a single transaction form an indivisible unit of work. While this definition is simple to understand within the confines of a single server, it gets a bit more complicated in the realm of e-business. After all, in today's e-based supply chain, we don't have complete control of the total "order" transaction. However, we do have the capability to compartmentalize a transaction.

In other words, if one of your e-customers is ordering a product online, you might want to consider each item ordered to be an atomic transaction. For example:

- Order an item through Web-server-based application.

- Pass the order request from the Web server to the order-processing system.

- Receive an acknowledgment of successful database completion back on the Web server.

- Respond to the customer through their browser—one item at a time.

While this approach certainly gives you the best assurance of transaction atomicity, it might annoy your customers because they have to wait between items. If the customer changes the items they've ordered, each change requires a similar transaction process to "back-out" their previous request, and another transaction to enter their new request.

This process creates significant network and database traffic, and some of that traffic might be unnecessary. Thus, to satisfy your customers' need for high-performance transaction speed, and to give you minimum network and database impact, you might decide to consider an entire shopping cart to be a single atomic transaction. However, if you show on-hand quantities to your customers as they order, you'll need to re-verify item availability once they've accepted their shopping-cart order and have made payment.

Consistency

Consistency is the characteristic that all data operations within a single transaction either commit to the database together or they abort together. In other words, when a failure occurs during a transaction (as they sometimes do), consistency ensures that there will be no "orphan" data operations within the transaction. No lost record locks (something a program does to a customer or item record prior to updating it), no partially updated vendor files, and no lost order detail records. Consistency makes sure that all data operations go forward into the database together or that they don't go at all.

Clearly, in the world of e-business, this requirement mandates the use of "packaged" transactions flowing between trading partners. Make sure the transaction completes correctly on your server before passing it on to the next server. Then, if there's an acknowledgment required (such as credit worthiness or item on-hand availability), set a timer and wait for the acknowledgment. If the timer expires before receipt, back-out the transaction on your local server. This is ACID consistency.

Isolation

Think of *isolation* as being the process of keeping data operations of one transaction completely separated from those of another transaction. Imagine the ability to keep your younger children from touching each other in the backseat while on a long family vacation. Better still, picture that imaginary line between your kids as being an impenetrable boundary. Nothing can pass from one child to the other—no touching, no words, nothing. Now that's a type of isolation I can get behind.

However, back to transactional isolation. For a transaction to pass the ACID test, you can't lock multiple, unrelated records. Neither can an update from one transaction overwrite an update from another. Isolation, particularly with databases that don't do record-level locking (like most of the unsophisticated databases), can be a real pain in the neck to get right. Isolation forces transactional separation, and thus ensures no inter-transactional corruption.

Now, if someone could just stop the kids from whining.

Durability

Guaranteeing that committed data is permanently stored in the database describes the concept of *durability*. Once all applications on all servers have blessed the transaction, durability ensures that this "committed" data will be permanently stored in all databases on all servers. In other words, you can be assured of finding and reconciling all data operations in the transaction throughout the IT infrastructure of all systems in all companies. It's a tall order to be sure.

Web-Facing to ERP Integrating

Now, I know it's a lot more interesting to build good-looking, flashy and glitzy Web sites than it is to worry about e-business transactions passing the ACID test. However, experience with lots of Web developers that don't care about

ACID testing tells me the look of a Web site is much less important than proactively protecting yourself from database corruption.

Make sure those in your IT department responsible for front-office (Web sites) to back-office (ERP systems) integration can pass the ACID test. You'll save yourself lots of grief in the process. Why? Business transactions in the '00s and beyond won't happen inside the cozy, comfy confines of a single IBM mainframe. Actually, in our interconnected, interdependent business world, at times the rules for a particular transaction are stored on multiple servers that probably are running different operating systems and potentially are even in different companies.

Figure 5.2 depicts the processes needed in an automotive manufacturing organization. The top section shows the internal processes—things like research and development, production, and marketing—while the processes external to the manufacturer are shown outside that box. Certainly, most of the processes are internal, but many of the most important processes are outside the box.

In other words, without strong integrity in the transactions between this manufacturer and their suppliers (in the boxes on the lower left of Figure 5.2), the entire business process model is suspect. Further, strong integrity is required in transactions with organizations that control the distribution channels (such as agents and dealers) in the automotive industry. The final result is the simple act of someone getting behind the steering wheel and driving off, but the transaction flow among organizations needed to get the car to the consumer is highly complex.

To further illustrate this issue, let's look at the major challenges facing an overall of e-business implementation and where integrity of the IT infrastructure is important. These major issues are:

- Collaboration
- Customer relationship management
- Globalization
- Electronic marketplaces
- Customer self-service
- Knowledge management
- Channel conflict resolution and channel expansion

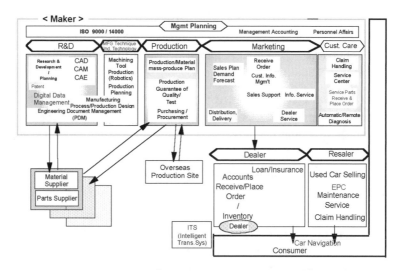

Figure 5.2: An example of automotive manufacturing organization processes that are needed in an automotive manufacturing organization.

Collaboration

Beyond simply working and playing nicely together, true collaboration requires deep and meaningful integration among business partners. To really collaborate, you have to trust the data you receive from your partners. In my view, that ultimate collaboration occurs in stock market where millions of individuals collaborate to create a free-market economy based on faith in our public accounting system and the laws governing reporting and compliance of our public companies. Without confidence in CPA audits and SEC oversight to ensure accuracy in public company reporting, our stock markets would look more like flea markets. True business collaboration requires this same level of absolute confidence in sharing order, inventory, customer, vendor, scheduling, and logistics information.

Customer Relationship Management

Customer relationship management (CRM) is one of today's hottest product segments in the IT world. Service becomes a major differentiator in a virtual business relationship, and effective CRM implementations assist greatly in this process. Furthermore, these systems offer your customers the capability to customize their experience with your company. Personalized, individual experiences—and the process of effective relationship management—create many points of integration between groups and individuals. Again, extreme care must be taken to ensure the quality and integrity of these transactions.

In my own experience, I trusted a well-known Web portal company with details concerning my stock portfolio. I read their privacy statement and researched thoroughly their approach to collecting and using their customer information. Finally satisfied, I allowed them to store my portfolio information. Well, due to some "unexplained" technology snafu, they lost my data.

Asking, "So, where did it go?" prompted some nervous and unintelligible babble from their customer-service rep. After hanging up the phone, I decided never again to trust that organization with my personal data. I now use a completely different organization. Furthermore, as a frequent speaker and author, I share my story with as many people as I can. Which company did this to me? Suffice it to say, I do not exclaim "Yippee!" (or something like that) anymore.

Globalization

In many respects, the Internet has definitely made the business world smaller. In the world of e-business, customers come from any time zone, correspond in any language, and want to pay for your products with various currencies. Making sure transactions flow across your intended boundaries of commerce is important to providing transactional integrity. If you can't support transactions in certain geographies, make sure your systems won't allow such transactions to occur. If you can't accept certain currencies, make sure your site won't take them. If delivery challenges create additional time or expense for shipping, tell your customers in advance. And most importantly, respect and proactively support interfaces to customs and other trade barriers.

Federal Express provides a good example of strong attention being paid to globalization in the world of e-business. A few years back, I had an interesting trip to take. First, I scheduled two weeks of vacation in Australia with my wife and children, and then I was off to England to make a presentation at an international computer users' group conference. I didn't want to bring my business clothes with me to Australia and then on to England. I thought I'd be smart and have my clothes shipped by FedEx to the hotel in Brighton, England.

Great vacation, with a *really* long flight (22 hours) from Sydney to London (via Bangkok), a bus, a train, and a cab ride—and I found myself in Brighton, looking for my business clothes. No clothes. Customs at Heathrow had inspected the FedEx package, saw my clothes (hand-tailored in Hong Kong), and assumed they were going to be imported into England. The British government wanted to collect some $400 duty. Things stalled. The first couple of days I had to make my presentation in casual attire. Finally, Federal Express came through, paid the duty, and my suits arrived at the hotel.

The two things I learned from this story are that (1) sometimes even the most innocuous-seeming transaction can be misconstrued when international rules are applied, and (2) make sure you deal with reputable organizations with high integrity in your global transactions. Federal Express did the right thing for me. They probably could have done a better job in informing me of the potential pitfalls with what I want to do but, in the end, they earned a customer for life.

Globalization and the need for transactional integrity turn out to be difficult issues to resolve. Again, set your own transactional boundaries and only accept and manage the transactions you desire. Oh, and be prepared for anything to happen anywhere at anytime.

Electronic Marketplaces

One of the newest aspects of e-business is the capability to form and grow electronic marketplaces or communities of interest. Some companies, like iVillage and eBay, have built entire business plans around just this capability. In the past, individuals with common interests in scattered geographies had few options for sharing virtual information, and often they waited for monthly or even more infrequent conferences. Or they relied upon telephone or fax contacts with each other.

Today, with electronic marketplaces, the need for transactional integrity is extreme. Trust is necessary for an electronic marketplace to be initially founded, and trust is vital for the marketplace's long-term survival. If a relationship is virtual (that is, without face-to-face contact), each party in the relationship demands trust in the shared information. Without confidence in the information, electronic marketplace participants will quickly defect to other communities, and the original site will fall apart (in a virtual manner, of course).

As shown in Figure 5.3, certain industries lend themselves more powerfully to
e-business electronic marketplaces. If you look to the right top corner of Figure 5.3,
you can see industries with highly digitally based products that have strong individual consumer dialogue. Overall, these industries are excellent candidates for
e-business and specifically for electronic marketplaces. If you are in one of these
industries and you've not yet jumped into e-business, now is the time. However, remember there are many other businesses competing for shares of these electronic
marketplaces. Clearly, one of the major benefits these marketplace constituents
have is their reliance on the quality and integrity of the data.

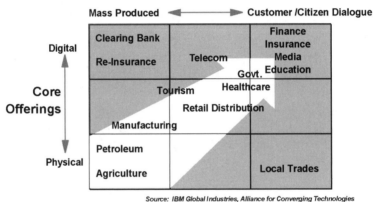

Source: IBM Global Industries, Alliance for Converging Technologies

*Figure 5.3: Certain industries lend themselves to e-business electronic market-
places.*

Customer Self-Service

Stories abound of companies saving millions of dollars by implementing
self-service, customer-service Web sites. Given the opportunity, many customers
will take over their own answer-finding tasks. This reduces or, in some cases, eliminates a company's need for customer-service personnel. I'm not now in a position
to recommend to your business a strategy whereby you might be able to save millions by having a self-serve Web site.

Perhaps you've heard a story about Cisco's $500 million-plus saved each year in
customer-service costs. But keep this situation in perspective. Who are Cisco's customers? Aren't they the people building the Internet?! They're probably pretty 'Net
savvy and are highly technical. As a result, Cisco isn't a good model to compare

with traditional businesses contemplating customer service done on a self-serve Web site. However, if you decide to employ a self-serve strategy, integrity in the data you offer at your self-serve site is essential.

Furthermore, much of the information you offer on your site might not be created or even maintained by your business. As a result, ensuring a high-quality interface between your business and those providing content for your self-serve Web site must be a priority. Remember that customers will be taking their own time and using their own resources to find information, solve a problem, or get answers to questions. If those customers at your site discover that your information or your business partners' information is out of date or inaccurate, you can quickly lose the trust you have with your customers. Transactional integrity on a self-serve Web site is mandatory.

Knowledge Management

Remember the phrase, "garbage in, garbage out?" GIGO! When I first heard this saying in the late '70s, it related to the quality and integrity of the data used to prepare good old, basic RPG or COBOL reports. Back then, we were concerned with things like sort sequence and proper collation in our card decks. The worst possible thing to do was to drop a card deck on its way to the reader. However, in today's Internet-based world, where we have almost everything known to humanity available at a click of a mouse, the integrity of the data used to prepare research or business intelligence potentially affects thousands or millions of decisions.

We've all heard about Internet or e-mail-based hoaxes and how people are all-too-quick to believe them. One of my favorites is the e-mail that instructs you to forward a message to as many people as possible. The message claims Bill Gates, himself, will write you a check for thousands of dollars if the message reaches *lots* of people. Of course, Bill Gates has no interest in the message, and this chain e-mail needlessly takes up billions of megabytes of storage on millions of servers. Trillions of bits are unnecessarily routed and transmitted by the communications infrastructure.

While things like chain e-mail can be categorized as a nuisance, I've seen situations where a lack of transactional integrity caused companies to lose millions of dollars once "GIGO-data" was used in data warehousing or knowledge-management tools. One example in particular relates to a traditional manufacturer who built a Web-based approach to quoting prices to its customers. For the bulk (more than 90 percent) of this manufacturer's items, a single commodity accounted for more than 50 percent of the cost. As a result, fluctuations in the futures markets for this commodity had a direct affect on this manufacturer's pricing (and profitability) schedules. Unfortunately, those developing this quotation system didn't make it Y2K compliant soon enough to mitigate a severe loss of transactional integrity.

Without a full, four-digit date, the futures prices for the commodity sorted in the wrong order, causing the prices for the Year 2000 to sort to the top. For customers, Year 2000 prices became the basis for the "today's pricing" information. The good news is this manufacturer received a record number of orders across its Web site the first day these "in Year 2000 commodity prices" were used in the quotation system. The bad news is that the Year 2000 commodity prices were much lower than the "what-we're-really-supposed-to-use" prices of the day. As a result, before this manufacturer literally unplugged the server running the quotation application, they believe they lost more than a $1million in profits. The quotation system had created binding quotes without human intervention.

In our Internet-connected world of e-business, garbage in, garbage out takes on a renewed significance. Your customers, your suppliers, as well as your internal staff are depending upon you to have integrity in your data warehousing, business-intelligence, and knowledge-management systems. In situations like the one I just described, many customers prevailed at the expense of the company. However, the longer-term ramifications of this information faux pas didn't manifest immediately. This company—as a result of the price quotation debacle—became somewhat of a laughing stock in the industry. It seemed customers didn't believe the company's data even if it was right. It took months to rebuild credibility with their customers even when so many customers had benefited from a lack of transactional integrity.

Channel Conflict Resolution and Channel Expansion

Trust is a weird and fleeting thing. As new business models manifest themselves, change creates stress on the status quo. Without question, the world of e-business is making even the most forward-looking business professionals ponder what's going on with their control of product distribution channels, sales and promotional activities, and geographic expansion procedures. The global reach of the Internet and the ever-expanding role of 'Net-based consolidators, auctioneers, and discounters, means increased stress for more than one product manager attempting to maintain brand quality and channel integrity.

The theme toward transactional integrity in channel conflict resolution—and this conflict is bound to happen—relates to proactive business rule enforcement, detailed record keeping, and exception situation handling. In other words, state clearly your expectations for your channel as you move toward e-business. If rumors run rampant surrounding purported changes in a well-established agent or dealer network, you'd be surprised at how fast these take on a life of their own. Therefore, be proactive, be specific, and build two-way communication.

Next, once the rules are established, make sure you collect high-quality transactional data surrounding your channel-related activities. Collect *all* the data (remember the words of Ross-the-visionary, if you've got the detail, you can recreate anything...), and then put the data through some sort of a filter. Look for exceptions to your rules. Once found, if you trust the data you're reading, you have the ability to take corrective action.

In some cases, corrective action may include cutting off supply to the violating member of your channel. Clearly, the entire notion of channel management strategies is worthy of its own chapter. Nevertheless, the message in this chapter relates to having integrity in the detailed transaction data that you use to monitor and manage exceptions. In my experience, when channel conflict occurs in established environments or when new problems arise as a company looks to establish new channels for their existing products (through Web-based consolidators, auction houses, or discounters), having clear, unambiguous rules makes resolution simple and straightforward. We need more, not less, straightforward e-business. It's complicated enough as it is!

Supply Chain Management

To me, SCM represents the top of the e-business pyramid as it relates to transactional integrity. SCM's capability to lower inventory levels, shrink working capital deployed, and reduce transaction costs (both internal to the business and throughout the supply chain) is directly affected by the quality and integrity of the transaction data flowing among trading partners. One data hiccup somewhere in the supply chain can translate into major delays, huge over-stock situations, and pointless wild goose chasing. The latter factor probably is where most of the intangible costs are lost.

SCM poses significant organizational and cultural upheaval to many businesses. After all, most companies don't even work well internally. SCM also puts total reliance upon fast, streamlined, IT-based transactions. Trust in SCM comes slowly, and only a few SCM implementations come close to delivering the overall potential they promise. Too often, human intervention intercedes to "oversee" transactions. This leads eventually to sloppiness and error-prone transactions negatively affecting the overall SCM implementation. Transactional integrity is the cornerstone of trust in the SCM world. You must have faith and confidence in the data you receive from your SCM partners. Don't underestimate this requirement. If you take it lightly, your partners will eventually suffer the negative consequences. At that point, your business runs the risk of forever alienating itself in the supply-chain network you've worked so hard to join. Even with high-quality data, effective supply-chain management is hard enough. Don't make it harder on yourself.

ACID Testing Revisited

Once again, the need for ACID testing in all of your applications is essential, but the world of e-business brings an entirely new level of negative consequence should inter-company transactions lack integrity. To illustrate this point again, Figure 5.4 takes Figure 5.2 (for the automotive manufacturer) and adds the e-business-related connection points (from Figure 5.1). And that is where transactional integrity comes into play.

Even a cursory look at Figure 5.4 tells shows that the world of e-business is highly interdependent. Successful e-business applications involve many organizations and each needs to be able to rely upon the quality and integrity of data it receives from the others. Once again, I believe it is of vital importance to the average non-IT professional to understand this issue. Figure 5.4 should provide a visual exclamation point on the topic. Every box that is touched represents a business process that is sending or receiving transactional data. Let's make sure they all pass the ACID test.

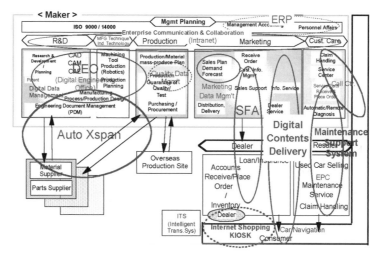

Figure 5.4: Interdependence is apparent in the world of e-business.

Summary

Clearly, e-business is rewriting much of what we thought we knew about business rules. One of these points relates to the level of knowledge the average non-IT (read business) professional needs to have related to IT issues such as transactional integrity. This chapter describes just how vital transactional integrity is related to overall quality in e-business. Furthermore, you've also earned a tiny propeller beanie (okay, I couldn't help myself!) related to ACID testing of database transactions. Once again, A is for atomicity, C is for consistency, I is for isolation, and D is for durability.

The next time you find yourself speaking to your IT staff about database and transactional integrity, ask them if they can define ACID. Then, to make life really interesting, ask them for a concise explanation of atomicity, consistency, isolation and durability—and how they've factored these issues into your e-business IT architecture. Atomicity is the process of keeping transactions small and atomic in nature. Consistency is the notion that all database updates in a single transaction either go into the database together or none of them go. Isolation is keeping the database activity from one transaction from messing in the other's sandbox. Durability means knowing that all the database transactions, in the entire transaction, are all written to permanent storage. This ensures your ability to retrieve and reconcile the entire transaction.

ACID is far too often overlooked in e-business application design. Once you've shown that you are ACID-savvy, I'd be willing to bet that you will have earned a much higher level of respect from the IT types. You'll probably intimidate some of them so much that they won't know what to say. Isn't it kind of nice to have the shoe on the other foot? Anyway, proper attention needs to be paid to transactional integrity in e-business and in all aspects of a professional IT architecture.

By the way, if you see an old-school IT guy named Ross Nelson, tell him thank you. He was a visionary well ahead of his time. Thanks again Ross.

Architecture is the learned game, correct and magnificent, of forms assembled in the light.

—Le Corbusier,
On the need for spaciously separated skyscrapers,
recalled on his death, August 17, 1965

6

The Anatomy of a Web Application

JENNIFER BIGUS

Whenever you talk about e-business, you are talking about putting business applications on the World Wide Web. But what does that mean? What does a Web application look like? How does it differ from a traditional application? This chapter explores the anatomy of a Web application by looking past the outer layer that is visible from a Web browser into the inner workings of the different components that make up the entire application.

Like the human body, a Web application is made up of many pieces or components that work together as a single unit to produce a specific function. Unlike the human body, however, these different pieces do not have to be part of the same physical system. One of the most common architectures of a Web application is the "logical" three-tier model. In other words, the three logically separate pieces that make up the application are the:

- Presentation or user interface.
- Business logic.
- Data storage and retrieval.

Editor's Introduction: Building architecture and the architecture of information technology serve similar purposes. They define a structure that is fulfilled by component materials and functions. Architecture is, at its core, the employment of forms, patterns, and components to achieve a desired functional structure. Those aspects are the same whether it's a building or an e-marketplace. In this chapter, Jennifer Bigus explains the architecture (anatomy) of a Web application. Understanding a Web application at this level is important to making business decisions about e-commerce.

–KR

Each of these tiers may reside on a physically separate computer system, reside on the same system as one of the other tiers, or even be distributed between systems.

Looking deeper into the anatomy of a Web application, you will find that the three tiers themselves are made up of many smaller components. The presentation components may include a Web browser, Java applets, HTML (HyperText Markup Language), a scripting language, or a number of other Web technologies. The business logic componentry may reside on the Web application server and use the services of an HTTP server, a number of application services, and a Java virtual machine. The data storage and retrieval components may include a relational database and triggers or stored procedures that work in conjunction with the database to ensure integrity or do additional manipulation of the data. The remainder of this chapter looks at each of these components in more detail as well as how they all fit together to make up a Web application.

Architecture Overview

A typical Web application consists of three logical tiers. The *presentation* or *client tier* makes requests on behalf of the user and displays the resulting information. The *middle tier* usually serves the Web application and contains much of the business logic. The *data server* provides for persistent data storage and often provides other application services like transaction processing. The high-level architecture of a typical Web application is shown in Figure 6.1.

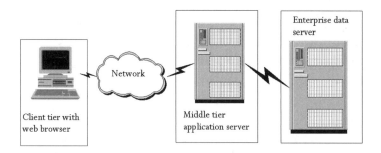

Figure 6.1: High-level Web application architecture consists of three logical tiers.

The Web client is often a thin client, meaning that very little of the application logic is on the client system. At a minimum, the Web client must include a browser that supports HTTP and can display HTML pages. Often the browser supports a scripting language, such as JavaScript, that lets you embed logic in the HTML page to add client-side functionality such as verifying user input or computing a simple math function. The browser may also support Java applets. Java applets allow more control over the user interface and allow the client to connect back to the server like a traditional client/server application. The application server in the middle tier provides the majority of the business logic and acts as the "middleman" between the client and the data server. The application server often provides security services to authenticate a user and grant the user authority to resources on both the Web server and the data server. The application server manages multiple client sessions and can connect to multiple back-end data servers to access enterprise data.

The data server contains the enterprise data for the business application. Because the heart of any business is its data, the data server must be protected from malicious or errant Web applications. But, at the same time, the data must be accessible so that real business can be conducted over the World Wide Web.

The remainder of the Web application architecture is the glue that holds everything together. This includes the physical network that connects the different computer systems as well as the protocols used to communicate over the network.

The Web Client

The Web client differs from the client in a two-tier or client/server application in that the Web client provides little or no application logic. The client's role is to receive input from the user and to present information to the user. The input received is called the *request*, and the results of that request are called the *response*. In the simplest case, the Web client sends an HTTP request to the server and receives an HTML Web page in response. This simple case is illustrated in Figure 6.2.

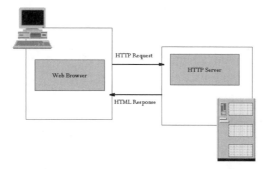

Figure 6.2: With an HTTP request and response, the Web client sends an HTTP request to the server and receives an HTML Web page in response.

There are a number of components involved in even this simple picture. Focusing only on the client, you can see that a Web browser is required. Two of the most popular browsers being used today are Microsoft Internet Explorer and Netscape Navigator. The Web browser is responsible for sending an HTTP request to the server. HTTP is the protocol used to communicate between the Web browser and the Web server. HTTP is a stateless protocol. Having a stateless protocol means that each interaction between the client and the server is independent. In other words, a new connection is created each time a request is made, and no information is carried over from one request to the next.

Part of the Web page request is the universal resource locator (URL) of the desired Web page. A URL can be thought of as the address of the Web page the user wants displayed by the browser. For example, the URL *http://www.as400.ibm.com* indicates to the browser that it should use the HTTP protocol on the file located at *www.as400.ibm.com*.

When the client sends an HTTP request, the server usually responds with an HTML Web page. HTML is a standard markup language used to describe the format of a Web page, including the placement of text and graphics on a page, fonts, colors, headings, tables, forms, and even links to other pages. In a typical scenario, the client would request a Web page from the server. In response, the server would deliver a Web page to the client through the browser. Often this Web page would contain forms to be filled in, buttons to be pressed, or links to other Web pages. Clicking on a button or a link would cause another HTTP request to be sent to the server, along with information related to this request. A simple example of the HTML used to describe a Web page and the Web page that would be displayed is shown in Figure 6.3.

As you can see, a number of HTML tags are used, even in a simple Web page. The parts of the page are defined using the <HEAD> and <BODY> tags. The text within the body of the HTML page is displayed by

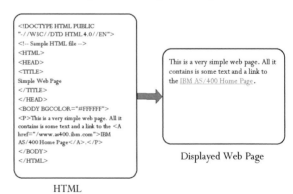

Figure 6.3: With a simple HTML Web page, the client requests a Web page from the server and, in response, the server delivers a Web page to the client through the browser.

the Web browser, and formatted according to the width of the browser window. Within the text, the <A> tag indicates a link to another Web page. The HREF attribute of that tag specifies the URL of the Web page to go to when the user clicks on the link.

One of the advantages of HTML is that it is an industry standard, controlled by the World Wide Web Consortium (W3C) and supported by any Web browser. It is a simple tag language that is fairly easy language for people to learn. Many tools, like IBM's WebSphere Studio, Netscape Composer, or NetObjects Fusion, make Web page development even easier by providing a visual or WYSIWYG editor that lets you compose your Web page visually and then generates the tag language for you. The simplicity of the language has contributed to its widespread adoption and has fueled the growth of the World Wide Web.

Simplicity, however, has its drawbacks. HTML can be used only to provide *static content,* meaning that the content of the Web page cannot change once it is sent to the browser. Even simple validation of user input cannot be done using HTML. In addition, HTML focuses on what the content should look like, not what it means. Providing tags to describe the semantics of the content would allow more useful and powerful search engines to be developed. As a result, searching on the Web would be a lot simpler, less time-consuming, and more fruitful.

Another drawback of HTML is that it is often too restrictive to describe the very complex Web pages that people want to publish on the Web. The various browsers available in the industry have often sought to overcome some of HTML's limitations by providing their own proprietary tags to extend the language. But, because these tags are not standard and supported by all browsers, they often are not used except in an environment where the user can be restricted, as in a corporate or departmental intranet environment, to a single browser.

The need to extend HTML has led to the development of XML (eXtensible Markup Language). Because XML allows you to create new tags, as you need them, XML is more flexible than HTML. These tags can be used to describe both the presentation and the meaning of the document content. But this extensibility also requires that the rules for the new tags be defined in a *document type definition* (DTD) so that other browsers and parsers can properly interpret the new tags. XML is still a very new language and not widely supported. In the future, it is expected to become the markup language of choice for the World Wide Web.

Another way HTML has been extended is through the use of scripting languages like JavaScript. A scripting language lets a Web developer define a sequence of commands that is run on the Web browser. A script can be run whenever the user enters data into a form, clicks on a button or image, or moves from one Web page to another. This gives the Web page developer a great deal of flexibility in the design of the Web page. JavaScript can be used to display different images based on the position of the mouse. Or it can be used to do simple validation of input entered by the user (such as checking for valid numbers in a date field). Math functions are available that allow calculations (such as a running total) to be displayed as the user enters data into an order form. It can even open new browser windows and point to other URLs.

One of the big advantages of a scripting language is that some front-end processing can be done on the client. Without a scripting language, data entered by the user must be sent to the server for validation. If the data is invalid, a new Web page indicating the error must be sent down to the client for correction. Similarly, even simple page formatting changes—such as displaying a pull-down list—must be done by first sending a request up to the server, and then receiving the newly formatted page to be redisplayed in the browser. With a scripting language like JavaScript, this processing can be done locally on the client without having to send anything to or from the server. This can greatly reduce the response time in a Web application.

But all this flexibility comes at a price. There is no industry-standard scripting language. Not all browsers support JavaScript, which was developed by Netscape and is supported only in Netscape Navigator 2 or higher. Microsoft's Internet Explorer 3 or later supports Jscript, which is similar—with a few exceptions—to JavaScript. Accounting for browser differences results in higher Web page-development costs. The pages need to be tested under different browsers and different versions of the same browser to ensure that the page will exhibit the desired behavior in all probable client environments.

Another drawback of JavaScript or any other scripting language is that the scripting commands are embedded in the HTML, resulting in a slightly longer time to download the HTML Web page from the server to the client. Once in the browser, the JavaScript must be interpreted, and the commands acted on by the browser. The Web pages also take longer to design and develop and require a more highly skilled Web developer.

Java applets are another way to make Web pages more dynamic. Java is a programming language developed by Sun Microsystems, and an *applet* is a small computer program written in Java. Unlike most other programming languages, Java does not get translated from its source code format into executable instructions for a particular computer platform. Instead, Java source code gets translated into a platform-independent format called *bytecodes* that are interpreted at execution time. What all this means is that a Java program is portable. In other words, a Java programt can be run on any computer system that supports the Java Virtual Machine (JVM). The JVM is the interpreter and execution environment for Java on any particular platform.

Both Microsoft and Netscape browsers support Java. A special HTML tag within a Web page is used to reference a Java applet that resides on the Web server. A URL is used to locate the code that is downloaded onto the client system. There it is interpreted and run by the Java Virtual Machine within the Web browser.

Because Java is a full-function programming language, it is more powerful than JavaScript or other scripting languages. It provides support for graphical user interface (GUI) development, audio and multimedia capabilities, and networking support, as well as features found in more traditional computer programming languages.

Nevertheless, using Java applets in a Web page has some drawbacks. Most Web designers are not computer programmers and do not know how to program in Java. Often, both a Web designer and a programmer must work together to develop a Web page that contains applets. Another problem is that Java is a quickly evolving language, and the Java support within a particular browser might not match the version of Java used by the programmer who developed the code. This leads programmers to only use the "lowest common denominator" when developing Java applets.

Also, the power of the Java language lends itself to using Java applets for more than the presentation or user-interface portion of an application. This moves farther away from the thin-client model and leads to the business logic being split between the client and the Web application server. If data is being updated within the applet, care must be taken to ensure that the data is kept in sync with the data on the server. Moving the business logic to the client also results in larger applets being downloaded in the browser, and that adversely affects the performance of the application. Web users get frustrated waiting for Web pages that contain applets to download into their browser environment. While Java applets are a powerful tool to be used in a Web application, they should be used mostly for presentation or user interface functions when HTML or scripting languages are inadequate.

The Application Server

The application server contains the business logic and is ultimately responsible for satisfying the client's requests. It interacts both with the client and with the data server. It must understand the requests coming from the client, process the requests, and format the response so that the client can present the results to the user. In processing the request, the application server can use resources available on the application server or on the data server. It is responsible for authenticating the user and accessing data and back-end applications on the data server on behalf of the user. As you can see, the application server must provide a wide range of services as part of a Web application.

With all the tasks the application server (Figure 6.4) must accomplish, it is not surprising that there are a number of components that make up an application server. An application server often contains:

- An HTTP server that receives requests and serves both static and dynamic content to the client.

- Security services that provide user authentication and control access to enterprise resources.

- Web application server software that contains the business logic and performs tasks on behalf of a client.

- Application integration software to connect to other applications that resides outside of the application server.

- Database connectivity services that provide access to object-relational database systems.

The HTTP server is the entry into the Web application. It is responsible for receiving requests from the client, processing the requests, and returning a response. Often the requests are as simple as a request for a static HTML page that resides on the server and is delivered to the client as the response to the request. In some cases, the HTTP server must authenticate the user before processing can continue. In some e-business environments, the HTTP server must be a secure server (HTTPS) and provide data encryption services as well.

Most e-business applications require more than page serving and security services. Many require business logic to be invoked in order to process the client's request. In the early days of the Web, this processing was done using the Common Gateway Interface (CGI). CGI is a way for a Web browser and a CGI program running on a server to communicate. The CGI program is referenced in the HTML file using a URL. When the server receives the request, the program is run, and the results are sent back to the browser through the server. Although this technology was widely used, the CGI programs often were not portable between server systems, and the performance was poor because a new process was started on the server each time a CGI program was invoked.

The next generation of Web application servers, such as IBM's WebSphere Application Server, provides a portable, Java-based solution for deploying business applications in a Web environment. The main technologies used in a Web application server are Java servlets, JavaServer Pages, and Enterprise JavaBeans.

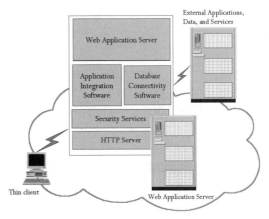

Figure 6.4: The application server must accomplish many tasks.

Servlets are server-side programs written in Java that run within a Web application server environment. Unlike traditional, stand-alone programs, servlets have no user interface and must depend on an HTTP server to pass information to and from the user. They also differ from CGI programs in that they stay "alive" on the server between client requests. A servlet can be started when the application server starts and will remain active until the application server is shut down.

A servlet is passed the HTTP request from the user, processes the request, and creates the HTML that is sent back to the browser and presented to the user. When processing the request, the servlet can access resources on the application server, as well as connect to other servers and services. A typical servlet-based Web application is shown in Figure 6.5.

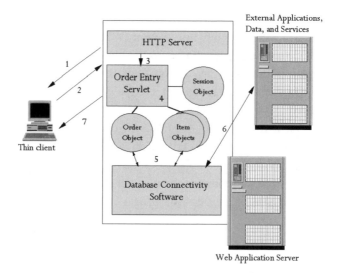

Figure 6.5: In a servlet-based order entry application, the servlet can access resources on the application server as well as connect to other servers and services.

The basic flow of the order-entry application is as follows:

1. An HTML order form is presented to the user by the Web browser.

2. The user enters the order data and submits the form, causing an HTTP servlet request to be sent to the application server.

3. The servlet business logic is invoked.

4. The servlet uses objects to represent the client session, the order, items within the order, and any other business objects needed in the application.

5. The business objects are stored using database connectivity software such as JDBC.

6. The database connectivity software may be connected to a remote data server.

7. After the order processing is complete, the results of the order processing are relayed, using HTML generated by the servlet, to the user.

JavaServer Pages (JSP) are another way to create dynamic Web content while separating the business logic from the presentation logic. A JSP looks very much like an HTML Web page that includes some Java code. A JSP file can contain the same tags that an HTML file can contain, plus a few new tags that deal with the Java code. The Java code is embedded in the JSP much like JavaScript can be embedded in an HTML file. The difference is that the Java code runs on the server while the JavaScript code runs on the client browser. A typical JSP-based Web application is shown in Figure 6.6.

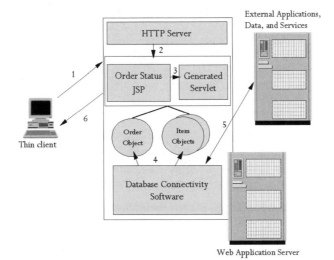

Figure 6.6: A JSP-based order status application looks very much like an HTML one.

The basic flow of the order-status application is as follows:

1. The Web browser sends a request for a JSP file.

2. The HTTP server sends the request to the Web application server.

3. The Web application server generates Java source code for a servlet that implements the JSP. This code is compiled and executed.

4. The servlet may use Java objects that are populated from database tables.

5. The database tables may exist on a remote data server.

6. The servlet returns the order status in the form of HTML, which is sent to the user and displayed by the Web browser.

Another technology available on many application servers is Enterprise JavaBeans or EJBs. EJBs are components or building blocks that can be used and reused by other Java applications or servlets. An Enterprise Bean can represent either a business entity (customer, address, order, item) or a business process (place an order, add a customer, pay a bill). Entities Beans are long-lived (persistent) objects that often represent rows in a relational database. Session Beans are short-lived (transient) objects that act on behalf of a client and implement the business process.

Enterprise JavaBeans execute on an application server inside what is called a *container*. The container isolates the EJB components from the underlying services such as database access, security, and transaction support. This frees the programmer who writes the business logic from having to worry about the "plumbing" and allows the programmer to concentrate on solving the business problem at hand.

Enterprise JavaBeans can be combined with servlet or JSP technology to provide e-business solutions. For example, an entity Bean could be developed that represented an order. This order-entity Bean could be used by both the order-entry servlet and the order-status JSP described previously.

Connecting to the Enterprise

Another key piece in any Web application is integration with the enterprise. In other words, accessing data and other systems within the enterprise so that the Web application is part of the overall work flow in a corporation. For example, an order-entry application could be available to customers on the Web. In addition to providing the Web interface, the application might need to access a customer database, look up item inventory, tie into an existing pricing system, and create an invoice that is then processed by a fulfillment system. Because there are many different systems and data stores that a Web application might need to access, a number of technologies might be needed to integrate the Web application with the rest of the enterprise.

One of the primary requirements of any business application is access to enterprise data. Because the Web application is written in Java, the main facility for database access is Java Database Connectivity (JDBC). JDBC provides a standard interface for database connectivity from within a Java application. Using JDBC, data can be accessed, updated, created, and deleted in a relational database. In addition, other data-processing programs called *stored procedures* can be executed using a standard interface. These stored procedures can be existing application code written in traditional data-processing languages such as C, COBOL, and RPG. Using JDBC and stored procedures are one way to access existing data and leverage tried-and-true business application logic. In addition, JDBC can be used to access data and stored procedures on remote systems as well as on the system where the business application resides.

Another way to connect to existing business application systems is through the use of messaging services that provide facilities to send messages to other systems to request services and receive messages. IBM's MQSeries is an example of a messaging service that provides reliable transfer of information between two applications, regardless of the type of system on which each application is running.

Connectors are another way to link Web applications to existing application software. Connectors are Java libraries that provide support access to a variety of data and application services. For example, the AS/400 Toolbox for Java provides connectors to AS/400 data and resources such as DB2/400, data queues, AS/400 commands, existing application programs, and other AS/400 system objects. The e-business connectors from IBM provide connectors for CICS, Encina, DB2 and other relational databases, IMS, Domino, and MQSeries. Connectors also can enable Web access to industry applications from vendors such as SAP, PeopleSoft, and Baan.

In addition, connectors can be used to integrate with services outside the enterprise to provide mail, newsgroup services, or even a payment server for e-commerce. Using these and other connectors can reduce the amount of time it takes to develop a Web application by reusing existing business logic. Reusing the existing application logic has the added benefit of reliability because the logic is already up and running in the traditional business environment.

System Management

It should be clear by now that a Web application and all its components can be a system-management nightmare. Fortunately, help is available. A Web application server such as the WebSphere Application Server has facilities to manage the resources under its control. Log files are available for errors and events that occur while the Web application server is running. Monitors can be run to monitor active sessions, database connectivity, exceptions, servlets that are loaded, and resources that are being used.

In addition to the services provided by the Web application server itself, services and tools are available to manage Web applications and all their components as a single entity. Within an enterprise, there are many resources to be managed. The network must be managed to maintain and monitor the underlying hardware such as routers and servers. The individual systems and their connections must also be managed. The HTTP servers, database services, mail, and application servers must all be configured, administered, and monitored. And, finally, the e-business applications themselves must be maintained and monitored.

System management services, such as those provided by Tivoli, will help you manage all of the technology components that comprise an e-business application. And, because these components may span multiple systems—especially when providing business-to-business Web applications—collaborative management systems are available to manage distributed data and applications. These services include deploying applications across a network, determining network and system problems that affect the availability of the application, and ensuring the security of the enterprise assets involved with the e-business application.

Summary

Using Web technologies like HTML, JavaScript, and thin clients, you can present your customers with information about your business and about your products. Because the Web interface is tied into your back-end, up-to-date information is always readily available. You can use server-side technologies, such as servlets, messaging services, and connectors, to access your enterprise data and processing systems. Your Web applications will fit your overall business workflow, providing an integrated business solution.

With technologies such as the WebSphere Application Server and Java, you can reduce the amount of time it takes to develop an e-business application. The component architecture allows the business logic to be separated from the presentation logic. The business logic can be developed as reusable components, which shortens the time it takes to develop an application. The applications can be deployed on a wide range of systems that range from a Netfinity server, to an AS/400 system, or a mainframe system. You can leverage and extend your existing applications and data through the use of messaging services and connectors, retaining their reliability, scalability, and security.

What does all this technology do for you? All the components that make up a Web application work together for one purpose. That purpose is to securely connect business applications to customers over the Web. The Web can be used to extend your internal business processes to your customers, your suppliers, and your business partners. You can make your customers happy by giving them what they want, when they want it. Customers can access your business and buy your products 24/7 over the Internet. This self-service model not only increases customer satisfaction, but also reduces costs. You also can make sure you have product to sell by providing Web-based procurement systems and other supply-chain management systems that can be accessed by your suppliers and distributors. You can use the Web to do business, keep business, and win new business, which is what e-business is all about.

The essence of workflow is the provision of electronic support for business processes previously accomplished by means of laborious manual procedures.

—Jeff Papows
Enterprise.com, Perseus Press (1998)

7

Lotus Domino and e-business

JELAN HEIDELBERG

Do you have a job that's hard to define? Do you have a fancy title with responsibilities that are broad and somewhat vague? Do you get to the end of a long, productive workday and wonder what you did and what you produced? When you're trying to tell someone what you do for a living, do you eventually shrug your shoulders and say, "whatever needs to be done?" If you're nodding your head and saying, "yes, that sounds just like my life," then you'll love Domino. It's just like you!

Since their creation, Lotus Notes and Domino have "suffered" from the label that they defy definition. But, in this discussion of Lotus Domino and e-business, I'd like to start from the premise that being difficult to define and categorize is exactly what makes Domino unique and powerful as an e-business tool. The most important, most creative, most productive work that we, as knowledge workers, perform is non-repetitive and highly

Editor's Introduction: Every successful business has one or more people who defy pigeonholing. These people have broad skills and capabilities that let them successfully tackle a wide range of tasks. They spend some parts of their business days doing things that don't appear on the job description but that are essential to the functioning of the organization. Domino and workflow are a little like that. It is a collection of functionality that helps people work together more productively. Like the folks described above, any brief description of what it does will leave something out. Jelan Heidelberg does an excellent job of explaining how to use Domino to improve your business. She links somewhat abstract concepts like groupware and messaging to real business improvements that your business can achieve.

–KR

unstructured. That's where Domino fits. Domino is an environment that makes it easier for us to productively perform unstructured work using information and knowledge that are hard to define. That sounds like a definition, doesn't it? But it's pretty broad— just like your job responsibilities.

Before refining that broad definition, I'd like to start with a bare-bones one, just to get the terminology straight. Lotus Notes is client software that runs on your desktop (your PC). Lotus Domino is software that runs on a variety of servers (NT, UNIX, AS/400, and others). It provides services for users who have Notes client software. It also provides services, such as Web browsers, e-mail software, and newsgroup readers, for other client software. What these services are and how organizations use them is the crux of this discussion.

A Brief History of Computing, and I Do Mean Brief

Often, when you're defining something, it helps to put it in a historical context. In the history of computing—at least the history I've lived through in the last 20-plus years—Lotus Notes and Domino gained popularity in about the fifth phase.

First, we had automation and batch processing of core business (or "back office") applications such as order processing, accounts receivable, accounts payable, and payroll. Data entry clerks sat at keypunch machines all day. The computers churned all night and spit out massive reports about the state of the business.

Next, batch processing was enhanced with online, interactive applications that gave users with "dumb terminals" direct access to up-to-the minute information. The immediate capability to see and change data interactively made profound changes in the way business was conducted.

Next, computing moved to the front office with the arrival of personal computers and productivity enhancing software such as word processors, spreadsheets, and personal database programs. All of these tools helped the knowledge workers who were not directly involved with the day-to-day core business transactions of the organization. Following closely on the heels of these front-office tools were local area networks (LANs). They provided a way to store and share the results of these new front-office productivity tools. But the basic capabilities of these early LANs were limited to sharing electronic filing cabinets and easy access to shared printers.

LANs didn't really provide a dramatic change in the way knowledge workers did their jobs and worked together.

Enter Lotus Notes and Domino. Lotus Development Corporation first made its name with a killer application for the front office called Lotus 123. It was the first industrial-strength spreadsheet. But Lotus had a vision that was bigger than a single killer app. They had a vision of a whole new category that became known as *groupware*, which was embodied first in Lotus Notes and later in Domino.

Groupware goes way beyond the simple physical sharing that LAN software facilitates. As its name implies, groupware is a software environment that makes it easier for groups of people—even when they're geographically dispersed—to work together efficiently and effectively. It provides knowledge workers with tools they can use directly, with no assistance from their IT department. And groupware provides programmers with tools to build the kind of applications that knowledge workers use.

The Foundations of Groupware

Groupware is a category or an environment; it's not a software application. I emphasize this because I want you to resist the temptation to pigeonhole Domino based on the examples in this chapter. Think about your job again. Do you have the problem that people will latch onto an example you give and assume that's all you do? I certainly have that problem. If I use this chapter as an example of what I do, someone will say, "Oh, you're a technical writer." Or if I talk about developing marketing presentations, I'll hear, "Oh, you're a speech writer." Technical writer and speechwriter are handles people can grab onto and categorize. Being a "technical marketing consultant" is just too vague and hard to define.

Domino and groupware suffer from the same identity crisis. People confuse what groupware is with the specific things you can do with groupware. Yes, you can build (or buy) many wonderful applications—such as human resources, or customer service, or IS9000 tracking—on top of a groupware foundation. Actually, thousands of applications are available that are built on the Domino environment. But groupware also includes important capabilities—such as e-mail, calendaring and scheduling, and workflow—that are broader than a single application and that are often incorporated into applications. So, just keep thinking about Domino in terms of your hard-to-define job: flexible, versatile, able to do many things.

To make sense of groupware as a foundation, think about the basic tools that you need to do your job. First, you need a good way to organize, store, and retrieve information—lots of information. Most of the information is unstructured and most of it originates as electronic data (spreadsheets, word-processing documents, e-mails, Web pages, etc.). Rather than printing this information and figuring out a way to file it, wouldn't it be nice to store it on your PC or a server (or both) and to be able to categorize it in multiple ways?

A Unique Database Architecture: Handling this wealth of information we deal with in our unstructured jobs is one of the foundations of Domino. Domino provides "related database" architecture (instead of a relational database). Domino databases are document-based databases instead of records-based databases.

This document approach to organizing electronic information makes perfect sense for the way we work. Think of those reports you've read, presentations you've built or reviewed, and letters you've sent or received. They're very different from customer master records or inventory balances that you store in relational databases. In a Domino database, you can combine structured data (traditional rows and columns) with unstructured data. For example, in a customer service database (built in Domino), you might have structured data (a name, address, and phone number) and unstructured information (a map to the customer location, a copy of the latest bid proposal to the customers, and electronic copies of faxes from the customer). Actually, a Domino document often more closely resembles a file folder that you have on your desk rather than a single document. And that versatility in organizing information is a key to Domino's strength and power.

By the way, you might have noticed by now that I'm using groupware and Domino interchangeably. With Notes and Domino, Lotus basically invented the groupware category. Other companies provide pieces of the groupware puzzle, but it's the integrated groupware solution that makes Domino so unique and successful.

World-Class Messaging: Domino's first cornerstone is its capability to organize and manage the diverse kinds of information you deal with every day. Its second cornerstone is the capability to help us exchange information and communicate better. In Domino terms, that's called a *messaging infrastructure*. Certainly, world-class e-mail capability is a given with Domino. But that e-mail capability is the visible evidence of the built-in capability to send anything to anyone. Sure, I can use e-mail to send you a copy of this chapter, an audio clip of a press event, or a picture of my kids. That's a simple definition of "sending anything." But with Domino, you can easily take advantage of its messaging infrastructure for applications. An application can send e-mail acknowledging receipt of orders or notifying you that a form is awaiting approval. An application can receive and process e-mail by perhaps scanning for key words and routing it to the correct employee or generating an automatic response. A Domino application can notify another application of an event or a required action.

This messaging capability seems so obvious because it's so fundamental to the way we work. We need to be able to share and exchange information easily in a variety of ways. Yet, Domino is really the only environment that has gotten this messaging capability fundamentally right—by making it fundamental. Messaging isn't a goal—an end application—any more than a phone system is a goal. A good messaging foundation is an essential tool for working and for building applications for the future.

Integrated Application Development: Cornerstone one is a unique, related database architecture. Cornerstone two is a world-class messaging infrastructure. Did you notice that the term "application" appears frequently in the description of both those cornerstones? Which leads us to cornerstone three: a built-in, integrated, easy-to-use application development environment.

Domino comes with ready-to-use capabilities right out of the box. Most people usually start with e-mail and calendaring/scheduling. Then they move to applications and get even more excited about Domino. Whether you're an IT person or a line-of-business person, you can probably think of applications that never quite seem to make it to the top of the "to build" list. Often, it's not for lack of desire or justification. It's because the application is just too hard to do with the tools you have today. That tough-to-crack application is hard to define and too unstructured. It's more "front-office" oriented without well-defined processes and procedures. Sounds like the perfect application for Domino, doesn't it?

The Domino family includes an easy-to-use, visual (point-and-click) application development tool called Domino Designer. Programmers and semi-technical, non-programmers can use it to design Domino databases and the logic that goes with them. With Designer, you can build electronic forms for creating and updating Domino documents (complete with edit rules). You can easily create views to sort and select your documents in different ways. And you can create programs (called agents) to perform a variety of tasks, such as generating e-mail reminders, updating pricing information, or archiving old documents from a database. Designer also includes templates of commonly used database examples so you don't have to build your Domino application from scratch. Customers and independent software vendors (ISVs) have used Domino designer to build thousands of applications.

The structure is now almost complete. However, unless you are building a teepee or a very unusual building, one more cornerstone is needed for our foundation. The fourth Domino cornerstone is a fundamental characteristic called versatility or adaptability. And that brings us to Domino and e-business.

Domino: Built for e-business

Actually, that subheading is a lie. Domino wasn't built for e-business. In fact, e-business wasn't even a glimmer in someone's eye when Lotus Notes and Domino were invented. But Domino's architectural foundations—those cornerstones—provide the adaptability and flexibility that Domino needs to morph as the IT landscape changes. From the beginning, customers have used Notes and Domino in ways that its designers never imagined. Similarly, the Lotus developers who work on enhancing Domino have been able to easily extend its solid architecture into new areas, including e-business and the Web.

Domino (the server part of Notes and Domino) actually got a name of its own because of the Web. Originally, the client software and the server software had the same name: Lotus Notes. But as the strategists at Lotus watched the Web gain popularity, they realized they had already built an architecture that was well suited for the world of e-business. They made their server and its capabilities accessible to users with Web browsers and gave the server its own name (Lotus Domino).

So where does Domino fit in the world of e-business? The truly passionate proponents of Lotus Domino (and there are many) might tell you that its role in e-business is pervasive. It fits everywhere. And there are organizations whose e-business implementations are testimony to Domino's strength and flexibility as an e-business infrastructure. But to say that Domino is a complete e-business answer isn't the norm or the conventional wisdom. A better answer is that Domino isn't the core of e-business but rather Domino is (or can be) everything surrounding the core.

The Core Can't Exist in a Vacuum

The core of almost any business is to process orders. Whether you're selling to consumers or to other businesses or whether you're selling services or physical products, you process orders. The fundamental transaction of almost any business is booking the order, delivering the product or service, and updating appropriate accounting records. Other transactions—such as forecasting, purchasing, resource planning, and scheduling—ripple out. All of these transactions make up your "line-of-business" applications that are often called Enterprise Resource Planning (ERP). The ripple-out transactions vary by industry, of course, but we all can relate to the fundamental order processing that makes up the core of a business.

Every businessperson knows that these core transactions don't just happen. Orders don't materialize out of thin air. Surrounding an order is a wealth of information and communications. Customers, distributors, and sales people need details about the product or service. They need updates about prices, promotions, and availability.

Customer service, before and after the sale, is essential to customer retention. Think about your own organization and all the communications and information—the knowledge—that goes into getting that order and keeping that customer happy. That's where Domino comes in. Domino isn't the tool you use to process the order. Relational databases and online transaction processing environments do order processing very well. Domino is the tool and the environment for all that other stuff that surrounds the order and is equally essential to your business.

Without e-business, front-office people, who are knowledge workers, do all that other stuff. They use tools such as Notes and Domino and applications built on Domino. Sales force automation that provides "road warriors" with up-to-date product and order information is one example of a front-office application. Another example is when customer service disseminates tips, techniques, and frequently asked questions, follows up on special requests, and tracks problems.

With e-business, you change how you do things and who does them. Whole functions or parts of functions move to the Web, and it's not just the core transactions of a business but "all that other stuff" that surrounds the core transactions. If you want to provide customer self-service on the Web, for example, then your Web site needs the same information and capabilities that your customer service representatives and sales people have today.

Building, Organizing, and Managing "Stuff"

Look at several of your favorite Web sites. Click on the links and surf through the sites. What you see is probably lots of great "stuff" (information) and very little hard-core data. In other words, the majority of any typical Web site is unstructured information. A Web site is a collection of Web pages. Each Web page is a document. The document is a collection of mostly unstructured information. You'll see text in different colors and fonts, graphics, animation, and even audio clips. And documents on a Web site are linked, letting you move from one to another with a click of your mouse.

Now think about what you've learned about a Domino database. It's a collection of documents. Each document is a collection of information that is structured and unstructured. The parallels are pretty obvious. A Domino database lends itself very naturally to becoming a Web site. Within the Domino database architecture you have all the tools you need to manage the documents on a Web site.

First and foremost, Domino provides *HTML conversion*. When you want to make a database available to Web browsers, Domino automatically creates the HTML for you. (Note that HTML is the markup language that browsers understand for paragraphs, headings, links, etc.). Your subject-matter experts can create Web content directly instead of having to send everything through technical Web people. Of course, you'll want professional Web designers to develop a graphic look and feel for your Web site and a template. But your own users can create the content—the tips and techniques, frequently asked questions, product details, and so on—within your Web site.

Sorting and Selecting: Managing information (documents) in different ways is easy with Domino. You can create views of the documents in your Domino Web database so that a Web visitor can view a collection of information by date, by category, by a specific subset, or by any criteria you specify that make sense for the information.

The capability to link from one document to another is built in to Domino. Your subject-matter experts who create Web content don't need to be Web wizards in order to build links between documents on your Web site.

Search Capability: The capability to search, so important on any Web site, is also built into Domino.

Security: Security is a fundamental part of Domino. You can easily control who can change documents on your Web site and even restrict who can view them. This gives you the choice to easily make parts of your Web site an extranet that is available only to authorized visitors with a user ID and password.

You can use Domino's workflow capability to institute an approval process for any new Web content. New documents in your Domino Web database must go through this process before they become part of a view that is seen externally on the Web.

And don't forget the messaging infrastructure that works hand-in-hand with the Domino database architecture. It provides the e-mail integration that any good Web site needs to get visitor feedback and to be responsive to current and potential customers.

The preceding list of features could be expanded, but you get the idea. The capabilities that make Domino such a complete groupware solution—supporting the unstructured jobs of knowledge workers—lend themselves naturally to moving "all that stuff" to the Web. Is Domino the whole answer for the Web? No. Remember the brief history of computing? Domino fits in the segments of your Web site that mirror the work done by front-office people.

The Tip of the Iceberg

By now, most business people agree that we're in the early stages of an e-business revolution. Many aspects of the way we conduct business are changing rapidly and dramatically. Most would also agree that we're nowhere near the final iteration of e-business. We're in a transition phase with much more change to come before things settle into anything resembling normalcy.

Domino has already proven its adaptability and flexibility to accommodate many different uses and applications within organizations and on the Web. But perhaps Domino's greatest strength in the face of today's changing business landscape is its capability to support groups of people as they invent new ways to work together. That's the secret of its leadership as a groupware environment. And now, we're seeing groupware reinvented as e-collaboration, with Domino in the forefront as the preferred environment.

While e-collaboration includes formal applications—notably Customer Relationship Management and Supply Chain Management—some of the ISV solutions for CRM and SCM are built on a Domino foundation. But e-collaboration also includes ad hoc, unstructured communities of people coming together for short projects or more permanent efforts. And by now you know that "unstructured" and "ad hoc" are terms that naturally lead to Domino.

As you build your Web site, these communities are already happening. Your knowledge experts are creating tips and techniques to put on your Web site. Visitors to your Web site are providing feedback about other information they'd like to see or even tips that you can post. Directly or indirectly, this is collaboration. Gradually, organizations will invent ways to make this collaboration more direct, more powerful, and more beneficial to both sides. With its track record for versatility, Domino is a great tool to enable whatever form e-collaboration takes.

Time for a Definition?

If you've reached this point and you think you can define Domino in a sentence, I've probably failed. If you think, "it's kind of hard to define … just like my job," I've succeeded. And why is your job hard to define? Because it's flexible, it changes depending on the current needs and demands of your boss, your coworkers, and your customers. It's unstructured, but vital to your organization. Just like Domino.

Is Domino the best tool for doing transactions on your Web site? Probably not. Is it the best tool for "all the other stuff" that is equally important for a good Web site? Yes. Domino's mission in life is to help you organize and manage and retrieve the "unorganizable" in your office and on the Web. And just as Lotus Notes and Domino invented the category of groupware a few years ago, they're inventing the category of e-collaboration today. As communities of people across organizations work to reinvent ways of doing business, Domino will be there providing the tools and the environment they need.

The particular need which all money, even fiat money which we now use, serves is to facilitate exchange. People accept money, even if it is not backed by a single grain of precious metal, because they know other people will accept it in exchange for goods and services.

—Robert Batemarc
Central Banks, Gold, and the Decline of the Dollar,
The Freeman, November 1995—Vol. 45, No. 11

8

Making Payments over the Web

KEITH RUTLEDGE

Making payments over the Web is an essential part of e-commerce. This chapter explains what a Web payment mechanism is and why Web payment mechanisms hold important promise for e-commerce and e-business. This chapter also describes two technologies that address current market requirements for electronic payments. First, *micropayment technology* provides a practical mechanism for making very small (pennies-to-dollars) payments. Second, *electronic payment technology* is built on *secure electronic transaction* (SET).

Some people would argue that there is already a widespread Web-payment mechanism in use: credit cards. A credit card, while useful on the Web, actually has the same relationship to the Web as cash. It is a proxy representation of transferable value that can exist in electronic form.

> **Editor's Introduction:** Every marketplace needs payment mechanisms. Societies of industrial specialization (the kind we have today) are not possible without reliable payment mechanisms using trustable mediums of exchange. The core function of money is to act as a repository of value that can be exchanged for goods and services. By storing the value in an exchangeable form, I can labor as a mason to create and store value (by saving money) and enjoy the results of a baker's labor. Likewise, the baker stores the value created by selling a loaf of bread and uses it to buy bricks. The Internet, because it is a totally new marketplace, will give rise to new mediums of exchange. This is inevitable and desirable. In this chapter, I explain how and why.
>
> –KR

Is It Safe?

Have you ever heard someone say, "You're crazy to give your credit-card number. I'd never give anyone my credit-card number over the Web!" In any discussion of buying over the Web, someone will make the point that it's not secure and that "they" can get your credit-card number and do whatever "they" want with it. Of course, these are the very same people who will hand their credit card to a waiter they've never seen before and wait patiently while the waiter takes the card to a back room to authorize payment for the meal.

Now, these folks are not simply technophobes who want society to return to the days of barter systems. They're just nervous about security and afraid that they will get ripped off in cyberspace. You can bet that paper money faced some of the same objections when it first appeared as a mechanism for exchanging value. And, just as with the Internet, some of the objections were justified. The U.S. Treasury currently is in the midst of a multi-year process of redoing most American paper currency to make counterfeiting more difficult. But a small risk of getting a counterfeit bill doesn't keep us from using money. We take reasonable precautions and go about our business. That's the subject of this chapter: reasonable precautions.

Understand that e-commerce payment mechanisms are only the latest step in a long series of payment mechanisms that have functioned as proxies for the underlying value of goods and services. Without these proxy mechanisms, modern life wouldn't be practical. Do you want to have to carry a bag of gold to the grocery store? It's much easier to write a check, and your check is a proxy for the value that you're willing to give the grocery store in return for the goods that you want to acquire.

Carrying Gold Nuggets Is Not Convenient

Do you want to carry a pile of cash when you travel? Credit cards offer a safer and more convenient alternative to paying all travel expenses in cash. Avoiding the risks of carrying large amounts of cash when traveling gave rise to a very common money proxy called traveler's checks. Traveler's checks can be replaced if lost or stolen. Credit cards can be disabled if lost or stolen.

As society has grown and developed capabilities such as printing, central banking, plastic, and electronic communications, value proxies such as paper money, checks, and credit cards soon followed. Internet payments are inevitable just as paper money was inevitable. Internet money will have its own set of advantages and disadvantages just like all other forms of money. Internet payment technologies have to satisfy the following criteria before they are usable for commerce.

- First, the technology must support verification of identity. (Are you who you say you are?).

- Second, the technology must provide confidentiality.

- Third, the mechanism must provide assurance to both parties that the transaction can be completed.

Buying involves commitment and any e-commerce mechanism must explicitly record that commitment.

Micropayment Technology

Micropayment technology is intended for use where consumers are making very small purchases. Examples include pay-by-usage software, music that is paid for as it is heard (just like old-fashioned jukeboxes), comic strips sold by the strip, and newspapers by the article. The very size of the purchases means that it is not economically viable to use existing payment mechanisms like credit cards or debit cards. The cost of processing a 1-cent credit card transaction exceeds by a considerable amount the transaction itself. Micropayment uses a "scrip" approach. One definition of scrip is "paper money issued for temporary use." In this case, the money is not paper, but instead is an electronic representation of the money for temporary use.

It works like this. You get a wallet (it may go by some other name) and fill the wallet with scrip from a broker. Then you spend that scrip on goods or services at a store (Web site) that takes the scrip. The Web site runs some server-side programs to validate your scrip, verify the prices, and complete the transaction. This is very similar, conceptually, to acquiring a Visa card, finding a store that takes Visa, and purchasing an item with Visa. The checkout clerk will validate your card, verify the prices by scanning the item bar code, and complete the transaction. The actual money changes hands behind the scenes.

On the Web, the wallet is analogous to a prepaid credit card (which isn't really a *credit* card at all). The wallet is client-side software that works with a Web browser to handle transactions on behalf of the user. The wallet can automatically approve a purchase or it can request approval for each transaction. Initially, you might think that you want to approve all purchases. But, in many of the intended uses of this system, you will not want to approve all purchases. One example could be network gaming, where you pay by time intervals. When your current interval expires, you might want the wallet to automatically pay for another round rather than stop your game play and get your authorization.

The scrip from the broker represents an account that a customer has established with a vendor of goods or services. Vendors have, at any given time, open accounts or outstanding scrip with their customers. When a customer makes a purchase, the cost of the purchase is deducted from the current value of the scrip balance and new scrip is returned to the customer as change. The customer can always get the unused portion of scrip back and close the account.

Scrip Is Not a New Concept

This might seem like a new payment model when described this way, but it isn't. Many examples of this model exist today. If you use a prepaid phone card, you're using essentially this payment model. You purchase a phone card with "real" currency and gain redeemable scrip in the form of telephone long-distance minutes. Airline frequent flier miles are a form of scrip as well. You "pay" for the scrip with your travels and then use the scrip to purchase plane tickets. Casino chips are a form of scrip that you convert, if you have my luck at such places, into a very few minutes of recreational wagering. If you have any chips left, you can "cash them out" and convert them into currency. And, of course, scrip has long been used as a military-occupation currency.

In this system, brokers function as trusted intermediaries much as credit-card companies and banks do. The broker server is server-side software that converts "real money" into scrip and issues scrip.

The vendor server completes the picture. The vendor server is actually server-side software that cooperates with a content provider's Web server to validate purchase requests and to complete the transaction. The vendor server takes the place of the checkout clerk and performs the price verification (analogous to ringing up an item) and completes the transaction by accepting the scrip in return for goods or services.

Secure Electronic Transaction Technology

For handling non-micro payments over the Web, you'll want to look at products that use secure electronic transaction technology. The SET protocol is built on the idea that to engage in a transaction with another party, you must be able to positively identify that party. Generally, SET payment involves four components, such as a:

- Wallet.
- Registry where certification of identity can be maintained.
- Payment gateway that bridges from the Internet to financial institutions.
- Payment server that bridges from the Internet to the merchant.

One key difference in this approach and the approach to micropayment technology is that generally the consumer explicitly authorizes every transaction. With micropayments, consumers may opt to not authorize every payment (remember the gaming example).

Here's how SET works. A wallet is launched when a consumer initiates a transaction through a Web browser. The wallet is client-side software that is a "helper" application or plug-in to a browser. The wallet sends messages to the merchant's payment server containing order information, digital certificate information from the registry, and payment-card information. A wallet can contain multiple payment types (or cards).

The payment server uses the order information to process the order and passes the certificate and payment-card information unopened to the consumer's bank (via the payment gateway) for credit approval. This way, the merchant never sees the consumer's credit-card information and the consumer's security and privacy are protected. The bank verifies the identity, authorizes the transaction, and sends approval back to the merchant. This is similar to a point-of-sale credit-card authorization today, but it is actually more secure. No one at the merchant ever sees the consumer payment information. After receiving approval (approval is really a commitment to transfer funds in return for the delivery of the product), the merchant completes the transaction.

You can get more information on how IBM's AS/400e server implements SET technology (using the IBM Payment Server) at *http://www.as400.ibm.com/ ebusiness/*. IBM's main e-business site is at *http://www.ibm.com/ebusiness/*. Information on wallet technology is available at the IBM e-business site.

Both SET and micropayment technology can use Secure Sockets Layer (SSL) encryption to open a private channel between the consumer and the merchant or service provider. Both methods provide for authorization of payment and verification of willingness (a.k.a. commitment) to pay. And, both methods provide an appropriate level of verification of identity.

Each method is aimed at a different market segment. The scrip method can be used to obtain a specific amount of spendable currency (such as chips in a casino) ahead of time. SET technology is aimed at larger purchases that occur among merchants. The method that your company uses will depend on the goods and services you offer across the Web and the price tag of those goods and services.

Internet payment methods are inevitable. If you provide goods and services to consumers, then you must find a way to accept payments over the Web or lose the customers. Micropayment technology and SET are market-ready Internet payment technologies usable now in your e-business.

Language is a process of free creation; its laws and principles are fixed, but the manner in which the principles of generation are used is free and infinitely varied. Even the interpretation and use of words involves a process of free creation.

—Noam Chomsky
"Language and Freedom"
Lecture at Loyola University, Chicago (January 1970)
Published in *For Reasons of State* (1973)

9

Java Technology

KEITH RUTLEDGE

There is no substitute for understanding technology. Even folks in the computer business sometimes wish for a substitute, but there simply is no substitute for an understanding of how something works. That is especially important when your career or your company's future depends on a technology.

The benefit of understanding technology is that you can make informed and reasoned decisions about the use of that technology. Combine a fundamental understanding of the technology with an understanding of the business environment and the goal to be achieved and you're prepared to make the best decision possible. If you don't understand the technology under analysis, then you have to rely on other people for recommendations and you must essentially trust others' judgment on crucial matters.

So, the point of this chapter is to arm you with a fundamental understanding of Java technology in a business context

Editor's Introduction: The Java programming language has been a uniquely publicized phenomenon in software. Today, people who haven't heard of any other programming language have heard of Java and know that it is associated with the Web. But Java is much more than just a programming language; it is a complete technology for creating and using programs on the Web. It reaches from the device on your desktop (or in your hand) through the network to the huge servers on the back end. Java is a very important development in the creation of software. In this chapter, I explain what Java is, why it's important, and provide a fundamental grounding in the technology.

–KR

so that you can make the best possible business decisions. To accomplish that, there is a lot of information in this chapter. Nevertheless, there isn't as much information here as you could find in one of the many books devoted to the topic of Java.

In this chapter, each Java technology topic is presented much as a newspaper presents stories. The first sentence or paragraph presents the core idea, including why the topic is important. As you read further, you find more detailed information about the topic until the topic is completely covered from a business point of view. When you feel that you sufficiently understand the topic, depending on your needs, skip ahead to the next topic. Don't feel duty-bound to persevere in any particular section after you have sufficient information. Do give each section a chance and read at least the first few paragraphs. Sometimes a business-level explanation is by necessity a long explanation.

Java: A Definition

Java is two things. Java is a general-purpose programming language and Java is a complete set of tools for using programs written in Java. The Java programming language is used to write programs for business ranging from general-ledger programs, to word-processing programs, to spinning logos for Web sites. Java is an object-oriented programming language. Because it is an OO language, program components written in Java can be used and then re-used again in different programs. The Java programming language is designed to understand and exploit the Internet. It works with the communications mechanisms of the Internet to make programs and information more usable than with other programming languages.

Tools for using Java include the Java Virtual Machine (JVM), the utilities and compilers that make up the Java Development Kit, Web servers and other computers that can run Java programs, and browsers that can run Java programs.

A JVM is a special program whose purpose is solely to run Java programs. A JVM running by itself wouldn't really serve any useful purpose. Instead, its *raison d'être* is solely to run Java programs. You can think of it as a container for Java programs that provides all the resources and services a Java program needs. It's sort of the same as what a family does for a teenager.

A Java Development Kit (JDK) is used to develop Java programs, to compile them, and to package them up for delivery. Web servers that can run special Java programs (servlets) on the server have become a very important Java technology. Browser programs that have the capability to run Java programs (applets) were the first important use of Java.

Write Once, Run Anywhere

A pressing need for the open community space of the World Wide Web (the Internet) is for a programming language that is universal enough to write programs that can be understood everywhere in that space. This need for a language that will let you write your program once and then run it anywhere has been a big problem for the computer business until Java.

Before Java was introduced, computer programs were restricted to the specific type of computer system for which that program was written. The restrictions originated because each computer had specific strengths; programmers for that computer type developed programming languages that took advantage of the strengths of the computer. They also found ways to program around the weaknesses of each type of computer. And, it wasn't considered important to run the exact same programs on computers of different types. Each computer was expensive enough, and the technology was new enough, that no one thought much at all about reusing the programs on different computers. The cost of the hardware was a more significant factor than the cost of the software. All that has changed.

As computers have become much more powerful, the cost of the computer hardware now is small in relation to the cost of the programs (the computer software) that your business uses on the computer hardware. And businesses have begun to recognize that the real value of the information technology asset to the business is contained in the software.

How does software contain value? It contains answers to business problems. It costs a lot of time and money to solve those problems. Why not reuse answers? To answer a question with a question: Why solve the problem twice, even if you can?

I've found as I have visited customers over the years that many of the detailed answers to their business problems are contained in their software. The documentation that explains the software or the business process that the software supports is always out of date (the only question is by how much). Most people in a business see only a small portion of the overall process, but the software supports it end-to-end and is as current as the process.

So, the "write-once, run-anywhere" need is for a programming language that will let you use that answer everywhere that the answer is needed. That means a program, once written, should run on any computer system on which you will need to run it.

Java does exactly that. Java programs run on any machine that supports Java technology. Today, all mainstream computers support Java.

Web Enablement

Most businesses have recognized that the Internet is an opportunity to dramatically improve many of their business practices. Java is a crucial component of using the Internet for business (often called e-business because of the electronic nature of the Internet).

Java does more than just allow businesses to run programs on different types of computers. When used to deliver programs across the World Wide Web (referred to as the WWW, the Web, or even colloquially as the Internet), Java lets programs run on other companies' computers and on computers whose type is completely unknown to the programmer who wrote the software. This addition of remote delivery and execution of programs on the Internet (also on your company's intranet) is one of the most important and exciting capabilities of Java.

Because of the capability to arrive from a remote location and begin work immediately, Java programs, called applets, are often used to add capabilities to Web tools such as browsers. A very common example today of adding capability is a small Java program that provides authorized, secure access to customer information upon request across the Internet.

Prior to the combination of Java and the Web, companies had to anticipate in advance who might need such capabilities and such information and provide them specialized access mechanisms. Now, you can write a small program and make it available over the Web, verify identity and authorization, as necessary, and anyone who's authorized can use the program to add capabilities to their computer.

It's like the difference in a telephone and an ATM. Just about everyone has a telephone and can call almost anyone they like (even if they usually get voicemail). To use an ATM, you have to travel to one and it has to be in your network. It's actually even better than that, because the requirements to keep the program up to date change dramatically with Java. If your company improves the program, they only have to post the improvement in one place. Because Java applet programs are loaded across the Web each time they are used, the user gets the new, improved capability the next time they use the program. To update an ATM (or older style program), each ATM (or each copy of the older program, which can run into thousands at many businesses) must be individually updated.

Java applets are one type of Java program used on the Web. They are the faces of the Web programming world. The heart of the Web programming world is another type of Java program called servlets. Servlet programs are the hidden partners of applets. Servlets run on servers on the Web. Servers do exactly what their name implies. They provide services to (or serve) the Web. The difference is analogous to that of waiters and chefs. Waiters often are the faces of a restaurant. Waiters take your order (request for service), relay it to the chef, and participate in the delivery of the results of the service request to your table. Chefs directly provide services to the waiters and, through the waiters, to you. Servlets running on servers, in a similar fashion, cooperate with applets to provide services that the applets helps deliver to you.

Another type of Java software, and one of the most important categories, is that of Java application servers. Java application servers use Java to create, in effect, a nervous system for the Web. Java application servers link applets, servlets, and other Web programs, Web-available data, and Web-available events into a structure that lets each program or event occur in a larger context. Actually, this word context is an important one in understanding Java. Dictionaries define context as the immediate circumstances or the background. That's exactly what context means here. An event that occurs in isolation can be very different than one that occurs in a particular setting. Java application servers let programmers create a context for Java programs and Web events in which to occur. This context, or nervous system, is an important capability as business build smart, Web-aware business processes.

What's important is that Java programs add capabilities at all levels of the Web. This changes the Web from a mechanism for just providing information electronically to something that resembles an interactive organism with the capacity to dynamically tailor its capabilities to the task at hand.

Software Reuse

One important business benefit of Java is that of software reuse. Software reuse is subtly different from write once, run anywhere. Write once, run anywhere is a statement about computer programs that run on different computers. Software reuse means being able to reuse the components of software programs to create new programs.

Using Java, once a component has been written, the component easily can be used again and again. Other computer languages have tried to achieve this and some have done it to a limited degree, but Java is the first one to make it practical. Component reuse is a fundamental capability in Java. Think of components as nuts and bolts that you use to build larger systems. You can create nuts and bolts that match your unique requirements when necessary. When possible, you can use standard components (nuts and bolts) that you buy from companies that specialize in creating standard components.

This reuse capability can be very significant. Intentia, a major ERP software vendor, recently rewrote its software in Java from RPG. The set of programs that make up the Intentia system is quite large. Written in RPG, it was 23 million lines of source code. After conversion to Java, the same system doing the same functions—exactly the same functions—was 8 million lines of code. Why? Code reuse! It's a big deal.

And, you can reuse the components on any computer system that supports Java. Just as a standard bolt can be used in many different mechanical contrivances, a standard Java component can be used on any computer system that supports the Java component mechanisms. This is one of the most important aspects of Java and a source of some of the most important business benefits.

The technical linguists have really enjoyed the Java phenomenon. Java is made from beans...get it? There's more; JavaBeans are stored in .jar files. But the business point is that it makes programmers more productive. In a 1998 survey, International Data Corporation (IDC) found that programmers are 25 percent more productive on their first Java-related project. And, that takes into account the learning curve inherent in any first-time activity.

Java Programs

Java programs come in several different forms and keeping them straight can be confusing. This section explains applets, servlets, applications, JavaBeans, and Enterprise JavaBeans. Each of these terms refers to a Java program with distinctive characteristics. It is important to understand these different types of programs. Decisions about what kind of program to use when and where affect your company from top to bottom. You might reasonably ask, how could such a simple decision affect an entire company? Because it affects the:

- Capabilities that can be delivered by that program.
- Capital assets required to support the program.
- Number of hours required to write the program.
- Time and expense of supporting the program after it's in place and in use in your company.

Applets

Applets are Java programs that are stored in one place (a server) in your network and retrieved when needed. After retrieval, the computer that requested the applet runs the applet using browser software and its own processor. Applets should be (sometimes they aren't) small programs because they must be retrieved across a network connection. Retrieving a program across a network connection takes longer than loading it from a computer's hard drive.

Applets are important because they can be used most easily (compared to the other Java program types) to extend your existing programs and computers into the Web space. Applets are the most portable Java programs. Applets run on computers that you might never see, that might not belong to your company, and that might not be anything like the computers in your company. Applets do this by using the Java capabilities of Web browsers. Browsers are themselves programs and have the capability to run Java programs. So, if a computer has a Java-capable browser, it can run Java applets and it doesn't matter where or on what computer the applets originate.

Applets are being used by businesses to extend existing programs out into the Web for use by people at other companies or by consumers. You can create an applet that communicates from outside your company to a program that you already have. This small program can make your program usable by many more people—such as traveling salespeople, suppliers, customers, and consumers—than you ever thought feasible. What this means to your business is that you don't have to rewrite the programs that support your existing business-process capabilities for use over the Internet. You just put a new face on them using an applet program.

Applets are less flexible than other Java programs. They also have some capabilities, like the capability to play sound clips or video clips, that other Java programs don't have. Table 9.1 lists the various capabilities of applets, servlets, and applications. Because the capabilities overlap, understanding the differences is important. As noted earlier, deciding to write a program one way or the other affects your company.

Applets also have a more rigidly defined life cycle. Applets don't get to wake up and do whatever they like with their day. They have a demanding, rigidly prescribed life. The life cycle of an applet is load; initialize; start; stop; and be destroyed. While I know that may sound like a typical Monday at your company, this rigid life cycle is unique to applets and is part of what makes it possible for any Java-capable browser to run them. The browser program controls the cycles and you can, for example, stop a Java program at any time by pressing the "Stop button" (the so-called *stop interface*) inside the applet. This is like pressing the stop button on a VCR. The browser can restart the program by pressing the "Start button." Stopping an applet doesn't necessarily rewind the applet just as pressing Stop on a VCR doesn't necessarily rewind the tape. To rewind (and eject) an applet, the browser presses the "Destroy button" inside the applet. This stops the applet if it wasn't already stopped and gets rid of it (e.g., ejects the VCR tape).

Your browser runs applet programs by retrieving them from a server (getting a video tape from the video store), initializing them (loading the video tape into the VCR and rewinding, if necessary), and pressing the "Start button."

Applications

Java applications are Java programs that reside on the hard drive of the computer that will run them. This is different than applets, which reside on a server somewhere else in the network. This "local" residence of Java applications is an important difference between Java applets and Java applications.

While there are many sources of confusion when it comes to computers and computer professionals, one particular source of confusion is the term application. *Java application* is a specific term that means a Java program that runs inside a Java Virtual Machine and not in a browser. *Application* is a general-purpose, catchall term widely used by computer professionals to describe a more-or-less complete collection of programs that support a business process. You'll hear the term used like this: "We use SAP's accounts receivable application..." or "What applications does your company run?" In each of these cases, the reference is to collections of programs that support a business process. The term "application" comes from the verb "to apply." The context is that software and computer technology has been applied to support the business process.

Java applications are important because they can be used without a network connection. Some programs must run when the network connection isn't available. An example would be during computer startup or when a phone line (or network connection) is not available. Java applications are less portable than applets but are somewhat more capable. Java applications don't run inside a browser as applets do, but instead run inside a Java Virtual Machine. Perhaps you have spotted the beginning of a trend here in that Java programs seem to always run inside something else. This is in actually true and is one of the sources of Java's portability. More about this later.

Java applications are more capable than applets, but the increase in capabilities carries a higher price tag. Applications can use files from the local hard drive of the computer that they run on, they can connect to any server in the network, and they use files from that server (assuming they have the necessary security authorization). Applications also can be programs without a face (the so-called *user interface*) in that they require no interaction or direction from a user to complete their work. These kinds of programs are far more common than most users realize. Actually, many of the most important programs in use in business are these kinds of "faceless" programs.

One of the most important aspects of Java applications, compared to applets, is that the life cycle of an application is completely under the control of the programmer who wrote the Java application. Remember that applets have a specific, rigidly prescribed (initialize, start, stop, destroy) life cycle. Java applications don't have this life cycle and can behave in any cycle or any way that a programmer decides is necessary to complete the task. For this reason, Java applications are used to support tasks, such as long-running server tasks, that applets can't support.

An example might be a program that raises every price in a product database by 3 percent. Nobody wants to watch a program like this do its work. Therefore, a command is issued and a faceless background program quietly goes about its work. Another example might be a *listener program* that listens for pricing requests and returns the result of a pricing calculation. This program might sit, listen, and calculate for days and weeks on end without either stopping or restarting. Obviously, a life cycle like that of the applet would not be appropriate for such a long-lived business function.

The higher price tag of applications is composed of two components: capital assets and support requirements. Java applications require more capital assets than applets. Java applications require a computer with access to long-term disk storage (like a hard drive) to store the program and require enough processing power to run a Java Virtual Machine (JVMs require more processing power than browser programs). In other words, applications require more powerful, hence, more expensive computers. And, because the Java program and JVM are both stored locally, any change or upgrade to the program or to the JVM requires direct access to the computer. Applets can be changed at a single, central location. Applications have to be changed on every computer on which they are stored. While this isn't necessarily difficult, it takes time and more computers take more time.

Having said all the above, the capabilities of applets and Java applications do overlap. Java applications can have a so-called *face* or graphical user interface (GUI) and can connect with servers over the network to perform many of the same functions as applets. Choosing to write a Java program as an applet or an application is a design decision that has consequences for the business. The decision affects capital asset requirements, software installation requirements, and support-personnel requirements. Design decisions should take these factors into account.

This capability of Java to centralize programs into one location and, thereby, reduce capital-asset requirements and support costs is one of the most exciting aspects of Java as a technology for business.

Servlets

Servlet programs are like applet programs with two key differences. They don't have a face and they run on a server computer instead of a personal computer. Actually, the term *servlet* takes the first half of the word from the word server. The suffix "let" denotes that a servlet is not a standalone program and so can be seen as a smaller program. The "let" in applet signifies a small program that has to run inside another program (a browser program). A servlet is much like an applet, but without a face. The servlet life cycle (initialize, service, destroy) is similar to the applet life cycle (initialize, start, stop, and destroy). Servlets run "inside" a Web server like applets run inside a Web browser. Servlets are often used with applets where applets provide the graphical face for the business process and servlets do the heavy lifting behind the scenes.

Servlets are important because of their effect on capital resources and personnel expenditures. Using servlets can dramatically reduce the need for expensive desktop PCs (capital assets). They do this by running the program on the server and showing just the results of the program to the user. Because the actual program is running on the server, users don't require as much processing equipment, computer memory, or hard-drive capacity. Potentially, you could save serious money on capital assets.

Personnel expenditures are favorably affected because servlets are stored in a centralized location and can be maintained, upgraded, and supported more easily than programs that are physically stored in every computer (wherever those computers are located). If you have a branch office in Kazakhstan and need to upgrade programs on that computer, you have to get access to that computer. And the programs have to be upgraded preemptively.

In other words, your support personnel must install the programs on the computer before your business people can use the upgraded programs. While that might seem obvious and perhaps even trite, in my experience it is a problem for business. Many times in business, the personnel who most need new capabilities must wait for a technical person to get to them and upgrade their programs before they can fully participate in the latest corporate business process. I believe that in corporations, with significant numbers of computers, the computer-using personnel are always behind on one or more aspects of software. It's just too time consuming and too hard to get a support person around to each machine to upgrade them. So, everyone is always behind; the variance is how much.

Contrast that with servlets. If you support your business processes with programs written as servlets, upgrading means changing programs only in a central location. Then, as your people use the program, they will automatically use the latest version. No installation required. No hardware tweaks required. No support people flying to Kazakhstan. (I'll bet that would be a ton of frequent flyer miles.) This centralization of programs is one of the most important benefits of Java and Java servlets.

Using servlets with applets means that computer users in your company can have the easy-to-understand graphical interface that they need to be productive without destroying the budget trying to support out-of-control computer hardware and software. This is really just a return to common sense. The logic of many personal computer folks, applied to other areas, would imply that you couldn't just get by with a telephone on your desk. According to their logic, you'd need an entire switch (a centralized telephone server) there to really get anything done. Your company doesn't do that because it's a bad idea. (Your telecommunications person could show you your switch located in a closet somewhere at your company.) The same logic works for computers. Your company has to settle on a controllable, usable delivery of business functionality to the users at your company. Over-equipping the desktop with programs and excessive computer hardware is not the answer.

Java servlets save your company money on computer systems and on support personnel by shifting programs to a centralized environment where computer-processing power can be used more efficiently and where programs can be supported more effectively and more easily. It is a programming model that your company should adopt. Is it the right programming model for every situation? No, but then such a model doesn't really exist.

Comparison of Java Program Capabilities

Table 9.1 lists the capabilities of the three fundamental types of Java programs. This might seem like a lot of detail for a business-oriented book. Nevertheless, it's important because the decisions about what type of program (applet, application, servlet) to use for a particular purpose affects the infrastructure that must be deployed to support that program and the potential support costs for that program. For example, a servlet can centralize capital assets. Applets can run on a wide variety of computer hardware without any installation or maintenance of that hardware by your support personnel.

I believe that servlets are generically the best choice for business programs and should be used where possible. It is not always possible, but servlets should be the default choice. Servlets lead to a reduction of capital assets and to reductions in software support and maintenance costs. Business people should review the program-level architecture of the programs that are written by and for their company with a view to the capital assets and support costs. Table 9.1 will help you understand the pros and cons of each program type.

Table 9.1: *Java Program Types*

Program Attribute	Applet	Application	Servlet
Program Location	Not resident on local system. Loaded from server at runtime. Requires high-speed network.	Installed on file system that is accessed as local. Doesn't require network.	Resident in central location on server. Requires network, but needs less network speed.
Method for Running Program	Loaded by HTML request in a browser.	Runs explicitly as a standalone program.	Runs on request from a Client or starts when Web server starts.
Required Environment for Program	Runs inside a JVM controlled by a browser program on a user's computer.	Runs outside a browser on user's computer.	Runs in a JVM controlled by a server; consolidates computer resources.
Program Life Cycle	Has well-defined life-cycle milestones (initialize, start, stop, destroy).	Starts at main method and has control of life cycle.	Has well-defined life-cycle milestones (initialize, service, destroy).
Access to External Resources	Runs in a "sandbox" (JDK 1.1 or less) or has policy-based security model (Java 2).	Security is according to the Java security model.	Security is according to the Java security model.

Table 9.1: *Java Program Types (continued)*

Program Attribute	Applet	Application	Servlet
Server Connections	Connections permitted only to the server that served applet.	Connections permitted to any servers.	Can connect to other servers.
Access to Machine-Specific Functions	Can't load native code (JDK 1.1 or less). Can load native code at Java 2.	Access provided to native code	Access to native code provided.
Sound Capabilities	Audio interface	Audio interface	No audio interface
Video Capabilities	Yes	Yes	No
Capital Resource Consumption	Processor (PC)	Processor (PC)	Processor (Server)
	Disk (Server)	Disk (PC)	Disk (Server)
JavaBean Capable	Yes	Yes	Yes
Enterprise JavaBean Capable	Yes	Yes	Yes

JavaBeans

So far, Java programs have been described as complete programs. JavaBeans are components that are used to build Java programs. Software components such as JavaBeans are really no different than components in other areas. A brick is a component of a house. Multiple bricks can be combined into a wall, which is a larger component of a house. Brick walls are combined with windows.

In computer parlance, a window would be defined as, "A visual-display device for outside visual imagery dynamically updated by the overhead passage of the Sun from the pre-visual period through the visual period into the post-visual period." In other words, a window will let you see the Sun rise, travel across the sky, and then set. Is it any wonder that computer-industry professionals have trouble being understood?

When constructing a house, combining sufficient numbers and types of components, such as walls, windows, floors, and roofs, eventually creates a complete

References

163

house. Software components like JavaBeans are used in much the same way to create complete programs. For example, a spreadsheet component can be combined with a component for retrieving information to create a complete program for information analysis.

JavaBeans are important to business because Java software written in the form of JavaBeans can be reused more easily than Java components that don't follow the Bean model. This reusability saves time, money, and maintenance costs. Reusability, like many things in life, is often something that can be measured in degrees. Whether they are Beans or not, Java software components are inherently reusable. Beans have a capability that makes them more reusable than regular Java components.

To be a Bean, a Java component must be able to tell a larger system about itself. A Bean can tell a larger system about the Bean's capabilities to take action and about its capabilities to store data. This important feature allows program designers and programmers to learn about and use the capabilities of the software component without dissecting the component.

Imagine if you had to disassemble your stereo and trace the connections from the buttons to the circuitry to determine the functions of the various buttons. If you had the necessary electronics knowledge, and an inclination to do so, you could do it. However, such a situation would definitely shrink the market for stereo systems. People prefer that stereo manufacturers clearly label the buttons and connections so that the components can be used as part of a larger system. Consumers don't want to dissect products to understand what they do and how to connect them to the larger system.

JavaBeans have a "self-announcement" capability that informs larger systems that use them what their buttons do and how to connect them into larger systems. This lets program designers treat them as black boxes with known functionality and known inputs and outputs. This *component model* is very similar in concept and function to stereo components or car components. For example, when you buy an oil filter for your car, you know that the component (oil filter) will have a standard connection that fits your car and it will have standard functionality (it will filter the oil). Competing oil filter manufacturers compete on the basis of quality. They don't attempt to lock you in by using nonstandard connections or functions.

This idea of standard components has become so pervasive in other areas of life that we mostly don't think about it. Do you know what the diameter and thread pitch of the base of a standard light bulb is? Did you know that light bulbs have a standard base diameter and thread pitch? Sure you did. It makes sense once you think about it. The point is that you don't really have to think about such details very often—if ever. That's the point of documented standards and component models. You can connect the components easily without understanding the innards.

Computer programs are moving to standardization. Much like what has occurred in other areas of technology, battles are being fought now over standards. Did you know that many leading industrialists, including Thomas Edison, once thought that direct current (DC) would become the standard for electricity? Instead, alternating current (AC) won out in the marketplace because, among other things, it transmits more efficiently over greater distances than DC.

In the computer business, the standards discussion is moving very rapidly. As Java becomes more pervasive, the Bean component model becomes much more important. Again, reusability built on the black-box method is the reason.

Enterprise JavaBeans

Enterprise JavaBeans (for simplicity, EJB) are JavaBeans that have additional capabilities that make them especially suitable and desirable for use in enterprise computing. Computer types use the term *enterprise computing* to refer to computing done in support of business processes. Although both can take place in the workplace, enterprise computing is held to be different than *personal computing*. Enterprise computing generally supports a business process that is used by many people (in parallel or sequentially), while personal computing generally supports one person's work. A spreadsheet is an example of personal computing. Accounts receivable is an example of enterprise computing.

A stated goal of EJB is to "... make it easy to write applications: Application developers will not have to understand low-level transaction and state management details; multithreading; resource pooling; and other complex low-level APIs. However, an expert-level programmer will be allowed to gain direct access to the low-level APIs."[1] In English, this means that programmers who write business programs will be able to concentrate on the business functionality of the program. An example of business functionality is debits must equal credits. The programmer simply expresses the business functionality in Java and then all the necessary plumbing and wiring to make the business functionality work is provided by the EJB infrastructure.

This is important because EJB explicitly provides a model (or structure) where programmers can concentrate on just the business part of the program and can let the computer worry about the rest. You might think that programmers do that now. Nothing could be further from the truth. Actually, programmers spend a lot of their programming time (some estimates say more than half) doing so-called *infrastructure programming*. They write code to open files, load the data from disk into memory, move data from one place to another, reformat data to make it useful in memory, reformat it again to store it on disk, and do a myriad of other tasks. Such work has plenty to do with computing but little to do with business.

Until now, infrastructure programming has been accepted as necessary overhead and has been regarded as unavoidable. The one notable commercial exception to this, IBM's AS/400e computer, is an object-based computer that has provided an environment where programmers can concentrate on business functionality and worry much less about plumbing-level issues. On most other computers, it's as if in order to write a note, you must first invent and then build your own pen and paper from scratch. What's most surprising about this is that business people have tolerated it. In other business areas, this situation would last about a New York minute.

Having written an Enterprise JavaBean, a company can use that component on any computers that support Java. And, the EJB can be used in differing systems. In this respect, it is much like a standard mechanical component (a bolt, nut, spring, or washer) that can be used in many different mechanical systems. Most new mechanical systems do contain more standard components than purpose-built components. Because doing so is expensive, new components are only designed, built, and used when they are pragmatically necessary. This also is true for software components. A new software component should only be designed and used when truly necessary because doing so is more expensive than using standard components.

The next few paragraphs get fairly technical and readers who are so inclined may skip ahead to the next section. Because I believe that Enterprise

JavaBeans are a very important development, I decided to explain them in quite a bit of detail. The following section on EJB is excerpted from an article entitled "Enterprise JavaBeans and AS/400e" that I published in *Midrange Computing* magazine in March 1999.

> Enterprise JavaBeans are enterprise Java components. EJB components can be used and reused in an organization as component parts of larger enterprise software systems. As component models, JavaBeans fall short when it comes to distributed systems architectures. While it is possible to run a Bean remotely, the JavaBeans specification offers no standards for such common behaviors as find, start, and stop. Nor does it provide standards for management. Enter Enterprise JavaBeans. The EJB specification provides component standards at a distributed level. These components implement specific interfaces and honor specific behavioral contracts (in other words, they behave as expected) to allow larger systems to find, start, stop, and manage them. In turn, the larger systems provide an environment for the component to operate and provide services to the component.

> EJB is also an architecture. The EJB architecture specifies a standard component architecture; addresses the development, deployment, and runtime aspects of enterprise application software; and defines the behavioral contracts that enable tools from multiple vendors to develop and deploy components that can interoperate at runtime. EJB defines roles for component providers, software developers who use components to assemble applications, software deployers, EJB server providers, EJB container providers (a container is the above-mentioned environment), and system administrators. EJB developers, users, and interested parties will want to get a copy of the EJB specification at *www.javasoft.com/beans/docs/spec.html* and read it.

What's the Big Beal?

The EJB component architecture is important because it builds on the JavaBean component concept to provide a practical enterprise mechanism for reusable binary-level components that will function on all the computing platforms in an enterprise. For example, you could buy a General Ledger debit/credit Bean and then use that debit/credit Bean without modification on your IBM AS/400e, your Windows workstations, your Windows NT Server systems, and your Sun server-based systems. This capability means savings in programmer time, savings in user training, and savings in software support costs. So EJB is important because it will make for better and more cost-effective enterprise software.

EJB also is an important software market phenomenon. Because EJB provides a platform-independent standard, software component developers can be sure that the components that they develop are widely marketable. In turn, a larger market draws more component developers leading to a larger selection of components for component users. Everyone benefits from an open-standard, platform-independent component market. Conversely, over time, components that are limited to proprietary platforms or single platforms will lead to a smaller market and to fewer components provided to that market by component vendors.

Finally, EJB is important because it lets business programmers work at a higher level. Most programmers now spend a lot of time doing low-level programming tasks. I've seen estimates that place the amount of time spent on things like file I/O, manipulating relational data, manipulation of data from disk into memory structures (arrays, vectors, etc.), and other low-level tasks at over 50 percent of a typical programmer's time. While this spent might have once been necessary, it sure wasn't productive. EJB lets programmers concentrate on their part of the task, and, for most business programmers, that means assembling pieces of business functionality into a functioning system. This ability to work at a higher level of abstraction will mean a large productivity boost for business programmers.

EJB and Child Behavior

EJB components are different from regular JavaBeans in some very important ways. They make some important assumptions about things like persistence, state management, transaction management, database services, and security. EJB assumes that they won't have to handle the details of accessing any of these or other platform services. They behave much as our young children do: They assume that all they have to do is ask and most of what they need will be provided. And, just as it is true for our children, as long as they are running in an EJB container, it is mostly true for Enterprise JavaBeans. This concept of a container is the key attribute of EJB that makes it possible for business programmers to concentrate on the business programming.

Logical Containers

EJB separates a regular JavaBean into two parts: the business logic part and the system services parts. The business logic part becomes the EJB components and the system services part becomes the EJB container. The business logic part is then portable form container to container, and the container can, in turn, run (or contain) differing multiple EJBs. In effect (and in technical terms), the EJB container is a portability layer of software that supports reuse of EJB components on different platforms. A container is where an EJB object "lives," just as records live in databases and files live in file systems.

EJB containers provide services for Enterprise JavaBeans. The services provided are detailed in the EJB specification (again, see *www.javasoft.com/beans/docs/spec.html*). The EJB specification services provided by the container are described as *contracts*. A contract is a predefined expectation of behavior. For example, when a client requests the location of an Enterprise JavaBean, the EJB container must behave as expected and provide the location. In the EJB architecture, contracts exist between the container and the Bean, between the container and the client, and between the container and the EJB server.

Services that containers must provide to the client are object-identity services, method-invocation services, home-interface services, and Enterprise JavaBeans creation and destruction. In other words, the container keeps track of what Beans are in it, how to invoke (or run) those Beans, how to find them, and how to create instances of and destroy those Beans.

Services that the container must provide to the Bean are life-cycle management, context services, state management, and environmental information. In other words, the container tracks the life cycle of the Beans, monitors and provides a description of the context that the Beans are running in, manages state information and provides access to environmental information.

Each bean is packaged in a .jar file that is known as an *ejb-jar* file. An ejb-jar file is the standard unit of packaging for EJB components and all EJB tools must support ejb-jar files. The ejb-jar file provides a .jar file manifest that describes the contents of the ejb-jar file. The ejb-jar file also contains Java class files for the Enterprise JavaBeans. These .jar files also contain EJB deployment descriptors. Deployment descriptors are a key attribute of Enterprise JavaBeans in that they let the Bean deployer control runtime attributes and requirements such as security or transactions.

Version 1.0 of the EBJ specification defines two types of Enterprise JavaBeans. *Session* Beans are typically short-lived (i.e., "just for this session") objects. *Entity* Beans are objects that survive this session and can be used again in future sessions. Relational database rows are an example that can be represented by entity beans. Actually, entity beans are most commonly persisted into relational database rows.

Session Beans execute on behalf of a single client. They can be transaction aware and can update data in a database, but they cannot directly represent the data in the database. Entity Beans, on the other hand, typically do directly represent data in the database. They are transactional, not just transaction aware, and they support shared access by multiple clients. Importantly, entity beans survive crashes of the server running the EJB container.

EJB Roles

The roles of the various participants in the Enterprise JavaBeans architecture are important to understanding and using EJB. There are five roles.

1. *Enterprise JavaBeans Provider.* Enterprise JavaBeans providers are typically experts in a particular software application domain (like General Ledger or Manufacturing). Providers implement a business task as an EJB component.

2. *Application Assembler.* Application assemblers take the EJBs provided by EJB providers and assemble them into business applications. The application assemblers must be familiar with the behavior of the Bean as specified in Bean interfaces but does not have to understand the inner workings of the Bean.

3. *Deployer.* A deployer strategically arranges Enterprise JavaBeans and their containers into a specific deployment environment (i.e., AS/400e, Sun, Windows NT). A deployer uses EJB tools to map security roles and may customize business logic using deployment descriptors.

4. *EJB Server Provider.* EJB server providers provide a platform on which to run EJB components. This platform (e.g., an AS/400e) will typically provide an EJB container (perhaps from an EJB container provider) and the necessary underlying services. Underlying services include transaction management, distributed objects, naming services, file systems, and other lower-level system services.

5. *EJB Container Provider.* EJB container providers do system-level programming focused on providing a secure, scalable, transactional container. The container must honor the contracts required by the EJB specification, but the underlying implementation of the services may vary by platform. Honoring the contracts required by the EJB specification ensures that EJB components are portable and reusable across platforms.

Java Development Kit(s)

A Java Development Kit (usually called a JDK) is a collection of programming tools for developing Java programs. Java Development Kits are important because the JDK that your company uses determines how capable your Java software can be. The JDK that your company uses also affects your company's use of Java software across a range of computer systems.

A Java Development Kit includes a runtime environment. A runtime environment provides the services necessary for a Java program to run on a particular computer system. This runtime environment is usually called a Java Virtual Machine. For Java programs, a compiler converts the source program statements into compiled Java byte code. Included are utilities for testing and packaging Java programs. JDKs are available free over the Internet from Sun and from other computer companies. One note that's often overlooked is that the free version you can download does not have unlimited distribution rights. When a programmer downloads the JDK, they agree to licensing terms that prevent them from freely distributing the JDK. There is a freely distributable runtime environment available from Sun for popular desktop systems.

Java capabilities have been provided in a series of progressively more powerful Java Development Kits. These JDKs are referred to by name as JDK 1.0, JDK 1.1.x, and Java 2 (this was known as JDK 1.2 until December of 1998). Each of these names is a reference to a version of the Java Development Kit. Each of these releases is known for major capabilities.

The following sections cover the major functions of the language in chronological deliver order. One could argue that the chronology doesn't matter; all that matters is what is present now. Nevertheless, I have found that it does matter. As programs are carried forward from one release to another, things change slightly and enhancements are available that might have obviated problems in previous releases. Knowing when features and capabilities became available in Java can help you understand why a programmer took one approach versus another and can help you decide when to change or replace a program.

Complete, pragmatic, and useful language technologies such as Java don't suddenly spring up. They grow and develop over time (though nowadays that time is very short). Knowing, or having a reference for how the development of the language proceeded, can be very useful in an overall understanding of Java.

Essentially, so far, Java has gone through three stages. Those three stages are applet Java, database Java, and servlet Java.

JDK 1.0

JDK 1.0 was the applet version of Java. It was widely used to create applet programs that have been used to automate the Internet. JDK 1.0 did not include access to corporate relational databases as a standard part of the JDK. For that, it was necessary to download an extension to the JDK.

Java 1.0 contained eight java packages. A package in Java is a collection of related functions. For example the networking functions in Java are contained in the Java.net package. Java 1.0 contained the functions necessary to:

- Write applets.
- Build graphical screens.
- Manipulate images such as maps, globes, and flames.
- Store and retrieve information on the hard drives of computers.
- Connect to other computers across the network.

And all the utility functions necessary to support these functions.

JDK 1.1

At JDK 1.1, Javasoft added a great deal of new functionality to the Java language. The number of packages grew from eight to 23. Some of the new packages had been available as standard extensions and at JDK 1.1 they became a part of the core language. An example of that is the Java Database Connectivity (JDBC) package. JDK 1.0 technically had no way to access relational databases, but JDBC was available as a standard extension (java.sql). The following major enhancements were added to Java at JDK 1.1:

- The architecture for JavaBeans. This is a very important addition for Java because it provides the platform-independent component architecture. This package is where the fundamental underpinning of JavaBeans is provided.

- Inner Classes are a somewhat technical addition that provides the capability to define a Java component (what Java programmers call a *class*) inside another component (or class). This is important because the structure of components in a Java program often should be hierarchical to match the business problem. Without the capability to define components inside components, Java artificially flattened the hierarchy. These inner components are invisible to other components. Other components "see" only the external component.

- Internationalization enhancements make it possible for Java programs to be aware of the world location in which they are running and to behave accordingly. Java programs can determine their locale, determine time in that locale, display the date and time with local conventions, and sort lists according to the preferred local sort sequence. (This is much more important than it may sound. Imagine if the phone book wasn't alphabetical). In addition, Java programs can display using local characters (i.e., Cyrillic, Greek, or English).

- At JDK 1.1, the I/O facilities in Java were enhanced to support character input and output. Character I/O is important because many international programs use different character-coding conventions than are used in the U.S. For example, Japanese and Chinese characters have a different internal structure than U.S. characters. Files that store these characters can have far different internal structures than ASCII files in the U.S. The new character-based I/O components (or classes) are also more efficient as they read and write data in larger chunks.

- A very important enhancement at JDK 1.1 is the Java Archive (JAR) file format. JAR files are the packaging mechanism for delivering multiple Java programs at program runtime. Jar files contain multiple Java programs and a single Jar file delivery to a running Java program can provide all the Java components necessary for the application (remember an application is a collection of program objects) to run completely. This can greatly reduce network traffic and improve the performance of the running Java program. JAR files also can be digitally "signed." This digital signature capability improves security and provides capabilities for "signed" programs that exceed those of "unsigned" programs.

- JDK 1.1 also added JDBC to the Java language. JDBC is a set of components for manipulating relational databases. JDBC uses Structured Query Language (SQL). SQL, invented by IBM, is a standard language for manipulating the data in relational databases. JDBC was a standard extension in JDK 1.0.

- Java math capabilities were enhanced at JDK 1.1, with decimal number formats suitable for monetary calculations and large integer number formats.

- *Object serialization* is the technical term for the capability to store an object directly from Java. Prior to the availability of object serialization, developers either had to write a storage routine or convert the object to another format such as relational data. Objects have structures that differ greatly from the two-dimensional table structure of relational databases. Being able to store objects directly and easily improves the performance of Java programs and makes them easier to write.

- At JDK 1.1, Java got a very useful program-to-program communication mechanism called *remote method invocation* (RMI). RMI enhances the capability of Java programs to work together. Java programs can communicate directly with each other using RMI, even though they might be on different computers. This interoperability enhancement greatly improves the capability of Java to build worldwide Java distributed computer systems. A Java program running on a computer in New York can communicate directly and easily with a Java program running on a computer in New Delhi, India (even if the computers are of different types).

Java 2 (a.k.a. JDK 1.2)

Java 2 introduced a number of important enhancements. The security model was further developed and performance was improved, Swing GUI components became available, and many other enhancements were delivered.

Enhancements to the Java Platform

Security: The security mechanisms in Java 2 build on those available in previous versions of the JDK. Java 2 introduces the concept of policy-based security with granular access control. JDK 1.0 used a "sandbox" security model where the type of java program and the origin of the program determined its capabilities at runtime. Under this model, Java programs from remote computers had only limited access to the local computer. JDK 1.1 introduced the concept of trust based on a digital signature where a Java program loaded from a remote system could be treated as trusted local code.

In Java 2, the policy-based security model introduces the concept of *permission*. When a Java program is loaded, it is assigned permission to do things (open files, run other programs, save files to the local hard drive, connect to other computers) based on the security policy in effect. A security policy can be bounded by several dimensions: a group of programs, time, location, program type, etc). The security policy itself is actually contained in a Java object (or a collection of objects) called a *permission object*. The security policy can be initialized from an external file.

This security model provides very granular access control. Computer folks love the term *granular*—as in grain of sand. With sand, you can deal with each individual grain of sand using tweezers. That would be very fine-grained control of sand. Or you can use a shovel for somewhat less granular control. The metaphor has a similar meaning in information systems. A tool that deals with the individual items (of programs, files, or whatever) is very granular. A tool that deals only with collections of items is less granular. Because the new security model in Java 2 is very granular, every single item (program, applet, servlet, Bean, EJB, file, server, etc.) can be individually controlled. Or you can implement a less granular approach by grouping things into collections and controlling the collections.

Java 2 also adds certificate interfaces, X.509 certificates, and some additional security tools for JAR files.

JFC (Swing): Swing is a set of building blocks for graphical computer screens (GUI components) that have a *pluggable* look and feel. Pluggable means that the building blocks look and behave much the same as other screen components on the system on which they are used. A Swing component used on Windows 98 will look like a Windows 98 component. That same Swing component in the same Java program used on UNIX will look like a UNIX component. These lightweight (meaning all-Java) components work the same way on all platforms. Previous Java screen componentry (the AWT) depended on the underlying operating system for part of its functionality. Swing removes (to the extent that it is possible) that dependency. Swing will make Java programs seem even more consistent to the program users.

Swing components also implement the Java *accessibility features*. Java's accessibility features make it possible for Java to support devices such as Braille readers, screen readers for computer users with impaired vision, and devices for computer users with impaired hand functions (for example, carpal tunnel syndrome).

Swing also supports mouseless operation. All Swing components can be operated using only a keyboard.

Java 2D: Java 2D is a set of Java programs for graphics and imaging. 2D means 2-dimensional geometry. Java 2D is part of JFC. Java 2D creates and manipulates shapes such as rectangles and ellipses. It also can do graphic operations such as union, subtraction, and intersection on shape objects.

Other Java Platform Enhancements

Other Java platform enhancements at Java 2 include:

- **Keyboard Navigation:** It is now possible to write Java programs that don't require a mouse. Java can substitute key combinations for mouse-driven events.

- **Multithreaded Event Queue:** Java 2 makes it easier for programmers to synchronize events.

- **Collections Framework:** There is now a unified framework for representing and manipulating collections of objects. This reduces programming effort and increases performance. It also fosters software reuse.

- **Extension Framework:** Java 2 supports the downloading and installation of extensions as JAR files.

- **JavaBeans Enhancements:** JavaBeans are enhanced at Java 2 with better design-time support and runtime services to make them more widely deployable.

- **Input Method Framework:** Adds enhanced support for Japanese, Chinese, and Korean text input.

- **RMI Enhancements:** RMI is enhanced to support persistent references to remote objects. In other words, it can remember where things are in the network.

- **Audio Enhancements:** Java gets a new sound engine at Java 2. Audio quality is improved with WAV, AIFF, AU, MIDI, and RMF files.

Extensibility

The idea of *extensibility* is one of the most important attributes of JDKs. Each release has the core JDK capabilities and then there are extensions. Extensions add additional capabilities without requiring a new release of the JDK. Standard extensions are available from Sun, but might not be supported on all platforms that support Java. Vendor extensions are additional capabilities provided by a computer system vendor that are written in pure Java, but are specific to a particular computer. For example, IBM's AS/400e computer system provides a set of components for accessing the AS/400e. These components, written in 100 percent pure Java, save considerable time for programmers who need to access the database or printer files (or many other areas) on AS/400e.

Nonstandard extensions are provided when necessary to accomplish something that the designers of Java didn't anticipate. However, the need for nonstandard extensions is decreasing as Java matures.

Java Virtual Machines

A JVM is a program that "runs" useful Java programs. In this manner, a JVM is as a book cover is to book pages. The JVM contains the useful Java program, provides a context for the program to execute in, and provides all the necessary services for the program to run. JVMs are very important because they make Java portable by providing a standard interface for Java programs.

Interface is a word that computer folks use frequently (mostly accurately). Used in the context of a conversation about computing, interface is a layer interposed between two dissimilar things at a joint boundary for the purpose of accomplishing something constructive. For example, shoes are interface technology between your feet and the ground. Shoes serve the purpose of cushioning your feet and providing protection from the elements. A JVM is exactly that; a layer of programs between your Java programs and the computer that you want to use to run your Java programs. An interface does for your programs exactly what your shoes do for your feet. It cushions the bumps and makes your programs usable in a wider range of environments.

JVMs are often referred to as a *portability layer*. A portability layer, in software terms, is a layer of software that makes some other software component portable. In other words, running this program makes it possible to run other programs on a wider range of computers. An operating system, like DOS or Windows 95, is a portability layer. Operating systems are closely married to the actual computer hardware and only run on specific computers. JVMs perform much the same function but isolate the Java programs from the computer hardware and make it possible to run the same Java programs on many different computers.

A JVM must be present on any computer that you want to use to run Java programs. JVMs are used in several different ways to support running Java programs in different places. A browser program uses a JVM to run applets. A Web server program uses a JVM that can run servlets. JVMs are available for most computers and can be used to run Java applications.

Application Servers

Application servers reflect such a hot market today that one might be excused for thinking that they are a new idea. Applications servers aren't new, but the realization of the concepts of an application server running on the Web by using Java as the programming language is new. Application servers have been around for a long time. IBM's Customer Information Control System (CICS, always pronounced "kicks") has been available for nearly 30 years and it is definitely an application server.

An application server is a software environment in which to develop programs. The application server provides standard mechanisms (or interfaces) for accessing the underlying computer and so achieves stability and portability in the business application layer of the software. The essential idea is to create a standardized environment no matter the underpinnings. Most people don't know how the foundation of a house is constructed, but they can use the stove and the lights and the heating system. So it is with application servers. Programmers writing the important part of the programs (the part that runs the business) have a set of services and resources they can depend on. They always know how to turn on the lights.

The idea of moving the application server to the Web was a great idea waiting for a language technology that could support it. One of the problems with application servers in the past was that it could be difficult to connect users to them. Web application servers fix that problem completely. Because Web application servers run on the Web itself, you easily can provide access to the set of users that need access.

Web application servers are important because they standardize the Web computing environment for business programmers to concentrate on the business task at hand. To accomplish assigned tasks at that level, business programmers cannot digress into low-level infrastructure tasks. This emergence of a set of Web operating systems is a major milestone in the progression of business computing.

Web application servers use Java as their development language. Using Java as the development language for Web application servers is important because of the open nature of Java. In the past, most application servers had their own software development language. The problems with that were program portability, programmer reuse, and customer lock-in (on several levels).

In the past, programs written for one application server would run only on that application server. Now, using Java and Java's component standards (JavaBeans and Enterprise JavaBeans), your company can achieve portable code across Web application servers. A similar problem existed in the past with programmers. A programmer who learned a particular application server might spend much of their career working only with that application server. With a standard language and similar architectures, programmers can now work with multiple application servers more easily.

Customer lock-in existed with previous generations of application servers on several levels. Once a customer went through the installation of an application server and got their programs running, they weren't likely to change things. The application server depended on a particular operating system, which depended on a particular computer, which was generally sold only by a particular vendor. Customers didn't change the pieces very often because it was too painful.

The standards conformance aspect of Web application servers is important to customers because it reduces the degree of lock-in. If a Web application server supports open standards, has an open interface for design and development tools, and generally doesn't do things in a proprietary manner, then program portability is enhanced, programmer reuse is enhanced, and lock-in is decreased.

Object-Oriented Software

Object-oriented software is an idea that has been kicking around the computer software community for many years. It had not been practical because of the computing requirements and the difficulty of the languages that supported it. With Java and the power of the computing platforms that can run Java programs, that's changing now.

Object-oriented programs are better than traditional (often called) *procedural programs* in the same way that prose written by William Faulkner is better than prose written by elementary school students. Object-oriented programs can represent the richness of the real world in a realistic, understandable, and readable fashion. Procedural programs treat and represent everything simplistically and, in the fashion of a beginning student, only think about one thing at a time. Procedural programs fool us about that because of the amazing speed of the computers that run them.

ORBs

Object request brokers (ORBs) are quite the rage in business computing right now and are actually quite important to the future of business computing. ORBs solve a large computing interoperability problem between programs running on different computers. If your program is ORB capable, then you can use an ORB to interact with other programs on other computers. Because that was already possible, you can be forgiven for asking why that makes ORBs important. ORBs are important because they provide a vendor-independent standard for programs (objects) to interact. Technical folks often call an ORB an *object bus*.

A bus is a multilayer metaphor that has been reused so much in computing that most folks have forgotten where the metaphor came from originally. The idea has been used in the hardware side of computing for years.

When you build a computer system, you can connect the devices in the computer system directly to each other. And that's how it was done originally. This quickly leads to problems with printed circuit boards. The wiring becomes too complex to complete and isn't cost effective. Hardware developers came up with the idea of a bus.

A bus is a standard path (a path for electrons, so the bus is made out of wire) that flows through a printed circuit board just as a street is a standard path that flows through a town. To quickly see why this is necessary, imagine having to define and build a direct path to every place you might want to go from every place that you might ever be. It's much easier and far more effective to go on a predefined road or path. This is true even though the path might not be the most efficient in terms of straight-line distance.

To move information from one device to another, you put the information on the bus and send it down the street to the device that needs the information. All the devices connected to the bus use standard connections (just as your driveway is a standard connection to a street) and know how to tell when information is meant for them. So, ORBs are an object (or program) bus. All programs can connect to the "street" using standards and can put information on the "bus" for movement to another program.

The implications of this object bus capability for business programming are huge. Programmers can stop building roads and start carrying (or at least using) the mail. Programming will never, thankfully, be the same. In the past, programmers defined a unique path for everything, built the road, and then did it again when they wanted information to "go" somewhere else.

CORBA

Common object request broker architecture (CORBA) exists so that software systems (the programs that you run your business on, for example) can interoperate. Many of today's business programs have limited capabilities to interact with other business programs. It's as if each program was an island with only limited shipping capability.

This is important to business because interoperability between business programs is a business requirement. The problem is often solved in business by putting people between the programs. People use the universal input/output media called paper. Did you know that most information keyed into a computer (some folks say upwards of 80 percent) is information that was printed out from another computer.

You've seen this many times, I'm sure, in your business. The accounting department prints a report that has information about the prior month's order entries and uses data to make general-ledger entries by hand. This approach has a number of problems associated with it. First, the information transcription creates errors. Next, because the information is usually summarized—don't have time to enter all that detail; got to get the financial statements out—much of the detail is lost. Lost detail makes data analysis difficult or impossible. And lost detail blurs audit trails. In addition, this approach is very expensive compared to having the machine do the work.

So, interoperability is a requirement for most business programs. Because CORBA provides a set of standard ways that programs can work with each other, programmers have to learn it only one time as opposed to figuring out a different method for each pair of programs that need to work together (interoperate).

Also, CORBA is object oriented, and that is a very good thing for business computing. OO programs behave in a more rational fashion due to their object-oriented design, support code reuse (reusing bits of programs instead of rewriting them—some folks call this not reinventing the wheel), and can more easily be distributed across the systems that you need to distribute them across. With apologies to Martha Stewart, OO is a good thing.

CORBA is a publicly supported standard and it increases the capability of your company's programs to work with programs at other companies. Doing things in a standard fashion is good; everyone doing things in a standard fashion is better. When an entire industry does things in a standard fashion (as it appears the software industry might in using CORBA), that's very good.

CORBA is a standard from the world's largest software consortium, the Object Management Group (OMG), and is supported by most of the other standard-setting organizations in the industry. CORBA is an important step along the road to creating standard thread pitches and nut diameters for the software industry. Imagine how hard it would be to build a car if every component provider had its own measurement system. It would be impossible. Imagine if there were hundreds or thousands of measurement systems in use and vendors of components refused to standardize. That's where software has been. CORBA is an important step out of that mess.

A detailed description of how CORBA works is beyond the scope of this book. For interested readers, I recommend *The Essential CORBA*.[2]

References

[1] Web site. Enterprise JavaBeans specification: *http://www.javasoft.com.*

[2] Mowbray, Thomas J., and Rob Zahavi. 1995. *The Essential CORBA*. New York: John Wiley & Sons.

The new electronic independence re-creates the world in the image of a global village.

—Marshall McLuhan,
The Gutenberg Galaxy: The Making of Typographical Man
University of Toronto Press (1962)

10

MQSeries Technology

MARK SCHREITER

Pardon the cliche, but no computer is an island. In the information-technology arena, you rarely see a computer that isn't communicating with another device or computer. Computers are constantly interacting with other computer nodes in a network, communicating with nodes in other networks, exchanging files and records to keep remote databases up to date, and doing all the necessary things needed to run a customer's business. Businesses must share information. However, it's typical of many businesses to have many computer models at one site, a choice of network protocols the computers can use (SNA vs. TCP/IP vs. IPX vs. NETBIOS), and a different set of communications APIs available for use on each different network protocol. Businesses easily can end up with major headaches in trying to provide a complete communications solution.

It's commonplace for a business application to be designed as a group of related programs, each of which handles a

> **Editor's Introduction:** In the networked Web world, computers function independently but require a reliable, assured, once-and-once-only delivery of information, requests, and messages from one program to another over the network. The mainframe in Delhi must have the capability of updating the marketing department's server in Los Angeles and know that the transaction went through. This is no different than real life. Delivery companies differentiate themselves on the reliability and the provability of their delivery of packages and messages. MQSeries provides this reliable, assured, once-and-once-only, delivery capability to electronically independent computer systems around the world. Mark Schreiter explains how in this chapter.
>
> –KR

single, well-defined component of the whole. Often, the programs that make up a business application run in a single environment on single or multiple processors. And sometimes they run in multiple, unlike environments. Many businesses go a step further and, rather than run them all on one processor, they distribute programs around the data-processing network. For example, a single application could be distributed between an AIX/6000 environment on a RISC System/6000 processor and an OS/400 environment on an AS/400 processor.

In this approach, most of the many advantages are related to making better use of resources. So that network traffic is kept to a minimum, it's often a good idea to put a program near the data it's processing. (My database is in Washington. Therefore, if I put my customer accounts program in Miami, my network is going to be kept busy just moving data between the two.)

Load balancing—rescheduling and relocating the workload to complete it as efficiently as possible—is another reason for distributing an application. (My London branch is running at capacity, but I've got an underused machine in Rome. Why can't I just move some of the work to Rome?)

Sometimes *rightsizing*—moving an application from one large machine to several smaller machines—is the trigger. (We've installed a midrange processor in each of our branches, so we need to share the workload among them.) Of course, when you distribute a single application, whether to unlike environments on a single processor or to different nodes of a network, you must have a way of getting the parts of the application to communicate with each other.

This can be challenging enough when the components of the network are from a single vendor, when there are no variations in the operating systems you're using, when programs are written in a single language, and when there's a single communication protocol. How much more challenging the problem becomes when the network components are from a variety of vendors, when different operating systems are in use at different nodes of the network, when the programs you're trying to connect are written in different languages, and when multiple communication protocols are being used. And yet, the interoperability challenge—the challenge of getting programs to communicate across unlike environments—could be the one facing you today.

So how do networks become so diverse in the first place? Perhaps, for your company, buying equipment and services from multiple vendors is simply a matter of policy. Or perhaps you have incompatible computer systems after changes to your business. If your company has merged with or acquired another, or if it has relocated or restructured in some way, the chances are that you've gathered an assortment of network components in the process. Perhaps you need to connect your applications with those of your business partners—your suppliers, your distributors, even your own customers—so that business procedures can be integrated and data can be shared. As the boundaries between businesses themselves are becoming less distinct, the need to connect computer systems across geographic and organizational boundaries is growing.

As more and more businesses attempt to associate related programs from unlike environments, some constraints are emerging. In particular, the time-dependent relationship between two communicating programs can impose artificial requirements. Typically, one program is executed while the other waits. Even though they take turns to run, both programs have to be available to maintain the conversation. Increasingly, businesses want to be able to run related programs independently of each other.

As the use of distributed applications has mushroomed, so too has the number of communication sessions in a network. Businesses that use a lot of distribution techniques can find themselves having to support thousands of dedicated network sessions. Such numbers may be manageable while the network is free of problems, even though long startup times are inevitable. But if the network fails, having a large number of sessions can cause performance problems simply due to the time it can take to restart a part or the whole of the network.[1]

Well, someone has given a lot of thought to the preceding dilemma and has come up with a solution that thousands of customers are using to exchange data within their corporate- computing environment. That solution, the MQSeries, is a communications software package available from IBM. The MQSeries runs on a variety of hardware and software boxes that includes anything from Windows 95 and Windows NT, to UNIX boxes, to AIX RS/6000 boxes, to AS/400s, and up to the System 390s.

MQ stands for Message Queues. The basic method by which MQSeries communicates to other platforms is by sending and receiving messages and taking them from or putting them to message queues. Think of a message in this context as an e-mail message destined for a target mailbox. MQSeries provides a common API set available on all these platforms. This is important from a business and cost perspective. Once the MQ technology is learned on one platform, the knowledge gained can be used to implement MQSeries-based applications on other platforms with little or no changes to the code that needs to communicate over the customer's network.

As of an announcement in June 1999, MQSeries is supported on over 35 different platforms. It is also the most widely used message-queuing software on the market. With more than 66 percent of the market share, MQSeries is used by more than 5,000 customers to solve their business integration issues. It is installed and running in 350 out of IBM's top 500 customers, and it is operating in two-thirds of the top 100 North American and European banks.

MQSeries Definitions

MQSeries is based on messages. A message is a "piece" of information that is sent between two or more programs. This message can be any mutually agreed-upon format for the communicating programs. For example, it can be

- A field of 80 characters to indicate a new record in a file.
- A multitude of records to indicate what part of a file might have changed.
- An array of binary values that is of some significance to both programs.

Messages in MQSeries have to go somewhere (ultimately to a destination). In MQSeries terms, when an application wants to send a message, it needs to specify a *destination* or *target queue* to which it will be sent. The queue in MQ is based on your standard queue as you know it from computer basics. It is an object onto which the user can "put" elements and "get" elements from as applications ask for these operations to be done.

Once a message has been put to a target queue, it's up to MQSeries to guarantee that the messages you put onto that queue will either be delivered to the target machine that this message is destined for or it will give you an error message. The error message will say something like, "Sorry—could not deliver this message."

Communicating some consistent terms associated with MQSeries is important. The terms used here are based on my knowledge and experience in using the MQSeries on the AS/400. Once the MQSeries technology is learned on that platform, it's easy to understand the implementation of MQSeries on UNIX, AIX, and WIN/NT platforms.

- **Queue Manager:** The Queue Manager is somewhat analogous to the "BOSS Program" of MQSeries on each computer where MQSeries is installed. It provides to the user a way to configure the various MQ elements, allows the user to start/stop MQSeries, and also provides status and diagnostic information to the user regarding any problems that might be encountered in communicating with other devices in the network using MQSeries.

- **Node:** A node in an MQSeries environment is a computing machine that has MQSeries software installed and configured on it. This computing machine will be communicating with the other nodes in the customer's network.

- **Channel:** A channel is a logical "pipe" for carrying messages between the nodes within the network. These pipes can be roughly equivalent to a freeway on which messages travel between nodes. These pipes are uni-directional. They can be defined as either a *sender channel* (used to send data out of a node) or a *receiver channel* (used to receive data into the node from other nodes in the network). Most nodes in the network, therefore, need at least two channels defined to allow them to send and receive messages.

- **Queue:** A queue is a first-in-first-out object onto which MQSeries will put on or take messages from on behalf of the applications that are using MQ. The queues defined on a machine can take on several characteristics. They can actually be defined as having a target node on the same machine as the sending application (MQSeries applications can talk to an MQ application on the same node) or the target node can be on a different platform within the network that is also using MQSeries. A queue also can have a special designation called a *transmit queue*. This type of queue is used to hold messages destined for a remote message-queue manager (basically, an outgoing-only message queue).

Process: An MQ process is an application on a target box that is using the MQSeries product on the target box. This is an especially important definition regarding the start up of MQ applications.

One of the key concepts associated with MQSeries is its consistent API set across the multiple platforms. This API set also is consistent across different networks. If your network is SNA-based and currently using MQSeries, and you decide to switch to TCP/IP based network protocol, the software running your business should not be affected when your network administrator switches to TCP/IP. The underlying MQ definitions will have to change (the capability to change/reconfigure MQ is provided using the Administrator Tools under the Queue Manager), but your software should not have to go through the cumbersome task of using another API set to communicate with other applications.

With its built-in knowledge of the differences between the platforms, MQSeries provides additional services on behalf of the applications using the API set. A most useful service is MQ's capability to convert text messages from one data format to another format (the dreaded ASCII-to-EBCDIC conversion).

Platform Differences

When viewing text, we know what the text is, we know what it is supposed to represent, and we know how to put letters together to form words. We know that an "A" is the first letter in the alphabet, "B" follows it, and that it is the first letter of the word Apple. Also, we know how to remember an "A."

Computers can represent an "A" in several different formats called *character sets*. PCs and most UNIX and AIX platforms use the ASCII character set. In ASCII, an "A" is represented as a hex value 41 in computer memory. Some of IBM's machines (the AS/400s and the 390s) usually use the EBCDIC character set for representing text data. In this character set, an "A" is represented as the hex value C1. When other applications (for example, FTP) send and receive text data between computers, using different character sets, the application must do the conversion from one character set to another.

At your request, MQSeries automatically can take care of this burden for you. MQSeries will convert EBCDIC text data from an AS/400 platform to the ASCII platform that a PC typically uses. Therefore, an example text message such as,

"Your account is overdrawn!" being sent from the AS/400 to the PC through MQSeries will appear as, "Your account is overdrawn!" once it has gone through the automatic character conversion that MQ can do for you.

Implementation Details

The first thing that the MQSeries application requires is a connection to the Local Queue Manager. Roughly, this is equivalent to picking up a telephone and getting ready to make a phone call. By picking up the telephone handset, you are telling the local telephone company that you are going to make a call and exchange some information with another person. With MQSeries, connecting to the Local Queue Manager gets the attention of the Queue Manager, and provides you with a handle (or Key) to using MQSeries services later in your application.

Once you have connected into the Queue Manager, you open the queue to which you want to send messages. MQSeries does some housekeeping tasks to see if this queue exists and whether or not it is writeable. If the queue is able to receive messages, you now have the capability to send one or more messages to your target queue.

When you have completed sending the message(s) to your destination queue, your program has several options available:

1. It can disconnect from the Queue Manager (if the program doesn't have any additional work to do).

2. It can start receiving messages from the application to which it had sent the messages (if it is expecting a response from that application).

3. It can choose to stop sending on this particular queue, open another queue, and start sending to different destination queues. (This application might be some type of broadcast-mode program.)

That's really all there is to it. It is up to MQSeries to reliably get that message across the network to wherever the target destination queue is. Not only will MQSeries ensure that the message gets to the target in a timely fashion, it can keep the message in the receiving queue at the destination node in case the receiving application is not yet ready to receive the data. In the latter case, perhaps the application hasn't yet been started or is temporarily busy doing something else prior to checking the incoming queue for messages.

For receiving data at the destination computer, a similar scheme is followed for the simplest case (starting the application manually). The application connects into the Local Queue Manager (telling it that this application will be doing some MQ-related operations), opens the queue from which it will be receiving messages, and then issues an MQGET command. Once the message has been received, the application can continue to receive more data, send a reply back to the sender if it wishes, or simply disconnect from the Queue Manager.

There are several variations associated with the preceding scenario to consider. The architects associated with MQ tried to make these solutions flexible and to take into account certain situations that might arise to prevent immediate reception of these messages.

Question: What happens if there is no data for the receiving application? (Either the sending application never sent data or the data hasn't arrived).

Answer: MQSeries allows the receiving program some flexibility in this area. The application can tell MQSeries to wait for either a predetermined amount of time for data before returning to the caller with a "No Data" indicator or the application can tell MQSeries to "wait forever." If so instructed, MQSeries will wait forever until either data does become available on the requested queue or the Local Queue Manager program is ended by a System Administrator.

Question: Does the receiving application have to wait for data to come in from the sending application?

Answer: That is not the case. MQSeries has some added flexibility with the definition of the Receiver Data Queues. There is an option to specify an MQSeries process (see the subheading, MQSeries Definitions) that should get started when a message comes in on a particular queue defined to use this approach. This is referred to as a *triggered queue*. MQSeries then tells the system on which it is running to start up this particular process.

In other words, the application can be written so that it has only the following purpose: Once it is started, it is to go to a target queue from which it is supposed to receive data, ask MQSeries for the data (the data should already be there, otherwise the program would not have been started), process the data, and then end. The next time more data comes in on that particular queue, the program should automatically activate.

The preceding examples are obviously very simple, but there are two key points to remember:

- A snippet of code for sending or receiving can be reused over and over on each platform using MQSeries. The only major difference might be what the target (destination) queue is for each application on each platform and the Local Queue Manager name being used on each platform.

- The programmer will not have to worry about sending a message to a destination queue. MQSeries will ensure data delivery and get your message through all the network "stuff" to the target queue. Pretty cool!

Transaction-Based Queuing

In the preceding example, the message to the destination queue was sent as soon as MQ was told to send it. What happens in the environment where an application might need to retrieve a sent message? First, keep in mind the following terms.[2]

- **Unit of work:** A unit of work is a recoverable sequence of operations performed by an application between two points of consistency. A unit of work begins either after an application starts or after an application has requested a syncpoint.

- **Syncpoint:** A syncpoint is an intermediate or end point during processing of a transaction at which the transaction's protected resources are consistent. At a syncpoint, changes to the resources can safely be committed, or they can be backed out to the previous syncpoint.

- **Commit:** A commit is an operation that applies and makes permanent all the changes made during the current unit of recovery or unit of work. After a commit is complete, a new unit of work begins.

- **Backout:** A backout is an operation that reverses or undoes all the changes made during the current unit of work. After the backout operation is complete, a new unit of work begins.

Within applications that access databases, message queues, and other IT entities in a computing environment, there might be situations (guided by a programmer's style or by real-life situations) where some actions might need to be retrieved or undone. A decision to retrieve a message might be based on some internal error that a program might have encountered or some external stimuli that would cause or force certain actions to be pulled back.

Once a message is retrieved, the state of the machine (databases, queues, etc.,) would be restored to the state these resources had at the last time a unit of work was started. On most platforms, there is a way to tell MQSeries to commit its events using an API call to MQCMIT. There also is a way to tell MQSeries to reverse changes using a MQBACK API call.

With some definitions out of the way, here's a concrete example of how these concepts can be used. Suppose you have an application running in a retail store. Its job is to help a cashier handle the transaction associated with having a customer pay for an item. In addition, suppose that you want to track—based on items are sold at the cashier's terminals in real time—what your inventory is. Here's a hypothetical sequence of events:

1. A customer brings an item to a cashier in order to purchase the item.

2. The cashier scans in the information for the item.

3. The item inventory count is then "decremented" by one locally, and has reached a threshold point where you need to tell our supplier (who happens to be listening for requests by way of an MQ application) that your store needs more of these items.

4. You send a message out to the Remote queue to request that the supplier send more inventory. But this message has not yet been committed (made permanent). Therefore, MQSeries has not yet sent it.

5. The customer attempts to pay by credit card.

At this point, one of two things will happen. If the customer's credit card is approved, then the customer can walk away with the purchase, and the application can then commit the MQ message. MQSeries will then make the changes permanent, and the message actually will be sent to the supplier.

Now suppose the customer's credit card is over the limit. Sadly, the customer walks away, vowing to address the credit problem, and the cashier routes the item back into stock.

At this point, the application determines that it doesn't want to have too many of these items in stock, and it does a backout. The backout tells MQSeries to undo the sending of the message to the supplier—so that the supplier never sees the message—and your current inventory remains at its current level.

Why not have the application wait until the credit check response comes back before it sends the MQ message out to the supplier? That could be done. However, 99 times out of 100, the credit check will be approved and you will have to send that message.

Why not just send the request to the supplier without waiting for the credit check? You could get a string of unapproved credit checks and, over the next couple of days, you would start receiving additional inventory. While this is somewhat of a mundane example, it should get the point across regarding how an application can undo or make permanent some transaction-processing events.

Dead-Letter Queue

Trying as hard as it can, MQSeries might not be able to deliver a message to the intended destination queue. There are several technical reasons that this might occur:

- The message might be too large for the channel that it is supposed to be sent across.

- The target queue to which you are attempting to send a message might be full and can't receive additional messages.

- There was a problem at the sending side of a connection in trying to convert your message from one data format to another.

- Et cetera.

In these instances, the message will go to a special queue called the dead-letter queue or undelivered message queue. When MQSeries can't get a message across the network to the target queue and does not know what else to do with a message, it gives the message back to the sending node. It is up to the sending node to take care of this situation.

When a message is queued, an associated reason code is also placed on the queue. Typically, at each node that has a dead-letter queue, there is a clean-up handler dedicating to taking care of problem messages. This handler will take a message off the dead-letter queue, examine the reason code for that message, and take appropriate action based on that reason code.

If the reason code shows that the destination queue is full, the handler could send a message to the local administrator with a note regarding some potential problems at the target node. If the message size is too large for the channel, the administrator could adjust the channel to increase its maximum message capability. As with other queues and queue handlers, the dead-letter queue handler can:

- Run as an application that will wait forever for messages to arrive to that dead-letter queue.

- Poll the queue once in a while for any messages.

- Run as a triggered application and be launched through MQSeries when a message does arrive at the dead-letter queue.

Summary

Most businesses have networks of diverse hardware interoperability and software. However, related programs in different parts of a network must be able to communicate in a way unaffected by variations in hardware, in operating systems, in programming languages, and in communication protocols. Moreover, businesses need to be able to run related programs independently of each other. And all this needs to be achieved with an overall reduction in the number of sessions on the network.

Complex though the problems may be, they need a solution that works equally well between programs on a single processor in all environments and between programs at different nodes of a varied network. MQSeries products provide just such a solution.

References

[1]   MQSeries. 1995. *An Introduction to Messaging and Queuing*. Document number GC33-0805-01.

[2]   MQSeries. 2000. *Application Programming Guide*. Document number SC33-0807-10.

Each problem that I solved became a rule which served afterwards to solve other problems.

—Rene Descartes
Discours de la Methode

11

IBM SanFrancisco: for Rapid Development of e-business Applications

VERLYN JOHNSON, PH.D AND THOMAS KONAKOWITZ

IBM SanFrancisco delivers Java-based business components, common business objects, and an object-oriented infrastructure for mission-critical commercial applications. The business components and common business objects are designed as frameworks. They contain a subset of the functions and business logic needed to build commercial applications such as the general ledger, accounts payable, accounts receivable, sales order processing, inventory management, and product distribution.

As frameworks, the components and common business objects are easily modified and extended. The objective of the product is to simplify and speed the move to distrib-

> **Editor's Introduction:** Speaking as a recovering programmer, I never wanted to write any piece of code twice. Once I solved a problem by writing a program, I wanted to reuse that program again and again (the program became a rule to solve other problems). However, in the past, the reuse of programs has been problematic. In most cases, reuse meant "copy and paste" and then tweak. That was better than completely rewriting the code, but not much better. The best case would be to simply use an existing component program as is without modification. By doing that, large business programs could be built mostly from existing components of known function and reliability. SanFrancisco is just such a set of existing Java components that can be used to quickly build large systems composed of highly reliable components.
>
> —KR

uted, flexible e-business applications by providing developers with an object-oriented infrastructure and a starter set of well-designed components that can be used as a base for their applications.

Motivation for IBM SanFrancisco

The development of IBM SanFrancisco began at the urging of IBM's partners called independent software vendors (ISVs). While the majority of these ISVs, who develop and sell applications, are small or medium-sized businesses, it became apparent that the problems they presented to IBM are problems that are common to many application developers and businesses.

For example, although they have highly skilled development staffs, most ISVs do not have the resources to continue to support their current applications and customer sets while enduring a long lapse in productivity needed to adopt to a new technology. At the same time, ISVs do recognize the need to enhance their applications to keep up with rapidly changing markets and that they need to develop new applications to exploit new opportunities.

ISVs also are searching for a development approach and tools that will allow them to rapidly embrace the concept of e-commerce and e-business. Because of IBM's reputation for reliable systems, and the large opportunity, the typical IBM business partner develops applications targeted at the commercial market (for example, general finance, enterprise resource planning, inventory management, human resources). Although many of the application developers are small in size, they understand the market trends and the value of technology. All of them are keenly aware of the need to enable their applications for e-business or face the prospect of becoming noncompetitive in the market place.

Historically, applications for the commercial market usually were written using a business-oriented procedural languages such as RPG or COBOL. Experts have estimated that 40 to 50 billion lines of RPG code have been written, and that there is an even greater amount of COBOL code. Much of this code is still in use today. The code ranges from well-structured, modular programs to unstructured, so-called spaghetti code. Usually, the older the application the less structured the code (if for no other reason than it has been modified over and over again). Most often, but not always, the applications use a relational database as the underlying data store.

Some of the applications have been updated to provide graphical user interfaces. Some also have been restructured to use client-server architecture.

In addition to modernizing the applications to support new technology and new market requirements, many need to be updated for a more global economy as e-commerce and e-business change the way business is conducted. It is estimated that more than 70 percent of business-to-business and consumer-to-business transactions will occur electronically by the year 2003. E-commerce is enabling more and more business to compete in international markets.

Most developers of small-to-medium-size application have a customer base that is regional in nature. These local customers want to expand their markets through e-commerce and e-business to an international scope. The internationalization of business will force the application developers to enhance their applications to support multiple languages, systems of additional weights and measures, and multiple currencies (including the new Euro currency).

Although highly skilled and knowledgeable in the application areas of expertise, internationalizing the applications is a new experience for many ISVs. In addition, the increased workloads resulting from an international customer set require applications that scale well. An important option for solving this problem, as well as expanding opportunities for marketing an application, is to provide the application on multiple hardware platforms and operating systems.

The preceding discussion provides the background for the capabilities the SanFrancisco product delivers to application developers. Major requirements include:

- The new or revised application must embrace the technologies to support e-business and e-commerce:

  > Adopt readily available, low-cost technology (e.g., the Internet for connectivity).

  > Use consumer-familiar browser technology for information presentation and data capture.

  > Allow any authorized user access to the application sever from anywhere in the world.

> ➤ Allow data and application logic to be located at the most optimum execution point.

> ➤ Support a distributed environment.

> ➤ Allow access to the application from a variety of user devices.

- Provide support for the commercial market opportunity.

- Provide international support.

- Provide support for multiple server platforms and operating systems.

- Reduce the time to market for the new application.

- Reduce development costs.

- Reduce long-term maintenance costs.

- Coexist with the legacy applications and data, including support for the prevalent relational databases in use today.

Meeting these challenges has proven to be a formidable task. It has required the use and integration of new and emerging technologies with proven concepts. At times, this has resulted in a product that moved ahead of the market and organizational standards. At other times, the result meant retrofitting the product as industry standards emerged. Nevertheless, the advantages to application developers are proving to far outweigh any migration costs.

Jump Starting Application Developers

In the purest sense, not all of the items in the preceding list represent current market requirements. Some are pleas from the application developers to create the tools and an application-development environment that would allow them to take advantage of the emerging commercial e-business opportunity. The concepts and technologies used in SanFrancisco were selected not only to help application developers improve their productivity, reduce their development costs, and reduce time to market, but also to meet the emerging commercial market opportunities.

Some of those infrastructure technologies and the rational for selecting them are as follows:

- Java and the Java related concepts to provide Application Server (platform) and user device (client) independence.

- Object technology to promote code reuse and to take advantage of the inherent distributed operation of both data and function (any to any from any).

- Internet technology as the readily available, underlying communications support.

- Application model that supports multiple types of clients, including browser technology familiar to developers and users.

- Application infrastructure that supports the distribution of data and function across a network.

It is generally accepted that the technologies, as mentioned in the preceding list, can reduce development time and costs. However, application developers have told IBM that even more is needed to be competitive. ISVs need a way to overcome initial barriers and costs that will prevent them from realizing long-term benefits.

Barriers to New Technology

The first barrier for developers to overcome is the retraining of their development staff. Since it was necessary to use object-oriented programming concepts and the Java object language to meet the requirements, the task is greater than just learning another programming language. Not only is it necessary to learn Java, but it is also necessary to learn how to analyze a problem in terms of objects and how to use that analysis to design an object-oriented solution. In effect, a whole new approach to developing commercial applications must be learned, and a whole new set of tools must be used.

A second barrier is the risk involved in moving to a new technology. Often, the first solution that is built with a new set of skills and a new technology is less than perfect. A poor design will manifest itself in problems such as code that does not function properly, poor performance, or a solution that is hard to use. These initial setbacks are a necessary step to learning how to apply a new technology, but the number and magnitude of the problems must be kept at a level that will allow a business to continue to support their customer base while the change to the new approach is learned.

A third problem that faces IBM's partners is the need—even as they begin to use new technology—to be highly productive. For many businesses, one factor is that the requirements of their customers are changing faster than the application developers are able to update solutions. New application requirements, additional hardware platforms and operating systems, the need to use the Internet and intranets, and the need to support various data-storage mechanisms all have major impacts on their application code base. Often it is difficult to customize ISV software to a specific customer's way of doing business.

Likewise, it is usually difficult to help customers combine software from different vendors—with in-house applications—into a workable solution. The larger the customer base for an application, the greater the potential for customer-specific customization. Most application developers do not plan for, nor do they design their applications for, a large amount of customer-specific customization. While there still is a need for customer-specific applications, there also is an increasing demand for custom solutions that is being fueled by the e-commerce phenomenon.

A fourth barrier is a resulting manifestation of the above three barriers. Application developers are finding that the ongoing maintenance and support is a greater part of their business than new development. This makes it much more difficult to adopt new technologies. The problem is to find a way to divert resources from an already stressed product-support team. These problems are complicated even more when some of the customers are slower to move to new technology than are other customers.

ISVs cannot just ignore the applications and databases that have traditionally been used. IBM's partners find that they cannot keep up with the requested changes, and that more and more of their development investment is being spent on support for infrastructure or on common business logic that all applications in the domain must have. Less and less of their development investment is being spent on functions that can give them a competitive advantage in the marketplace.

The final barrier is one of cost. Small and medium-size companies do not have the financial resources to purchase new tools, new development platforms, and support contracts. They want a way to defer these costs until they have an opportunity to complete their development work and to begin deployment of their application. Larger companies are able to support up-front costs, but need to be assured that the required investment will be in proportion to the usage and benefit that is gained.

Overcoming the Barriers

The current SanFrancisco products (and the WebSphere Business Components that will soon follow) not only help application developers meet crucial market requirements for e-commerce but also help them address several internal concerns and issues. The following is a summary of the major concepts and technologies of IBM's component products and their benefits to application developers.

- Extensive education support and documentation are available.

- Consulting support is available for initial projects.

- An infrastructure layer is provided so programmers developing applications can concentrate on application functions. Code reuse is extensive since common business objects and business components are available. The use of a code generator greatly reduces the amount of code that needs to be addressed manually.

- Productivity gains allow smaller teams to focus on new projects, allowing support of existing systems and customers.

- The business model lowers up-front costs.

One of the original objectives for SanFrancisco was to reduce the learning curve typically associated with adopting and using new technology for the first time. SanFrancisco helps with this by allowing developers to modify existing designs and code rather than starting from scratch. SanFrancisco makes it easier to learn to build object-oriented applications because developers can design their solutions using a proven and well-tested application design instead of developing their own unique approach. This provides consistency in how applications are designed and makes it easier to recognize and understand what a particular piece of code is doing. Extensive documentation is provided on how to design and program using SanFrancisco, and how the common business objects are designed. In addition, IBM classes are available that cover the basics of object-oriented design, coding in Java, and how to use SanFrancisco.

Even with all of this, there is a large learning curve associated with moving from procedural languages and design to the use of SanFrancisco. Much of this learning process is associated with learning to design objects. Experience shows that application developers are most successful (especially if they are just starting to use object-oriented technology) if they have skilled mentors (consultants) to help guide them through initial projects. SanFrancisco is working with a number of consultant groups to provide this expertise when needed. A testing lab also is available where applications can be brought in for final tuning and testing. This allows direct access to skilled SanFrancisco developers who can help ISVs achieve the best possible results with their applications.

SanFrancisco provides an infrastructure that provides the complex functions necessary to support mission-critical commercial applications. For example, all commercial applications require transaction-processing capability, recovery, communications support, and many more functions. Extensive work has been done in areas such as thread management at the object level, and in query support and optimization to provide an infrastructure that includes necessary functions that will perform well. The infrastructure has been designed to allow interoperability with existing databases and applications. It also is designed so that different relational databases can be used for persistent storage without having to change the application code.

SanFrancisco also is providing object models for specific domain business processes and default business logic that can be used to start building applications in these domains. The domain specific models have been designed as business frameworks so that they can be easily extended and modified. Use of a shared architecture also makes it easier to integrate components from different software developers into overall solutions. The design patterns and the infrastructure capabilities, such as multithreading and locking at the object level, allow components to interoperate with each other. SanFrancisco recommends using a three-tier application architecture. This supports the use of many different clients and also allows an application developer to rapidly adopt to new types of clients.

Developers who are now using SanFrancisco are finding that they are better able to meet customer demands. In part, this is due to being able to use the infrastructure and application content that is provided by SanFrancisco. Developers can choose how much or how little of the technology to use when they build their applications. At the highest level of reuse, SanFrancisco provides a base object-oriented analysis and frameworks for business components in application domains such as business financials, order management, and warehouse management. The models include basic business logic for each domain. Some developers will choose to implement their application by enhancing and extending these components instead of building their entire application from scratch.

Other developers will choose to build applications by using some of the common business objects and not using the business logic contained in a specific domain framework. And some will choose to use only the distributed-object infrastructure and build all of their objects, components, and business processes themselves. In all cases, SanFrancisco allows developers to apply more resources on the functions that will give them competitive advantages because it supplies the common function that is required.

Whatever a developer chooses as the degree of reusability, the application—when completed—can be deployed in a variety of topologies without special considerations. The SanFrancisco infrastructure was designed knowing full well that customer business processes are imposed over a wide variety of physical topology and organizational structures. SanFrancisco applications can be deployed with a central application and data repository, a totally distributed application and data repository, or in any configuration between these extents without special design or programming considerations.

Developers also are finding that the use of a code generator speeds development by reducing the amount of time needed to build new functions and by reducing testing time by reducing the number of bugs that are produced in the new code. As a result, they are able to both support existing customers and applications while developing their new products.

The SanFrancisco Business model further reduces the application developer's initial investment. For developers who are building applications that will be resold, the business model does not require any out-of-pocket cash to get started and to use SanFrancisco. The developer pays IBM royalties based on product sales. The royalty rate agreed to by the advisory ISVs and IBM was very low. Developer's who are building applications for their own company's use initially only need to pay for development platforms. At the time the application goes to production, additional runtime fees are paid based on the size of the deployment.

Summarizing the Value of SanFrancisco

Frequently, these days the industry buzz is about *application servers*. Along with other products in the market that use Java and OO technology, SanFrancisco can be called an application server . However, as the following examples show, SanFrancisco brings more to the table.

1. **Java:** Application servers running on different operating systems and hardware platforms use Java.

2. **Object Oriented (OO):** Object-oriented technology has been around for a long time. The cost of information technology is now low enough to use it everywhere. OO is the first level of code reuse. While all the new application servers use OO, some use the technology more effectively than others do. The team that developed SanFrancisco—the first cross-platform, OO-based application server in the industry—had more experience developing OO platforms than anyone in the industry. They also did the AS/400 operating system.

3. **Programming Model:** The programming model provides programming discipline without interference. It ensures a consistent approach and structure for the resulting applications. Well-structured code is easier to modify, change, and support. All the popular application servers have a programming model. Whose is better can be debated. The programming model define by SanFrancisco is well suited for the commercial application market. Others may be better suited for different market opportunities.

4. **Infrastructure:** Among technologists, infrastructure is also called the plumbing because it provides the services and functions necessary for a

disciplined operating environment and application-market segment. The term *disciplined operating environment* describes those functions necessary to ensure good coding practices and techniques. SanFrancisco does this automatically for the programmer. The functions provided by the SanFrancisco infrastructure are designed to support the application server. Functions targeted at the personal productivity application market would offer a different set of functions. IBM has more experience in the commercial market than anyone in the industry. The application severs following after SanFrancisco are building their infrastructure to a proposed industry standard called Enterprise JavaBeans. SanFrancisco will also become EJB compliant when the standard has enough function defined to adequately support the commercial application-market segment. Currently, it is easier for those application servers targeted at other market segments to become EJB compliant. If ISVs are willing to invest the time and effort to include the missing infrastructure as part of their application, application severs that are EJB compliant can participate in the commercial market.

5. **Code Generators:** Code generators are a very good way to improve productivity. To be effective, code generators depend on a well-structured program model and design. The infrastructure and application frameworks built into SanFrancisco improve the quality and amount of code that can be generated from modeling tools. It is a simple case of the more tools there are to work with the better the results. With SanFrancisco, the modeling tools have more to start with than other application servers. The SanFrancisco product is also open to all tool providers. Because ISVs can select the tools most familiar to them, the need to learn new tools from different providers is reduced.

6. **Legacy Coexistence:** The SanFrancisco product was conceived knowing full well that conversion of all applications and the migration of all customers to e-commerce is neither practical nor desirable for IBM, the ISVs, or customers. For this reason, coexistence with legacy applications and data always has been a major design consideration. IBM has the largest commercial application customer

base in the world. Customers and ISVs can benefit more from
SanFrancisco than any other application server.

7. **Reusable Business Objects and Components:** The ultimate in programmer productivity is to have much of the code already done for you.
There is no better way to get an application to market faster. Design, development, testing, and debug are already done. SanFrancisco has more
reusable business objects and components than any other application
server.

8. **Application Framework:** The SanFrancisco reusable Business Objects
and Components are designed as frameworks. A framework can be easily modified and extended while maintaining its intended design, functionality and integrity. No other application sever has the repertoire of
application frameworks as SanFrancisco.

9. **Affordable Business Model:** The entry into new market opportunity is
sometimes beyond the affordability of small and medium ISVs. The
SanFrancisco business model delays much of the financial burden until
the ISV is generating revenue using the SanFrancisco application server.
The key point is that SanFrancisco is a royalty-based payment scheme.
The royalty rates are very low. No other application server product in
the industry has a more competitive business model for the small and
medium ISVs, or for that matter large ISVs, than SanFrancisco. In addition, the SanFrancisco business model allows ISVs to price their products in the way that is most appropriate for them and their customer set.

10. **Alliances between Partners:** Using SanFrancisco, multiple ISVs can
cooperate on larger and more lucrative projects than any of them could
do on their own. The SanFrancisco frameworks, program model, tool
sets, and infrastructure were all designed with cooperation between
ISVs as a major consideration. That cooperation is already beginning
to happen between the SanFrancisco business partners.

11. **Maturity:** E-commerce and e-business is a whole new opportunity for
everyone. SanFrancisco has brought the most to the table two years
sooner than anyone else. That two-year period is immeasurable in
terms of function, quality, and market preparedness. All the other ap-

plication servers are trying to achieve the same stature as
SanFrancisco through acquisitions and alliances.

12. **Deployability:** SanFrancisco has the most flexible deployment capability of any commercial application server in the market. The
same applications can be deployed in any customer organizational
structure and physical topology.

SanFrancisco Design Principles

Most approaches to object-oriented design assume that the result of the process
is a finished application that is used in the operation of a business. However,
the application software built in the SanFrancisco project has a different design
point. It is not intended to be a finished application. Instead, it is intended as a
starting point for developers who are building e-commerce enabled applications. In designing SanFrancisco code to be modified, the SanFrancisco designers and developers added steps to the usual object-oriented design processes.

The initial steps in the design are the same as any other OO project. The design
process began by capturing the requirements for the vertical domain that was
being examined. Multiple applications were looked at and typical task flows in
the domain were documented. These were verified by domain experts (in our
case, from several companies) to ensure that we had representative coverage
from several industry experts.

The second step—developing an initial class model for the domain—also was
typical of object-oriented analysis and design. Again this was reviewed by object-oriented and domain experts to ensure its completeness and quality. It was
at this point that additional analysis was needed before proceeding with the development of the frameworks.

The first additional process of this new design analysis was to identify the parts
of the domain design that someone building an application that is based on a
framework would typically want to change, enhance, or override. The term *extension points* is used to describe the places where modification is expected.
Examples of reasons for changes include:

- **Internationalization:** Changes required due to the country or countries in which the finished application will be used.

- **Industry Specific:** Changes needed due to the industry the finished application will support.

- **Customer Specific:** Changes needed to support the business and organizational structure of the customer of the finished application.

- **E-commerce:** Changes to support the e-business of the target customer.

Equally important, it is necessary to identify those areas of the design that should be reserved for application developers. Therefore, developers receive help with applications rather than competition in the marketplace. By providing only the most basic functions, IBM's business partners can continue to add their value to the frameworks to produce finished applications. Examples of these areas include:

- **User Interface:** The final look and feel of the application.

- **Industry Algorithms:** Embedded logic that allows one application to function better than another.

As was the case with the extension points, the final design must have changes that can be integrated easily into the function provided by the frameworks.

Working with our partners, we made sure the design was exactly what they needed by reviewing it with them. We asked them to verify that we had found the correct extension points and that we were not providing function that would compete with what they wanted to produce.

The second part of the additional analysis done for the framework design was targeted at reducing the interactions between the various classes in the frameworks. Grouping the classes that cooperated to perform domain tasks started reducing interactions. The design of these categories was then reworked to ensure that there were no two-way interactions between categories.

For example, some two-way interactions could be removed by simply moving a class from one category to another. At other times, it was necessary to add an additional category to change a two-way interaction into one-way interactions. This approach had two benefits. First, the categories become candidates for replacement by a developer who is using the frameworks. They have a clearly defined, finite set of interfaces that they must meet to be able to do this. Second, we could organize the categories into blocks of work that could be developed independently of other, unrelated categories. This aided us in structuring our development plan.

Use Patterns for Quality and Consistency

Application designers and developers have recognized for many years that they revisit similar problems over and over again. The same types of problems occur in many different domains, and in many different applications within those domains. If the problems encountered are the same or similar, it makes sense that the solutions to those problems can be the same or similar if the appropriate technology is applied properly.

The concept of design patterns has evolved to help designers and developers solve these similar problems by reusing structures that have successfully been applied in other situations. This approach improves the quality of the solution because proven design concepts are being reused and because the consequences of those design decisions are well understood. In addition, it is easier for developers to understand the system. Rather than having to understand unique designs in each solution, developers can learn a handful of patterns. The method also provides greater consistency and quality across solutions because the same proven techniques are used over and over.

Design patterns have been found to be very useful in the SanFrancisco project. We began by examining the patterns that were available in print. These had evolved primarily by studying productivity applications of user interface systems. Some of these patterns continue to be useful in the development of the non-GUI business application frameworks. A good example is the concept of Abstract Factory, which allows distribution of persistent data and eliminates the need for an application developer to code directly to underlying persistence interfaces. However, in designing easily extensible business logic, we also found several reoccurring design problems that benefited from a new design pattern. Examples of patterns include:

- **Atomic Entity Update:** Support grouping of updates of multiple business objects into atomic transactions.

- **Property Container:** Support dynamic properties/attributes on business objects.

- **Controller:** Allow partial sharing of business object properties/attributes across an organization.

- **Chain of Responsibility Driven Strategy:** Allow a flexible way to change and select which domain specific algorithms are applied.

- **Policy:** Allow easy customization of volatile business algorithms.

The atomic entity update pattern is a very simple one that will help to illustrate the concept of design patterns. Often groups of updates to multiple business objects must be considered as a single transaction. In other words, either all of the updates must be applied or none of them should be applied. In the SanFrancisco frameworks, we have used the command as a way to group these updates, and then establish transaction boundaries around the whole command. This gives us a simple structure, which achieves the objective and that can be applied in many situations.

Another simple pattern that we use is the property container. The problem to be solved is that businesses need to be able to add properties/attributes to business objects at execution time. This allows them to enhance the system without having to change code, recompile, and reinstall. The pattern accomplishes this by associating a set of property objects (Name/Value pairs) with entity business objects. For example, a user could add the property "Second Fax Number" with the value "123-456-7890" to an object representing a partner with which they do business.

Provide for Application Portability and Flexibility

The SanFrancisco infrastructure is designed to help developers build applications that are portable and flexible without requiring changes to the application code itself. In part, this is achieved by the SanFrancisco Programming Model, which provides the necessary operations for distributed business objects such as object creation and retrieval, transaction begin and commit, and security. These objects are presented in a way that gives better ease of use than other distributed-object technologies because the operations integrate a number of services.

Application developers do not need to have a detailed understanding of low-level object services and do not need to assemble them themselves. For example, application developers can access a persistent business object by using a single factory interface. They do not need to write the code that uses the naming service to locate the object, the container service to activate it from the particular type of persistent storage, and the locking service that ensures data integrity while the object is in use.

The infrastructure also insulates business objects from changes in specific technologies. For example, object request broker operations do not appear in the programming model. Therefore, changes in this technology will not impact the business objects. Likewise, the infrastructure provides separation of programming and administrative roles so that areas like object location and security can be administered separately from the program flow. Also, the infrastructure masks any platform-specific function, which increases the portability of applications and business objects.

Another important part of portability and flexibility is to use three-tier architecture as the overall architecture for the application, and SanFrancisco has been designed to support this type of design. This design has all application data (the model) separated from the information about how it is presented to the user (the view). In addition, the application logic, which defines the flow of an application based on user interaction (the controller), should again be separated into a separate part. An application is built by associating all three—model, view, and controller—with each other. Conceptually, an application can be split into three tiers.

The first tier contains the view (the presentation information). In traditional applications, the first tier is built using a library of GUI components. In thin-client environments, where no application software is installed and where the client communicates with the server through the Internet or an intranet, the first tier is typically represented by a browser. The browser displays Web documents that provide the application interface. These documents are typically written using HTML or Dynamic HyperText Markup Language (DHMTL).

HTML and DHTML are standards that have been adopted to facilitate the electronic exchange and display of simple documents.

The second tier in the architecture contains the logic that controls the flow of the application and the flow with the browser. A controller or application server can be used for the application flow. This code acts as a client to the persistent data and uses Bean or command interfaces to interact with the persistent objects.

By providing different modes under which a Bean can operate, a Bean hides the complexity individual objects from the client. It can access a business object through a controller, or directly by getting it from its owning business object, without any impact on the client interface of the Bean. Moreover, each Bean can represent an individual business object as well as an entire collection of business objects. In a thin-client environment, a *view server* might also be used to handle—because they are running in different processes on different machines—the data traffic between the view and the controller. For example, a servlet can play the role of a view server.

The third tier contains the model (the application data). The model knows nothing about how the data is presented to a user and, in many cases, it is designed and developed independent from any actual application. In a business application environment, the model describes the business domain model, which contains business data as well as the processes that control the data.

For example, the SanFrancisco frameworks contain business objects as well as business processes modeled for specific business domains (general ledger, warehouse, and order management). These domain-specific objects and processes are fairly stable; in contrast, the client application requirements change very often. Also, different client applications, without knowing about each other, may share the same server-side business object. Figure 11.1 shows the WebSphere and SanFrancisco infrastructure.

Once the three tiers have been identified and designed, the actual application can be implemented for a particular target environment. In other words, all three tiers can run on the same machine or they can be split up over several separate machines and processes. Access to server-side business object data can be optimized by caching some of the data in the Bean. If and how this is done is transparent to the client of the Bean. There is no impact on the client interface that the Bean provides.

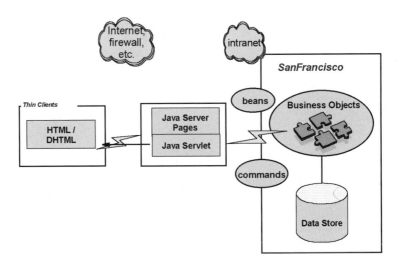

Figure 11.1: The WebSphere and SanFrancisco Infrastructure has three tiers.

Architecture Overview

The SanFrancisco product includes three layers of reusable code for use by application developers. The top layer consists of business process components for key business activities. These are called the Core Business Processes and each provides business objects and default business logic for a particular vertical domain.

The second layer, called the Common Business Objects, provides definitions of commonly used business objects that can be used as the base for interoperability between applications.

The lowest layer, called the Foundation, provides the infrastructure and services that are required to build industrial-strength applications using distributed, managed objects, on multiple platforms.

Application developers can choose to use SanFrancisco at any or all of the three layers. For example, they could choose to build directly on the Foundation and develop their own frameworks and business objects. Or they could choose to use the Core Business Processes and just make the extensions needed to complete their application.

Figure 11.2 shows a diagram of the SanFrancisco architecture.

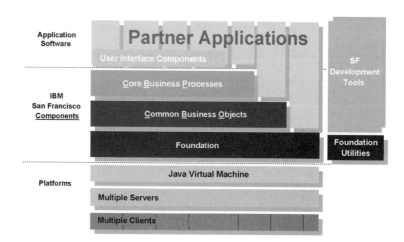

Figure 11.2: Using the SanFrancisco architecture, developers can choose any or all three layers.

Core Business Processes

The Core Business Processes form the top layer of the SanFrancisco architecture. They provide components complete with default business behavior in a sound, well-designed, object-oriented architecture. They have been designed as frameworks that include extension points. These extension points make it easy to extend their function, and they override the default behavior. Initially, three application domains have been designed. They are:

1. Business Financial.
   a) accounts payable.
   b) accounts receivable.
   c) general ledger.

2. Order Management—several variations of sales and purchase orders.

3. Warehouse Management—receiving, storing, and shipping of materials.

In all cases, it is expected that the frameworks will be extended and changed. They are not intended to be finished applications. Estimates are that the frameworks can provide up to 40 percent of a finished application. A majority of the remaining work will be in the area of the user interface. This estimate is based on feedback received from partners working on the project. However, the exact percentage will vary depending on the specifics of the application being built.

Common Business Objects

The Common Business Objects (CBOs) are a set components that fall into three general types:

- Business objects commonly used in multiple application domains.

- Business object interfaces that provide interpretability between applications.

- Objects that implement frequently useful design patterns for business applications.

During the requirements and analysis phase of the project, many business objects were identified that are common to more than one vertical application domain. Providing these objects in a common layer, for use by multiple applications from different vendors, enables these applications to share the information and logic encapsulated in these objects. This enables a company running multiple applications to maintain this information in a common way and have a common database for all their SanFrancisco based applications. Examples of these business objects include:

- **Address:** Format control; relate address to locale and language.

- **Business Partner:** Customer or supplier information.

- **Calendar:** Natural and period-based calendars.

- **Number Series:** Generates serial sequences of alphanumeric strings for identifying objects, documents, etc.

- **Currency:** Supports arithmetic and logical comparisons of currencies, exchange rate conversion, etc.

The next type of function found in the CBOs enables application interoperability by providing interfaces to core business processes. These CBOs allow independently developed SanFrancisco applications to work together and allows SanFrancisco applications to interoperate with legacy applications. This is done by creating an interface—such as the interface to post an entry to the general ledger—to a desired business process. The implementation for the business process can be a SanFrancisco-based application or a legacy application. The interface for the general-ledger posting can then be used by independently developed SanFrancisco applications or legacy applications.

The last type of mini-framework in the CBOs layer supports design patterns that have been found to be useful in many different application domains. The objects in these frameworks are generally not business objects visible at the domain level, but are finer-grained objects that flexibly implement some part of another business object or business process. Examples of these are:

- **Keyables:** Used to create composite keys and to support balances across different composite keys.

- **Classification Types:** Used to represent user-defined types that modify business policies.

- **Result Messages:** Used to accumulate multiple warnings or errors from complex validations.

Providing the CBOs layer for reusable business objects, cross-application interfaces, and design pattern implementations allows application developers to concentrate on building function into their applications that will differentiate them in the marketplace but still work well with other vendors' solutions.

Foundation

The lowest layer of the SanFrancisco frameworks is called the Foundation. It provides the infrastructure that is used to build the CBOs and the Core Business Processes. The Foundation includes two sets of interfaces that are visible to application developers. The first of these is the Object Model Classes. These base classes provide a consistent programming model for use by application developers. Examples include:

- **Entity:** Support for independent, shareable objects.
- **Dependent:** Support for objects that must be owned by an Entity.
- **Command:** Support for a group of operations on one or more objects.
- **Factory:** Manages lifetime and access of instances of objects.

Regardless of the platform on which the application will eventually execute, application developers use the same interfaces. This means that developers can write their applications once, deploy them on many different platforms, and use many different persistence mechanisms.

Developers use a second set of application utilities called the interfaces application. These utilities provide services that will be needed by most applications built using SanFrancisco. Examples include:

- **Administration:** Maintaining the SanFrancisco logical network.
- **Configuration:** Location of objects and persistence storage mechanism used.

Many of these services are implemented using functions that already exist in operating systems or other products. SanFrancisco ensures that the functions are well integrated and have a consistent look and feel for developers and administrators.

Tools for Building SanFrancisco-Based Applications

SanFrancisco is an open initiative that is designed to work with a wide variety of tools from multiple vendors. The vision for SanFrancisco application development is to evolve a broad set of integrated development tools that span the entire life cycle of an application. These tools will help developers understand and find the extension points in the frameworks and help produce the code that is needed to build or complete an application.

The vision is being implemented in stages by leading Java tool providers such as IBM, Inprise, Rational, Midcomp, Metex, and Symantec. Their tools support many paradigms and users. For example, object-oriented analysis and design tools are available to help business analysis and developers understand and extend SanFrancisco content. Code generators transform this design into Java source code that is based on the SanFrancisco programming model and Foundation. Links can be built between relational databases and the associated SanFrancisco objects. Java development tools are available to complete and test the application code. Wizards help developers to quickly make needed changes or to build new objects. Also, deployment tools help install the finished application into the environment where it will execute.

Future Directions

Working with Sun and others in the industry, IBM is driving the use of Java for enterprise e-business solutions. The Enterprise JavaBeans (EJB) specification defines the server-side component model for robust e-business solutions, application servers, and object servers. Many of the ideas and interfaces in the Enterprise JavaBeans specification are derived from IBM's work in its SanFrancisco and WebSphere products. The WebSphere product family is the key element of IBM's Enterprise JavaBeans strategy.

IBM is building a large set of cooperating application business components for application developers. This set will include versions of the business content available in the SanFrancisco products today. The Common Business Objects (CBOs) and Core Business Process components (CBPs) will be migrated so that they become EJBs that run on IBM's WebSphere family of Enterprise Java servers (EJSs). IBM will transform the SanFrancisco programming model into an EJB-compliant component model as part of this effort. Transforming the business content into WebSphere EJB components will provide many benefits. This approach provides customers more choices in databases, hardware, and operating systems. It also provides more options in server scalability and performance. For example:

- WebSphere business component solutions will be able to easily combine components with Enterprise JavaBeans from other vendors.

- Tight integration with Web-server environments and new tools for building e-business solutions should result from the industry's wide adoption of Enterprise JavaBeans as a server component model.

- CBOs and CBPs will continue to provide prebuilt application content that can be used to speed the development of applications.

- Different qualities of service—such as replicated naming for continued operation during network failures or automatic workload balancing across servers—will exist in choices of Enterprise JavaBeans servers. IBM believes its WebSphere Application Servers will provide leadership in the server marketplace by delivering a high quality of service for customers and their applications.

In parallel with the WebSphere business component effort, IBM will continue to maintain ongoing service and support for application developers and SanFrancisco customers who are already developing and deploying applications based on IBM SanFrancisco. This includes automating, to the greatest degree possible, the migration of existing applications to WebSphere business components. IBM intends to maintain the SanFrancisco open tools strategy and encourage a choice of application-development tools. This migration will enhance the choice of tools by enabling additional development tools to use WebSphere business components. VisualAge for Java will continue to be the IBM application development environment for SanFrancisco.

Conclusions

The SanFrancisco project has teamed with industry-leading software companies to develop a functionally rich set of infrastructure, CBOs, and business-process components aimed at helping application developers migrate to building applications based on distributed-object technology. Because our business objects are written in Java, they will be able to run on many different platforms without code changes. Using SanFrancisco as the base for building applications shortens the time needed to develop new systems because developers can learn to build systems by modifying consistently designed, well-tested code, instead of having to start from scratch. In effect, we have already encountered, and fixed, many of the coding and design mistakes that would be made by developers trying to learn to use a new technology from scratch.

The first installment of SanFrancisco became available in August 1997. Over 1,000 companies have licensed the code, and over 2,100 downloads of the evaluation code have taken place since then. Work is underway to determine what additional business-process components and infrastructure enhancements IBM's partners and customers need. In addition, work is under way to further integrate the WebSphere and SanFrancisco products. The goal is to replace

SanFrancisco infrastructure with WebSphere, and to allow SanFrancisco content to run on the enhanced WebSphere platform.

For more information on SanFrancisco products and partners, visit:

www.ibm.com/software/ad/sanfrancisco

For more information on WebSphere business component products, visit:

www.ibm.com/software/webservers/components

The value of a network increases as an exponent of the number of users connected to the network.

—Robert Metcalfe
Founder of the 3Com Corporation

12

TCP/IP

CHRIS PETERS

The creation of a means whereby two devices could communicate with each other (for example, a CPU and a printer) was almost simultaneous with the early development of computing machines. The means of doing so took the form of arbitrarily fashioned agreements or specifications for electronic signals traveling over a piece of wire. Taken together, the agreements are called a protocol. There are many communications protocols in use today; *Transaction Communications Protocol/Internet Protocol* (TCP/IP) is one of them.

The protocol originally established for IBM equipment is called Systems Network Architecture (SNA). Initially, SNA was an IBM standard for communications between a host (mainframe) and peripheral devices. SNA later grew in function to include support for communications between whole computers and is widely used today. Microsoft estimates that over half of the world's electronically stored data resides on SNA-based systems. SNA, however, was an IBM convention and not the

> *Editor's Introduction:* TCP/IP networking is the nervous system of the Web. In our body, nerves transmit low-level electrical impulses that are converted at the brain or at the limb to useful tasks or information (wow, that's hot ... press the "h" key, etc.). TCP/IP serves a similar purpose in the Web world, and it's useful for people who make business decisions about IT technology to understand how it works. TCP/IP functionality and technological components are part of every e-business and e-commerce project. Understanding TCP/IP, as you will after reading Chris Peter's chapter, will help you make sound business decisions.
>
> –KR

communications specification used by non-IBM communications platforms such as ARPANET (the forerunner to the Internet).

TCP/IP is the communications protocol of the Internet. The booming popularity of the Internet (the number of Internet users doubles about every 10 months), has assured the future of TCP/IP as the de facto communications standard for the majority of networked installations. IBM has extended communications support within their operating systems to include TCP/IP.

> **Note:** Although you have to use TCP/IP to communicate over the Internet, you do not have to use the Internet to communicate with TCP/IP. TCP/IP is used with great success in closed-communications networks called intranets.

What Is TCP/IP?

When broken down, the term TCP/IP might make more sense if taken as "Communications Agreement for Transaction Processing Over a Communications Link" (the "TCP" part) and "Communications Agreement for the Internetwork and Intranetworks" (the "IP" part).

TCP/IP is a term that represents a group, or family, of agreements about telecommunication services. In other words, TCP/IP is a set of specifications about how data communication will take place between two computers over an electronic link. Once these agreements have been struck, a productive dialog of electronic messaging can take place.

Of this family of communications protocols, TCP (Transaction Communications Protocol) and IP (Internet Protocol) are the most widely used. Therefore, the term TCP/IP has come to represent all the protocols in the family. Bear in mind that there are other protocols in the family and there will no doubt be more added in the future.

TCP/IP is a specification for peer-to-peer types of communications. Specifically, TCP/IP provides support for communication between two programs written at the application level. The two programs can reside on physically separate computers or on the same system.

What Is a Protocol?

To provide a more straightforward definition of the term TCP/IP, the words "Communications Agreement" could be substituted for the word "Protocol." "Protocol" means there is an agreement between two linked participants that allows electronic communication to take place.

As an analogy, consider the communication mechanism used when you place an ordinary voice telephone call. You perform the physical addressing required when you dial the phone number of the person you wish to reach. You first wait for the physical communications routing to take place (although you probably aren't aware of how the routing is accomplished and you probably don't care). You then wait for the phone on the other end of the line to ring and thus announcing an incoming call. You also wait for a person to pick up the phone receiver to complete the physical connection, and for someone to say something like "Hello."

If you don't wait for the preceding steps—you just start talking immediately after dialing, and if you're already talking when the other person says "Hello"—only confusion can result. So you don't just start talking; you observe the communications agreement established for voice telephone calls. That communications agreement could be said to be the "Voice Telephone Protocol" had we the need of such a term.

There might be more to this protocol business than you realize, however. For example, by agreement, telephone numbers in the U.S. are 10 digits long. There are three digits of general information (the area code), three digits of more specific information (the prefix), and four digits of specific information that exactly identifies an endpoint within the network. You could think of the overall telephone system in the U.S. as a collection—each with its own area code—of smaller telephone systems. This same scheme of subdividing addresses is used in TCP/IP networks to route communications.

Low- and High-Level Communications Support

The TCP/IP family of specifications contains a seemingly odd mix of low-level and communications-support structures like those that packetize data and route transmission through a network, and high-level applications of communication support, like Telnet remote logon and FTP. Remember, however, that TCP/IP is a set of communications specifications that define what TCP/IP is and what a TCP/IP-compliant operating system must do. Indeed, some systems don't comply completely with the full set of TCP/IP specifications.

The TCP/IP Protocol Stack

In any network communications platform, a number of tasks must be performed; things like matching communications support to physical hardware, error checking and recovery, and preparing data for transmission. The tasks are handled by multiple support layers that work together. The group of support layers is called a *stack*.

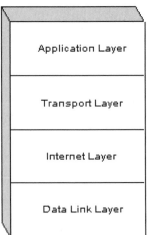

TCP/IP too operates in a layered arrangement of support mechanisms—a stack. The TCP/IP protocol stack is a model for the division of responsibility for network communications tasks. The TCP/IP stack is represented in four layers (see Figure 12.1).

The layers make the following contributions:

Figure 12.1: The division of labor in a TCP/IP protocol stack has four layers.

- **Application Layer:** Forms the interface between a TCP/IP application (like Telnet or a sockets program) and low-level TCP/IP support layers. This layer of the stack enables you to write a TCP/IP client/server program.

- **Transport Layer:** This layer is responsible for preparing data for transmission and making received data available.

- **Internet Layer:** The Internet layer provides the information required to route data from one node to another within a network until it reaches its destination.

- **Data Link Layer:** This layer serves as the interface between the physical hardware used in a network and the higher-level layers. The hardware in a network is of no concern to the TCP/IP applications that use the hardware because the data link layer provides a transparent interface.

TCP/IP Utilities

As an experienced IT professional you might well ask yourself, "This is all just grand but what can TCP/IP do for *me*?"

The TCP/IP specification calls for implementation of certain communications management functions as well as high-level applications. These high-level applications are called *TCP/IP utilities*. The most common TCP/IP utilities include:

- **FTP:** File Transfer Protocol is support for bulk transfer of program and data files from one computer to another.

- **Telnet:** Telnet is support for remote logon services.

- **HTTP Server:** This server program sends multimedia documents (like HTML) and attendant graphic and data files to a remote computer's Web browser in response to requests.

- **DNS:** Domain Name Server is a TCP/IP utility application that provides addressing information to computers in a network. A DNS server allows the network administrator to control IP addressing for multiple computers from a single host system.

- **SNMP:** Simple Network Management Protocol is a means of collecting information and conducting management tasks across a network.

- **SMTP:** Simple Mail Transfer Protocol provides support for the exchange of e-mail.

- **POP:** The Post Office Protocol mail server performs e-mail routing functions for clients that support the POP3 interface.

- **LPR and LPD:** Line Printer Requester and Line Printer Daemon are the client and server portions of data transfer for printer output.

- **BOOTP:** Bootstrap Protocol allows a controlling host to dynamically associate a server with workstations, to assign IP addresses to workstations, and to supply sources for booting a network client type of PC.

- **TFTP:** Trivial File Transfer Protocol is similar to FTP in that it supplies files across a network, but it does so without any authentication. Together BOOTP and TFTP provide support for network client.

- **RouteD:** The Routing Daemon provides routing information for RIP and RIP2 (Routing Information Protocol). RIP technology assists TCP/IP in dynamically routing transmissions across networks.

- **DHCP:** Dynamic Host Configuration Protocol enables you to send configuration information to remote computers on a TCP/IP network.

> **Note:** You do not need to know how to use all of these TCP/IP utilities in order to take good advantage of TCP/IP. IBM has provided support for all of these varied utilities in an effort to more completely comply with the full TCP/IP communications specification.

TCP/IP Routing and Data Delivery Support

TCP/IP communication support also provides the network management and data-delivery mechanisms required to identify endpoints in a peer network and to route data between those endpoints. TCP/IP network management software can monitor the network connections and congestion and route traffic accordingly.

Data transmitted from one computer to another moves through the network according to TCP/IP routing support. TCP/IP routing keeps track of actual physical hardware information as it relates to IP addresses.

TCP/IP routing can be direct or indirect. *Direct routing* is used when the two computers are on the same physical network (like Token Ring or Ethernet). Each computer on the network knows its own IP address. When a data transmission is placed on the network, its destination address is sent with it as a header. Each computer on the physical network will examine the header and accepts a matching transmission, thus taking it off the network.

Indirect routing supports for data transmission when the two computers are not on the same physical network. A router or IP forwarder must be present between two physical networks to accept transmissions intended for a host on the other network. The routers are made known to the sending computer by entries in its routing tables. Date transmissions are then sent to the router, which places the data on the proper physical network.

Packets

TCP/IP sends data through a network in packets. When you send data through a TCP/IP network, your data is broken into chunks, wrapped with identifying information, and then sent. Together, the data and its attendant identifying information is called a *packet*. A packet is a proscribed number of bytes of data wrapped in an "envelope." The envelope identifies the sender and the intended recipient of the data.

Naturally, when your data is broken into chunks, there must be some way of putting it back together again before your application can make sense of it. Packets also carry information that TCP/IP support can use on the receiving end to put the data back together.

The exact route that each packet takes to its destination is determined by TCP/IP network management software. Packets travel through a TCP/IP network according to data traffic algorithms that assess link types, transmission priorities, and congestion, and determine the best route. Indeed, two packets transmitted at nearly the same moment to the same destination could conceivably take different routes.

Hosts

In a TCP/IP network, each computer is called a *host*. It doesn't matter that one computer is a server and another is a client; in a TCP/IP network each computer is still a host. Each host can represent one or more *nodes*. A node is a labeled endpoint within a network that is capable of receiving addressed transmissions.

Internet Protocol Addressing

Of the more confusing concepts regarding TCP/IP is that of Internet protocol addressing. First, there's that word *Internet*. It sounds like you have to be attached to the Internet to be concerned with IP addressing, but you don't. Beyond that, the notation used to describe an IP address, such as 123.123.12.1, has contributed to the confusion.

When you set up your own closed TCP/IP network, or *intranet*, you must make decisions regarding assignments of host IP addresses. You have a great deal of latitude when your network is closed, but not so much when you're connecting to the Internet.

IP Address Notation

You must understand what an IP address represents so that you can take full advantage of TCP/IP's capabilities. A typical IP address looks like this:

```
68.76.95.97
```

There are four sets of numerals separated by three periods. Have you ever noticed that a set of numerals in an IP address never exceeds a value of 255? Read on.

TCP/IP network-management support keeps track of the hosts in the network by number. Each host identifies itself to the network by number, and that number will be used by TCP/IP to direct transmissions to each host.

The number used to identify a host in a TCP/IP network is 4 bytes in length, which means that the IP address number must be less than 4,294,967,295. That is the largest number you can represent in 4 bytes. While 4 bytes of data is 32 bits, each byte is 8 bits long (called an *octet*). If all 8 bits in each of the 4 bytes is set to "1," the resulting binary value is:

```
1111 1111    1111 1111    1111 1111    1111 1111.
```

The decimal representation of this binary value is 4,294,967,295.

It is important to understand that these two notation methods—one in binary using zeros and ones and the other in decimal using zero through nine—are simply two ways to represent the same numeric *value*. In other words:

```
11111111 11111111 11111111 11111111 (bin) =  4,294,967,295 (dec)
```

However, IP addresses, although they are numeric values, are neither truly binary nor decimal. A slightly different notation is used because of the a bit-pattern logic scheme used in subdividing IP addresses (*subnetworking*).

Recall that there are 4 bytes in an IP address. If you consider each byte on its own, even though it's part of the overall address, you can describe the numeric value of each individual byte as a decimal number from 0 to 255, the binary equivalent of 00000000 to 11111111. That's how IP address are represented. Each individual byte of the 4 bytes used in an IP address is represented as if it stood alone. That's why there's a "dot" between each of the four decimal values—to separate the individual bytes of the overall four.

Consider the IP address 68.76.95.97. In binary, it would be represented as follows:

```
decimal 68  =  binary 0100 0100
decimal 76  =  binary 0100 1100
decimal 95  =  binary 0101 1111
decimal 97  =  binary 0110 0001
```

Now put all of the binary representations together. Not added, just set side-by-side:

```
|   byte 1   |   byte 2   |   byte 3   |   byte 4   |
   0100 0100    0100 1100    0101 1111    0110 0001
      68           76           95           97
```

This binary value 01000100010011000101111101100001 is the real IP address value as used internally by TCP/IP support. It's equivalent decimal notation is 1,145,855,841.

Network ID and Host ID

By convention, a 4-byte IP address is usually broken into two logical parts: a network ID portion and a host ID portion. This arrangement allows improved transmission routing by TCP/IP support.

Consider, again, the voice telephone system. A telephone endpoint's 10-digit phone number consists of parts. There is an area code that is analogous to a network ID, and the local phone number within that area code is analogous to a host ID.

The division of an IP address into network and host IDs follows a rather arbitrary specification called *IP address classes*.

IP Address Classes

By agreement, IP addresses are divided into network and host ID portions. There are five classes of IP addresses, or methods by which the network portion and host portion of the overall address are determined. Each class is assigned a letter designation, A, B, C, D, or E. Of these five, classes A, B, and C are for use in ordinary TCP/IP applications.

The point within the overall address at which the division takes place is determined by the value of the first byte. Five ranges of values are used, each corresponding to a class (see Table 12.1).

Table 12.1: *IP Address Classes.*

Class	Value of First Byte	Network ID Bytes	Host ID Bytes	Networks	Hosts per Network
A	0 - 127*	1	2, 3 & 4	126	16,000,000
B	128 - 191	1 & 2	3 & 4	16,000	65,000
C	192 - 223	1, 2 & 3	4	2,000,000	254
D	224 - 239				Multicast
E	240 - 255				Reserved

* Network ID 127 is reserved for loopback testing

Class Divisions of IP Addresses and You

For all but very large TCP/IP installations, the network ID and host ID divisions of an IP address provided by simple class designation will do. There will be a great many wasted network and host IDs but so what? They're just numbers. Most likely, selecting a class A or B IP address will meet your needs.

In large networks, the simple division of an overall IP address into network and host IDs by class does not provide enough capability. Either too many network ID numbers will be wasted, too many host IDs will be wasted, or both. So, a method of further dividing an IP address, called subnetworking, was devised.

> **Note:** The next Internet standard (IPv6) specifies a 128-bit IP addressing scheme, among other things. Also called "IP Next Generation," IPv6 will be phased in over the next few years.

Subnetworking

Subnetworking provides a means of dividing an overall IP network into smaller subnetworks. Or, looking at it from the other side, subnetwork masking provides a means of bringing multiple small networks together into a larger one. So, with subnetworking, you have a network ID, a subnet ID, and a host ID. IP address classes A, B, and C are capable of being divided into subnetworks.

Consider the telephone system analogy again. The first three digits (the area code) of a local phone number define the exchange, or local switching office, to which the local telephone is attached. The telephone's exchange is similar to a subnet ID. Under this arrangement, telephone-switching equipment can be made to perform more efficiently.

A given telephone call can be routed first to an area code facility without regard for the rest of the number, then to the local exchange office based on the next three numbers, and then finally to the individual telephone. The switching equipment operating at the area code level is only concerned with the 250 or so area codes, not the entire network.

So, if an IP address is divided into a network ID and a host ID portion is based on the IP address class, how is subnetworking accomplished?

Using a Subnet Mask to Define a Subnetwork

Even if you will not be in need of division of an overall IP address beyond that specified by the IP address' class, you'll need to understand how a *subnet mask* works. At the least, you will have to specify a subnet mask just to tell TCP/IP support that you're not going to use subnetworking.

A subnet mask is a number represented in the same manner as IP addresses as nnn.nnn.nnn.nnn. As with IP addresses, each set of numerals represents the decimal value of 1 byte of the 4 bytes used, and is in the range 0 to 255.

> **Note:** Your subnet mask must at least match the IP address class. That is, a class A IP address requires a minimum subnet mask of 255.0.0.0 (see Table 12.2).

The subnet mask is a pattern of binary ones and zeros that defines the parts of the IP address to be considered as the subnet ID. Each position of the 32 bits in an IP address is compared to the corresponding position in a subnet mask. If the subnet mask contains a one at a given position, the bit position is part of the network or subnetwork ID. If a given position in the subnet mask is zero, the position is used as part of the host ID.

Table 12.2: *Minimum Subnet Mask Values.*

Class	Minimum Subnet Mask Designation
A	255.0.0.0
B	255.255.0.0
C	255.255.255.0

Consider the IP address 68.76.95.97. Because 68 is in the range 0 to 128, this is a class A address. Class A addresses have 1 byte for the network ID and 3 bytes for the host ID.

The network ID is 1 byte in length and has a value of 68 in decimal, or 01000100 in binary. The host ID is 76.95.97, or 01001100. 01011111. 01100001. As is, this arrangement will allow a maximum of 254 networks. This arrangement should use a minimum subnet mask bit pattern of 11111111 00000000 00000000 0000000 or 255.0.0.0 in IP notation.

Because all of the bits in byte one of the subnet mask are set to one, all bits in the corresponding first byte of the IP address will be considered part of a network ID, according to the convention set by the class. If, however, one wants to use some of the host portion of the address as a subnet ID, a change to the subnet mask will be required.

If you apply a subnet mask bit pattern of 11111111 11111111 00000000 0000000 (or 255.255.0.0 in IP notation) to a class A address, you are declaring that all bit positions in the second byte of the overall IP address designate a subnetwork. All bit positions in the first byte are still used as the network ID, but now there are only two bytes' worth of bit positions to use as the host ID (see Table 12.3).

Table 12.3: *Subnetwork Masking Examples*

With Subnet mask 255.0.0.0:

	Network ID	————————Host ID————————		
Position:	Byte 1	Byte 2	Byte 3	Byte 4

With Subnet mask 255.255.0.0:

	Network ID	Subnet ID	————————Host ID————————	
Position	Byte 1	Byte 2	Byte 3	Byte 4

If the whole first byte of the host ID portion of the IP address (byte 2 overall) is used to represent a subnetwork, you can identify up to 254 subnetworks within each of 254 networks.

Using Part of a Byte in a Subnet Address

You don't have to specify that an entire byte of an IP address is to be included in the subnet ID. Instead, you can designate just part of a byte. For example, a subnet mask of 255.240.0.0 has a binary representation of:

255	240	0	0
11111111	11110000	00000000	00000000

All bit positions in byte 1 are set to one, so all corresponding bit positions of IP address byte 1 are part of the network ID. In byte 2 of the subnet mask, however, bits 1 through 4 are set to one, while bits 5 through 8 are set to zero. This means that half of the byte will be assigned as a subnetwork, while the other half will be part of the host ID.

> **Note:** While it's possible to use noncontiguous bits to define a subnet mask, the practice is strongly discouraged because the values assigned to host IDs will be intermingled with the value of the network ID.

Domain Name System (DNS)

An IP address represented in the form "nnn.nnn.nnn.nnn" is a handier representation than its binary equivalent but it's still not the sort of thing users will take to. Instead, names can be associated with an IP address, such as *www.ibm.com* or *www.as400.ibm.com*. This practice of associating an IP address with a name is called the *Domain Name System* (*DNS*)

Besides being easier to remember, using a name to identify a host allows the underlying IP address to be changed without inconveniencing the user. For example, the physical server for the Web site as400.rochester.ibm.com can be changed, and a different IP address associated with the name, without the knowledge or concern of the user.

Domain and Host Names

The name that is associated with an IP address consists of two parts: the domain name and the host name. Together, they're called a *fully qualified host name*. Each name segment, or *label*, of a fully qualified host name is separated by a period:

S1099999.SEATTLE.YOURCOMPANY.COM

The domain name is intended to specify how a given network fits within a larger network or group of networks. The name segments go from the specific to the general, from left to right. For example, in the fully qualified host name S1099999.SEATTLE.YOURCOMPANY.COM, S1099999 is the name of an individual host, SEATTLE is the name of a division of the overall company where the host is located, YOURCOMPANY is the name of the company, and COM is a designation for the commercial segment of Internet users. There are some rules for making up domain and host names:

- Name labels are separated by a period.
- Upper- and lowercase letters are equivalent.
- The first letter of each name label must be a letter.
- The last letter of each label must be a letter or a number.
- Blanks are not allowed.
- Special characters "_" (underscore) and "-" (hyphen) may be embedded within a label.
- Each label can not exceed 63 characters in length.
- The fully qualified host name can not exceed 255 characters in length.

In a small network that has no aspirations of joining the Internet, the domain name can be very simple. For example, the domain name can simply be the system name—S1099999, in this example. When dealing with a larger network, however, simple names might become inadequate.

> **Note:** Important. If you intend to attach your AS/400 to the Internet, you will want to consider making the AS/400's name unique. That is, come up with a name for your AS/400 that is unique within the Internet. That way you can register your AS/400's name to the Internet servers through an agency like InterNIC to make your AS/400 available to Internet users by name, rather than just IP address. You can check the availability of a domain name by accessing the InterNIC Web site at www.networksolutions.com.

It is common practice to divide responsibility for domain and host naming into parts called *authorities*. In this example, suppose that the authority referenced by YOURCOMPANY is responsible for naming each regional location within the network. They named the organization in Washington State "SEATTLE." The organization in Seattle is responsible for naming all hosts in their area, so they name each of their AS/400s by system name in the form "S1099999."

Using an IP address or a host name is equivalent. Try this the next time you're on the Internet: Start an MS DOS session on your PC, and key the following command:

```
ping as400.rochester.ibm.com
```

(or any other valid host name).You should get a display like the one in Figure 12.2.

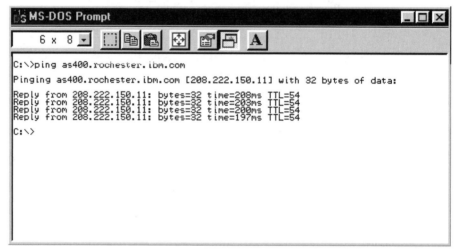

Figure 12.2: As a test, you can ping as400.rochester.ibm.com from an MS DOS session.

Note: Ping is a TCP/IP utility used to test connections. Four or five test transmissions are sent, and the result of the efforts is displayed along with the response time.

Notice that even though you specified a host name as a parameter on the ping command, the responses reference the IP address 208.222.150.11. That's because the name is merely a convenience, a cross-reference to the actual IP address. When you ping a host by name, a translation from name to IP address must take place. TCP/IP routes transmissions to a host by that host's IP address, not its name.

Try the ping command again, this time using the IP address 208.222.150.11. You should get nearly the same result shown in Figure 12.3.

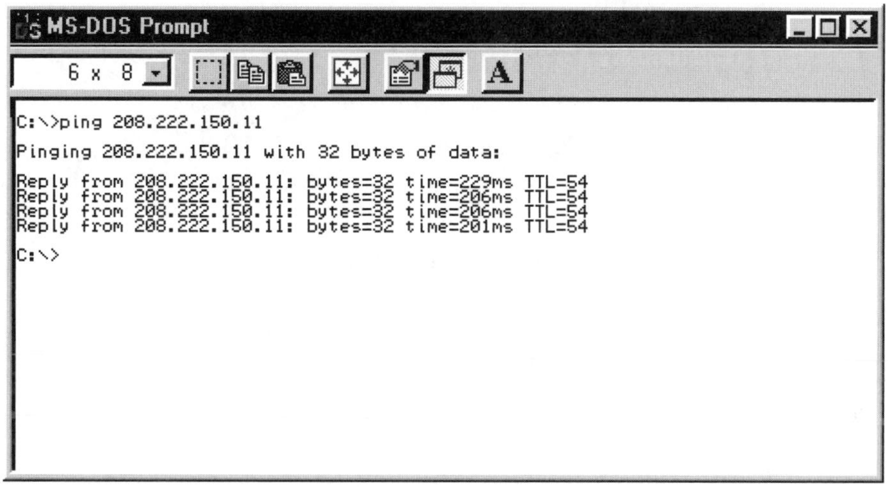

```
MS-DOS Prompt                                          _ □ ✕

  6 x 8 ▼   [] 🖻 🖺  🔲  🖻🖪  A

C:\>ping 208.222.150.11

Pinging 208.222.150.11 with 32 bytes of data:

Reply from 208.222.150.11: bytes=32 time=229ms TTL=54
Reply from 208.222.150.11: bytes=32 time=206ms TTL=54
Reply from 208.222.150.11: bytes=32 time=206ms TTL=54
Reply from 208.222.150.11: bytes=32 time=201ms TTL=54

C:\>
```

Figure 12.3: Here are the results from pinging 208.222.150.11.

Notice, though, that the reverse of cross-referencing a host name to an IP address did not happen. Specifying an IP address did not bring up a corresponding host name. One reason for this is you can assign more than one host name to a given IP address.

Assigning IP Addresses to Host Names

Generally, there are two methods used to assign an IP address to a host name:

- Explicit assignment through use of a *hosts table* at each host.

- Assignment from one or more other servers within the network, such as a DNS (Domain Name Service) server or WINS (Windows Internet Naming Service) server.

Hosts Tables

A host table is simply a text file containing a list of IP addresses and their corresponding host name. On a Windows PC, there is a hosts sample file named hosts.sam located in your Windows or WinNT directory. This sample text file, shown in Figure 12.4, indicates how entries that cross-reference IP addresses and host names are specified.

```
# Copyright (c) 1994 Microsoft Corp.
#
# This is a sample HOSTS file used by Microsoft TCP/IP for Chicago
#
# This file contains the mappings of IP addresses to host names. Each
# entry should be kept on an individual line. The IP address should
# be placed in the first column followed by the corresponding host
name.
# The IP address and the host name should be separated by at least one
# space.
#
# Additionally, comments (such as these) may be inserted on individual
# lines or following the machine name denoted by a '#' symbol.
#
# For example:
#
#      102.54.94.97      rhino.acme.com           # source server
#       38.25.63.10      x.acme.com               # x client host

127.0.0.1        localhost
```

Figure 12.4: The sample hosts file on a Windows PC indicates how entries that cross-reference IP addresses and host names are specified.

IP addresses are matched to the fully qualified host name on the same line. Comments begin with a pound sign (#). TCP/IP support will look for this file and, if present, will use its entries to find an IP address.

> **Note:** IP address 127.0.0.1 is a special designation to test for active TCP/IP support on a local host.

If you were to use the explicit method of cross-referencing host names to IP addresses on your PC, you would have to copy the hosts.sam file to hosts and place an entry in the hosts table file using a text editor like Notepad. Note that the hosts.sam file is a sample. The real hosts table file will have no extension at all.

When using the explicit "hosts table" method of looking up IP addresses, the hosts table on each host system must have an entry for each of the other hosts to which it wants to communicate. In a large network, then, simply adding a new host to the network means you have to add an entry to each PC or AS/400's hosts table.

Domain Name Service

Obviously, in a large TCP/IP network, keeping all of the hosts tables properly updated could become quite a chore. That's where Domain Name Service comes in. DNS is a service provided by TCP/IP support where a host can request an IP address lookup on another host. Very handy. You can tell all of your PCs to use your AS/400 as a DNS server. The AS/400 keeps entries that match IP addresses to host names. An individual PC can then contact another by name, and the DNS server will supply the IP address.

Ports and Sockets

TCP/IP communication takes place over logical conduits called *ports* or *sockets*. Ports exist within TCP/IP software support only. They are not actual physical places to connect cables. Ports are necessary to allow multiple TCP/IP applications to be running at the same time. The jobs and the data traffic are kept separate and managed by port assignment.

There are 65,535 logical ports to which you can send a packet for each of the two connection methods that TCP/IP supports. The packet carries a 16-bit port assignment number that is used to map the packet to the proper port.

Within TCP/IP there are two types of packets: those addressed as *UDP* (User Datagram Protocol) and those addressed as *TCP* (Transaction Control Protocol or Transmission Control Protocol). A given TCP/IP application will use one or the other of these protocols. Each of these protocol subsets has its own set of 65,535 ports.

TCP/IP Utilities and Their Well-Known Ports

There are numerous standard utilities that provide services that are commonly included as part of TCP/IP (FTP, Telnet, DNS, etc.). Each of these client/server applications runs over its own port assignment. The port assignments used have been established and agreed upon by the TCP/IP development community, and are the same on most platforms. These ports are called *well-known ports*.

For example, FTP services run over port number 21. Telnet runs over port 23 and DNS over port 53. That means that there is a program that is active and "listening" to the port, waiting for an incoming request.

In TCP/IP client/server applications, the server program must be active and listening first, before the client program can make contact. When you issue a command to start a TCP/IP server (HTTP, for example), what you're doing is starting a system-supplied server program and attaching it to its well-known port.

Reserved Ports 1 Through 1023

You would not write a client/server application that uses port 21 because that is the well-known port for FTP services. Actually, you shouldn't use any of the port numbers 1 through 1,023 as they are reserved for TCP/IP utilities, existing and future.

The concept of well-known ports extends beyond the system-supplied TCP/IP utilities. An application that runs over TCP/IP support might very well have its own "well-known" port, albeit one numbered above 1,023.

What You Need to Know about TCP/IP

TCP/IP is an evolving technology with ever-improving standards and services and is indeed the "language" of the Internet. You do not, however, need a doctorate in TCP/IP theory to make good use of its capabilities and features. A solid understanding of TCP/IP basics is sufficient to make accurate evaluations and effective implementations of the technology within your organization.

Furthermore, what TCP/IP is and what TCP/IP can do for you is a moving target as new specifications for the platform are developed. You will do well to keep tabs on TCP/IP as it evolves in the future.

Summary

- Because of the impact of the Internet, the principle implementation of TCP/IP, TCP/IP has become the standard for communications between computers.

- The developers of TCP/IP-compliant operating systems have endeavored to make their server a viable player in the network server arena. To that end, server users have seen increased and improved TCP/IP server capabilities.

- TCP/IP is an agreement regarding communications standards within a network. TCP/IP is made up of families of communications standards. A communication standard is called a protocol.

- TCP/IP support is made up of a set of technologies working together in a TCP/IP protocol stack. The stack is responsible for bridging the gap between the physical hardware and the user-level applications that use that hardware.

- TCP/IP utilities such as Telnet or FTP are TCP/IP programs written at the application level to provide user services.

- Routing of data within a network can be direct or indirect. Direct routing takes place when hosts are attached to the same physical network. Indirect routing is required when data must cross from one physical network to another.

- Packets are encapsulated chunks of data as prepared for transmission within a network. Packets carry additional information, beyond the data itself. Packets must be reassembled into meaningful data once received at the destination.

- Each computer in a TCP/IP network is called a host, regardless of its position in a client/server application. A host can represent one or more nodes, or addressable endpoints in a network.

- An endpoint in a TCP/IP network is identified by its IP address—a 32-bit value that is usually represented as four octets, each separated by a period. The next generation of IP addresses will be 128-byte values.

- The overall IP address can be divided into a network IP portion and a host ID portion, as defined by a network mask. The more networks you have, the fewer hosts within each network, and vice versa.

- Classes of IP address have been created based on the portion of the overall IP address devoted to the network ID portion. All Internet addresses are class C addresses.

- Subnetworking is a scheme to divide an IP network into smaller subnetworks. Subnetworking is used to more efficiently route IP packets.

- A host name is a more easily remembered representation of a TCP/IP node than an IP address, and so is often substituted. A host name must be associated with an IP address.

- A host name is associated with an IP address with a hosts table or by a name server like WINS or DNS.

- Domain Name Service (DNS) is a TCP/IP application that associates IP addresses with a name as a service to other hosts in a network.

- A fully qualified host name is comprised of a domain name and a host name.

- A TCP/IP port is a logical segmentation of the communications link into assignable values.

- Ports numbered 1 to 1,023 are reserved for TCP/IP services and are called well-known ports. If you write your own TCP/IP program, it will use a port numbered above 1,023, and that port will be the well-known port for your applications.

To honor Tim Berners-Lee for his notable achievement (the invention of HTML), some have urged his nomination for the "Duke of URL."

—Many
Anonymous

13

HTML

MARIAN O'SHAUGHNESSY

To send information globally on the Internet, a universal language all computers and all browsers understand is needed. The publishing language used by the World Wide Web is HTML (*HyperText Markup Language*). Figure 13.1 shows what the start of this paragraph would look like without a markup language:

> HTML To send information globally on the Internet, a universal language all computers and all browsers understand is needed. The publishing language used by the World Wide Web is HTML (HyperText Markup Language). Here is what the start of this paragraph would look like without

Figure 13.1: Display text without HTML shows the results of no formatting for fonts or paragraphs.

Fonts (such as italics and boldface), new paragraph marks, and spacing information would be missing without a markup language. Things like highlighting, color, and images are also described with markup languages. If a display can't handle color, what should happen? If images can't be displayed, that needs to be handled also.

HTML has been developed with the goal that all types of devices should be able to make use of information available on

Editor's Introduction: The face of the Web is created using HTML. The appearance of your business, the effectiveness of your business, and maybe the responsiveness of your business is encoded in HTML and transmitted around the world via the Web for everyone to see. If you are responsible for the appearance of your organization on the Web, or just want to gain an understanding of how the stuff you see in your browser gets there, Marian O'Shaughnessy's chapter is a good start on understanding and maybe even coding HTML.

–KR

the Web. PCs should be able to access graphics displays of varying sizes, resolution, and color depths, and you should be able to use cellular telephones, hand-held devices, text-to-speech devices, Braille systems, text-only devices, and computers with high or low bandwidth.

HTML allows you to publish pages containing different headings, fonts, colors, tables, pull-downs, buttons, and pictures. Using HTML, you also can include sound, video, spreadsheets, animated images, and Java applets on a published page. HTML forms can be used to search for information and order products. In addition, you can click a button to retrieve other pages of information using hypertext links.

HTML pages can be very impressive and are usually the starting point for any Web-development effort. Pages of static information can be shown quite nicely using just HTML. A computer professional usually learns the HTML basics in less than a day. Even novice computer users can become proficient in this markup language.

The History of HTML

HTML was derived from a standard that was written, in 1986, with a goal of not allowing system and display differences to affect the final document display. The standard was ISO Standard 8879:1986, "Information Processing Text and Office Systems; Standard Generalized Markup Language" (SGML).Tim Berners-Lee originally developed HTML from SGML. While working with colleagues at CERN (the physics research center based in Geneva, Switzerland), Berners-Lee needed a good worldwide communications mechanism. His group had members around the world and the group had a high turnover rate. In 1990, Berners-Lee's cross-platform communications system, using HTML at its core, was named the World Wide Web (WWW). Toward the end of the CERN project, HTML 1.0 was a draft documented as published by Berners-Lee. While use of the Web exploded during this timeframe, so did the makeup of HTML. In the original HTML 1.0, there were only 20 tags. It has since grown to over 90 tags.

Because the WWW depends on authors and system vendors using the same standards for HTML, in 1995 the Internet Engineering Task Force (IETF) developed HTML 2.0. HML 2.0 was the standard for much of the initial Web explosion. The success of the WWW is due mainly to interoperability across different browsers and platforms—which was the basis of the original SGML standard—and is the primary advantage of the HTML markup language. An industry consortium, known as the World Wide Web Consortium (W3C), developed HTML 3.2 (January 1997) as the next major standard.

Today, HTML 4.0 is the recommended standard. Each HTML version contains more function and reflects greater consensus among the industry developers. Also, backward compatibility has been factored into each version so that the development investment is not lost and documents do not become unreadable.

Why Use HTML?

To present information on the Web, it should be obvious by now that you have little choice but to use HTML. It is the standard language accepted by all Web browsers. Any information sent to a browser has HTML at its core.

Because the browser is the lowest common denominator for Web usage, it is important to understand this technology. You could develop a proprietary system that allows you to send and receive information across the Web without a browser, but that would require special client code on all users' systems. The client code would have to be distributed and maintained for each user. Most people would agree that this approach is too costly. Nowadays, it is safe to assume that most people have a browser and, if they don't, they can obtain one for free. You can't beat that for a great value proposition!

How to Code HTML

To develop HTML, all you need is a text editor such as Microsoft's Notepad or WordPad, and an HTML specification. Create a file with an extension of *.htm* or *.html*. A very simple example is shown in Figure 13.2.

```
<html>
Hi beautiful!
</html>
```

Figure 13.2: A simple example of HTML can be used to create a Web page.

After creating the file, open it in a browser (look under File pull-down on your browser and open the one you just created).

HTML tags are shown with brackets around them. In Figure 13.2, <html> is the tag indicating the start of the HTML language and </html> indicates the end. Other common tags are <title></title>, <b></b> for bold, <i> </i> for italics, and <p> to indicate the start of a new paragraph. It really is easy.

One of my favorite things about using HTML is that you can easily copy it. When you find a page you like, you can select FILE, SAVE AS, and save it to disk. Then use your text editor to modify it. With most browsers, you also can view the page source to see what HTML tags have been used.

You can find a good, very easy tutorial at *www.htmlgoodies.com*. At the Web site, go to PRIMERS, THE BASICS.

HTML Generators

Even though HTML is easy to code, many people don't want to have to get down to the level of coding brackets and <P>s for every paragraph. There are numerous HTML editors available that let you type information exactly how you would like to see it and they generate the HTML for you. You can simply draw a box where you would like a picture or a video clip to be shown. You can change colors and select predefined templates with images and buttons for your pages. A number of these HTML editors are available on the Web for free. IBM sells a product called NetObjects TopPage that allows you to create animation and other special affects. It has an interactive audio tutorial that makes understanding each step effortless.

HTML and Browser Compatibility

When developing Web pages using HTML, you must first ask yourself which devices, which browsers, and what level of browsers do you need to support. For example, coding HTML tables or images without descriptions can be a problem for the visually impaired. Some devices have limited or no color choices. Browsers behave differently. Most browsers have defined their own extensions which, for the most part, are ignored by other browsers. Examples include Marquee and Blink tags.

If you need to support all browsers, the safest bet is to use the HTML 3.2 standard. HTML 4.0 is pretty well supported by Netscape 4.0 (June 1997) and Internet Explorer 4.0 (October 1997). While these are the top two browsers in use today, most users could be expected to have new browsers or new versions within three years.

As you develop pages using HTML, it is important to test them against the browser(s) and version(s) you intend to support. Also, some good test vehicles are available to ensure that you are following good coding practices and correct standards. These include:

www.websitegarage.com

www.siteinspector.com

www.netmechanic.com

and the W3C standard validation site, *validator.w3.org*

What's New

Cascading Style Sheet: Proposed by the W3C, Cascading Style Sheet (CSS) language allows you to add style (font, color, and spacing) to your Web pages. Instead of putting font tags and background color tags on each page, you simply include a style sheet (.css file) at the top of your page to describe how you want each item to look. For example, you would indicate that all heading 1 items (<h1>) would use an Arial font size 20. Style sheets allow you to separate page content from page appearance, and easily can be modified. Therefore, you can change all your pages with a single update of the .css files.

Another advantage of using style sheets is that you can manage the look and feel of a large, sophisticated site by enforcing a small number of style sheets. Internet Explorer 3 and 4 and Netscape 4.0 provide support for style sheets. Figure 13.3 shows a sample style sheet.

```
<STYLE TYPE-"type/css">

<!-
BODY {background: #FFFFFF}
A:link {color: #FF00FF}
A:visited {color: #8000FF}
H1 {font-size: 20pt; font-family: arial}
H2 {font-size: 18pt; font-family: arial}
H3 {font size:13pt; font-family: helvetica}
->

</STYLE>
```

Figure 13.3: With a style sheet, you can manage the look and feel of a large, sophisticated site.

Dynamic HTML: Dynamic HTML (DHTML) is a vague term used when referring to style sheets, layering, JavaScript, and positioning functions to create movement and interactivity on the HTML page.

HTML and the Future

Released in 1997, XHTML 1.0 (proposed by W3C 8/99) is the first major change to HTML since HTML 4.0. It merges the existing HTML 4.0 standard and XML (eXtensible Markup Language), which is another SGML derivative that is more restrictive but less complex.

As Web usage interact with such diverse devices as cell phones, wireless pocket devices, televisions, and cars, XHTML becomes important. A cell phone doesn't have enough memory to load complex HTML pages. Therefore, a subset of the language or a module is needed.

The main benefit of XHTML is its capability to modularize new extensions. For example, you could create a module used for cell phones that would subset the existing tags and add a few more. Then you could possibly translate between the cell phone module to the television module when switching devices. Translation utilities can be used to translate existing HTML pages to XHTML.

Slang is a language that rolls up its sleeves, spits on its hands, and goes to work.

—Carl Sandburg
Describing poetry, The New York Times (February 13, 1959)

14

JavaScript

MARIAN O'SHAUGHNESSY

Have you every filled out an Internet form with your name, address, phone, etc., and then been presented with a page telling you that one piece of information is incorrect? Upon attempting to review the data, did you discover that all your information was blank? Doesn't that drive you crazy? Tell the developer about JavaScript!

If the form developer had coded some simple JavaScript with the HTML page, an invalid field-error message would be displayed in a warning box and the form would be redisplayed with the cursor positioned to the incorrect field. All the other fields would still contain your data.

Besides validating fields, calculations can be made and other feedback—such as help text—can be presented to users. Pop-up windows can be shown. The user can see customized displays containing their name or greetings depending upon the time of

Editor's Introduction: JavaScript is not Java. JavaScript is the blue-collar "roll-up-the-sleeves-and-go-right-to-work" cousin of Java. It looks like Java but it has a specific craft or purpose. And there are computing applications where Java treads confidently that JavaScript dares not go. But JavaScript is less costly in computational terms and can be easier to use. JavaScript is a special-purpose tool used to add functionality to HTML pages. Java is a general-purpose programming technology that can run inside a Web page and can run directly on almost any computing device. In this chapter, Marian O'Shaughnessy explains what JavaScript is, compares it to Java, and shows you some examples of how JavaScript can make Web pages more exciting and more useful.

–KR

day. JavaScript can determine the browser's capability and play a sound/video or not depending upon the capability.

JavaScript is a scripting language that is object-based and very easy to learn. JavaScript is an extension of HTML and is embedded in HTML pages. Like HTML, JavaScript is platform independent and it will run on most browsers, including Netscape Navigator 2.0+ and Microsoft Internet Explorer 3.0+. You can think of JavaScript as a coding language for HTML pages. It runs on the client and is especially useful for validating user input.

JavaScript is a key technology to employ to improve the usability of your Web site. Plus it is easy to learn and fun to use.

The History of JavaScript

JavaScript was created at Netscape and was originally called LiveScript. At the same time, Sun was developing Java for doing the server-side work (which might have been done with a server-side scripting language). However, Sun was finding that a client-side language, such as LiveScript, would be complimentary. Therefore, Netscape partnered with Sun to rename the language JavaScript.

JavaScript was submitted to the European Computer Manufacturers Association (ECMA) and was adopted in June 1997 as standard *ECMA-262*, currently in the second edition. It also was standardized as ISO-16262 by the International Organization for Standards.

Microsoft's Internet Explorer supports JScript, which is compatible with JavaScript. As with HTML, there are differences; any code should be tested on the browser(s) with which they will be used.

About JavaScript

JavaScript is embedded in HTML. For example, Figure 14.1 shows HTML with embedded JavaScript in boldface.

```
<html>
<body>
<br>
Regular HTML.
<br>

  <script language="JavaScript">
   document.write("Inside JavaScript.")
  </script>

<br>
HTML again.
</body>
</html>
```

Figure 14.1: An example of embedded JavaScript in HTML is shown here in boldface type.

The browser output would look like the example shown in Figure 14.2.

```
Regular HTML.
Inside JavaScript.
HTML again.
```

Figure 14.2: This is the output from the HTML and JavaScript shown in Figure 14.1.

Figure 14.2 is not a very useful example. JavaScript usually gets called when events happen while using your browser. Common examples are when a button is clicked, when a page is loaded, or when a mouse rolls over an image. Buttons, pages, images, forms, documents, and windows are all objects. Because JavaScript works with objects, it is an object-oriented language. If you have never programmed in an object-oriented language, JavaScript would be a good place to begin. The only requirement is a browser and a simple text editor. The example:

```
document.write("Inside JavaScript.")
```

uses the document object. It uses the write method associated with the document object to write one or more HTML expressions.

JavaScript *methods* are used to perform the work. Other examples of methods are alert(), open(), submit(), random(), prompt(). Figure 14.3 shows a simple, more useful example of JavaScript using the alert method associated with the window object.

```
<input type="button" value="Order" onClick="alert('This function is not yet
available.')" >
```

Figure 14.3: This example of JavaScript uses the alert method.

The alert method will show a pop-up error message that looks like the example shown in Figure 14.4.

Besides using the methods defined for each object, you can also write your own functions or section of code. Figure 14.5 shows an example of the onClick event calling a validateDate function that I wrote instead of the alert method.

Figure 14.4: A pop-up message results from the alert method.

```
<input type="submit" value="Order" onClick="return validateDate(this.form)" >
```

Figure 14.5: You can write your own functions or section of code. This sample code can be used for an example event.

OnClick, onLoad, and onMouseOver are examples of events that can be used to trigger JavaScript functions. In this example, the button's onClick event is used to call my validateDate function. Figure 14.6 shows a sample section of code I would include at the top of the HTML form for my validateDate function:

```
<script language="JavaScript">
.
.
.
function validateDate(form)
{
        // check that start date is a valid date
        if (!isDate(form.STRDATE.value)){
                alert("Start Date is invalid")    // pop-up error
message
```

Figure 14.6: You can include HTML code with the validateDate function in JavaScript at the top of the HTML form (part 1 of 2).

```
                form.STRDATE.focus()          // set cursor on
start date field
                return false;
                }
        else
                {return true;
                }
}

</script>
```

Figure 14.6: You can include HTML code with the validateDate function in JavaScript at the top of the HTML form (part 2 of 2).

So, now you know about the key elements of JavaScript: objects, elements, functions, and events. Next, consider how JavaScript compares to other technologies.

JavaScript vs.
Java Applets vs. Java Programs

It is easy to get confused about the differences between JavaScript and Java. They are really different languages like C and C++. The syntax is similar, they are both object-oriented and can, if desired, both access the same objects. Java was built as a robust, general-purpose development language. JavaScript was designed to be similar to Java, but to be a quicker and simpler language to enhance HTML for use with Web pages. Using Java, you can write both Java applets and Java programs. JavaScript is it's own language separate from Java.

JavaScript, Java applets, and Java programs all can run on the client. JavaScript and JavaApplets can be embedded in HTML forms. However, client-side Java programs typically are started as a program and run in their own window—not in the browser. Figure 14.5 shows a diagram that helps to clarify these three flavors of Java-type clients.

Both Java applets and Java programs must be compiled before you can run them. They are compiled into byte code, which can run on any client. Each client interprets the byte code into it's own native machine code and then runs it. In other words, when the browser sees the <applet> tag it must download the byte code (which is often quite large). If you have applets on your HTML page, it usually loads much slower than if you have JavaScript code embedded for a similar operation.

Because Java programs are compiled, the compiler can check to see if variables exist and have been declared. Java also is much stricter about data typing. For example, it will not allow characters to be assigned to numeric fields. In some ways this is good because it is more reliable. In some ways this is bad because it is much less forgiving when you are coding. JavaScript lets you

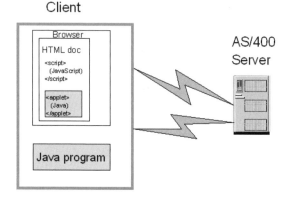

Figure 14.5: Java programs typically are started as a program and run in their own window.

do things like writing an integer out as a character. JavaScript assumes that you know what you are doing and converts before displaying. Java would force you to cast the integer into a character type first.

With JavaScript, there is no compiler. The code is interpreted line by line and evaluated. This means that the functions you use, such as validateDate(), need to be inserted into the HTML page before they can be used.

JavaScript is dynamic. Because it interprets the HTML line by line, JavaScript can be used to examine data a user types in. It can be used to change the page or form. Because data items might not be available at compile time, a Java program is not as dynamic.

Why Use JavaScript?

Here are some of the things I have seen successfully accomplished using JavaScript:

- **Navigation:** Cascading menus, pop-up menus, right-click menus, moving circle of images with links, tree outlines, and tabs that pop out with links.

- **Text manipulation:** Snaking text around on a display following mouse movement.

- **Images:** If the image doesn't load due to network timeouts, reload them automatically.

  ➤ Magnify sections of an image using a magnifying glass that moves with the mouse.

  ➤ Plot graphs, pie charts, etc.

  ➤ Toggle the image as the mouse rolls over it.

- **Checkboxes:** Turn on/off depending upon status of other check boxes.

- **Detect User Information:** Plug-ins loaded; browser.

- **Special Effects:**

  ➤ Have the H key, when pressed, always take you home.

  ➤ Play sound when a form is loaded

- **Utility:** Calculators, calendars, etc.

- **Cookies:** Use a cookie to recall what the user previously has entered.

Consider using JavaScript whenever you need to perform work with objects on the client that cannot be accomplished with HTML alone.

Helpful Links

My favorite link for JavaScript education/reference is:

www.developer.netscape.com/docs/manuals/communicator/jsref/index.htm

Useful freeware can be found at:

www.zdnet.com/devhead/resources/scriptlibrary/javascript

www.dhtmlzone.com

HTML—the HyperText Markup Language—made the Web the world's library. Now its sibling, XML—the Extensible Markup Language—is making the Web the world's commercial and financial hub.

—Charles F. Goldfarb,
XML in an Instant: A Non-geeky Introduction
http://www.xmlbooks.com/press/nongeeky.htm

15

XML:
Universal Data for the Internet

DON DENONCOURT

For years, IT departments have dealt with the problem of disseminating information between dissimilar platforms. Data files were batch transferred from OS/400 to AIX, from OS/390 to Windows, and from OS/2 to Solaris. Why? Because information captured by an application on one system was required by an application on another system. Complete databases were transferred between systems for two reasons: one, communications between the systems was slow, and, two, the data had to be converted from the format of one system to the format required of the other system. It would have been better if the disparate applications could dynamically access the information residing on remote platforms. Although some companies have been able to implement such systems, the complexity of developing distribution protocols prevented most companies from using such a strategy.

Editor's Introduction: XML is a due-diligence issue for any businessperson responsible for exchange or trade with other businesses. XML is several things but, most importantly, it is a method for specifying the structure of information. And the information itself is not dependent on any particular computer system. XML provides several other capabilities and, while each of the other capabilities is important, none are as significant as separating the structure and the information from the underlying system. In this chapter, Don Denoncourt explains XML from the perspectives of structure, content, and presentation. It's must reading if your business uses information in any form.

–KR

To share information between systems, many companies transferred complete data files on a regular basis. These companies then wasted valuable IT resources synchronizing those redundant databases. One solution to the problem of timely sharing of information was Electronic Data Interchange (EDI). Although the cost benefits of EDI have been proven, EDI has not been widely adopted (only 1 percent of IT shops use EDI today).

Another popular mechanism for the exchange of information was SQL through one of a variety of subprotocols: Call Level Interface (CLI), Open Database Connectivity (ODBC), and, more recently, Java Database Connectivity (JDBC). The big problem with SQL, however, is the data format (the database schema) has to be published to clients so that they can customize their applications to use the proprietary data format of the server system. SQL works fine when the network of applications is under control of one IT department, but it is unacceptable in a business-to-business scenario where the supplier base is dynamic.

The solution to information sharing is to use a common data format (something everyone agrees on). That data format is Extensible Markup Language (XML). XML, without question, is the common information distribution protocol for today's e-business applications. As a result of XML's broad acceptance, it is now being referred to as the universal data format for the Internet.

What about HTML?

But what about HTML? After all, HTML is the well-known mechanism for the dissemination of information across the Internet. While no one can argue that HTML wasn't a hugely successful technology, HTML was designed to format information for presentation in a browser. It was not designed to describe the content of the information it contains. Web developers dynamically construct HTML from information residing in a relational database for presentation in the user interface of a Web browser. Business-to-business applications, to be able to process information, need to send and receive information in a fixed data format that is not available with HTML.

Even as the descriptive language for the user interface of Web browsers, HTML is showing its age. E-business experts believe HTML is being used past its original intent. They argue that HTML was designed for the dissemination of static, not dynamic, information. Today, almost all Web applications—such as Common

Gateway Interface (CGI), Java servlets, or Microsoft's Active Server Pages (ASP)—use some mechanism that dynamically constructs HTML.

The problem with HTML, however, is that to support various Web browsers, the HTML requires constant tweaking. You might be thinking that support for multiple browsers is becoming less of an issue with Microsoft (*www.microsoft.com*) winning the browser war over Netscape (*www.netscape.com*). Realize, however, that the new Web browsers are being developed to run on a broad range of the latest electronic devices ranging from portable phones, to shop-floor devices, to wristwatches.

XML, coupled with another language called Extensible Style Language (XSL), is poised to replace HTML. XML doesn't describe the presentation—as does HMTL. XML describes the data and a different XSL file is developed to describe the presentation of the data contained within an XML file for each of the various devices on which the XML is to be presented.

For example, consider an invoice. Using HTML, it's easy to picture a Web page that presents that invoice. What if you want to print that invoice? The format of the invoice, as shown in a Web browser, is not suitable for a formal hard copy of an invoice. If the invoice was packaged, not into an HTML file but rather in an XML file, that XML file could be used to display the invoice in a Web browser. You could print the invoice on a laser printer and process the invoice with a remote application program.

Will XML completely supplant HTML? Probably not. There are too many instances where the data being captured for presentation does not have enough "structural value" to justify the added cost of developing the DTD and XSL. But for e-business applications, which require complex data formats, XML is already being used heavily.

Structure, Content, and Presentation

Any stored piece of information, whether in the form of a relational database file, a text document, or an HTML Web page, has content, structure, and presentation. With a relational database such as IBM's DB2 UDB, information content is retained in a table and the structure of that data is maintained in schemas. The presentation of RDB data is typically enabled with a high-level language such as COBOL, Java, and C++.

With HTML, information content, structure, and presentation are all maintained in one file. HTML tags such as <HEAD>, <P>, and <TABLE> demarcate the structure and presentation of an HTML file, and the content of an HTML file is maintained between those HTML tags. The problem with HTML is that the content of a document is tightly coupled with its presentation. Furthermore, none of the tags of an HTML document describes its content—only its presentation.

XML resembles HTML in that it also contains tags that enclose data content. Yet, XML differs from HTML in that its tags describe the structure of data. Furthermore, those tags do not specify anything about the presentation of an XML document's data. The following HTML header tag, for instance, displays what is obviously somebody's name:

```
<H2>Don Denoncourt</H2>
```

The following shows the same piece of information but within an XML tag that explicitly describes the information:

```
<AUTHOR>Don Denoncourt</AUTHOR>
```

The HTML <H2> tag described, not the information, but how to display the data contained within that tag (as a header in a large, bold font). On the other hand, the XML <AUTHOR> tag describes the information, but it doesn't describe how to present that information. By describing the structure of the information that is contained in the XML document, but not the presentation, the XML document, unlike an HTML document, is not limited for use in a Web browser. Figure 15.1 shows an example XML document for a simple purchase order XML language that I "invented" called POXML.

```
<?xml version="1.0"?>
<ORDERS>
  <ORDER>
    <ORDERNO>11</ORDERNO>
    <CUSTNAME>Exxon</CUSTNAME>
    <DATE>01151998</DATE>
    <POLINES>
```

Figure 15.1: XML tags define the structure of an XML document (part 1 of 2).

```
    <POLINE>
       9832</PARTNO>
       <QUANTITY>7</QUANTITY>
    </POLINE>
    <POLINE>
       3241</PARTNO>
       <QUANTITY>4</QUANTITY>
    </POLINE>
    </POLINES>
  </ORDER>
  <ORDER>
    <ORDERNO>12</ORDERNO>
    <CUSTNAME>Disney</CUSTNAME>
    <DATE>01121998</DATE>
    <POLINES>
    <POLINE>
       7391</PARTNO>
       <QUANTITY>2</QUANTITY>
    </POLINE>
    </POLINES>
  </ORDER>
  </ORDERS>
```

Figure 15.1: XML tags define the structure of an XML document (part 2 of 2).

Notice that, unlike HTML, the structure of the information—two purchase orders complete with line items—is contained within the XML document. Because the syntax of XML is both simple and extensible, you can easily "invent" your own language. Alternatively, you can use an industry-specific XML language published by organizations such as those shown in Table 15.1.

Table 15.1: *Organizations That Have Developed Sophisticated XML Languages*

RosettaNet	www.rosettanet.org/
Open Application Group	www.openapplications.org/
XML.Org	www.xml.org
BizTalk	www.biztalk.org
Commerce Net	www.commerce.net
Ariba	www.ariba.com
OTP	www.otp.org
Data Interchange Standards Association (DISA)	www.disa.org

Presentation

One of the strategies that enable the presentation of information contained within an XML document is to use an Extensible Style Language (XSL) document. A different XSL file is developed for each of the various devices that you want to support for your XML documents. Those devices can be Web browsers, printers, or any of the latest Internet-enabled gadgets such as portable phones.

The problem with this XSL strategy, however, is that each of those devices has to support XSL. And XSL is not yet recommended or ratified by W3C or any other standards organization (for more information on XSL, visit *www.w3.org/Style/XSL*). Even without the standard, as of early 2000 there were two prevalent XSL languages: IBM's LotusXSL (*www.alphaworks.ibm.com*) and Microsoft's XSL (available from *www.microsoft.com/xml*).

If you use Microsoft's version of XSL, you can deliver your XML documents directly to Internet Explorer 5.0. Version 5.0 of Internet Explorer uses XSL documents that are associated with an XML to present the information contained within the XML document. Until XSL is ratified by the W3C and other Web browsers support a standard XSL, you need to consider the implications of tightly coupling the use of Microsoft's version of XSL with your Web documents.

An alternative to directly delivering your XML documents to the Web is to run your XML documents through a utility that uses your XSL documents to dynamically generate HTML. Those HTML documents are then used for Web delivery. Both IBM and Microsoft have these tools: IBM's LotusXSL and Microsoft's MSXML. Figure 15.2, for example, shows the LotusXSL document that was used to convert the POXML document of Figure 15.1 into the HTML document shown in Figure 15.3. Figure 15.4 shows how the resulting HTML looks in a Web browser.

```
<?xml version="1.0"?>
<xsl:stylesheet xmlns:xsl=
                "http://www.w3.org/TR/WD-xsl">
  <xsl:template match="ORDERS">
    <HTML><BODY>
      <H1>Open Purchase Orders</H1>
        <TABLE>
```

Figure 15.2: Lotus's LotusXSL is an XSL processor that converts XML to HTML (part 1 of 2).

```
                <xsl:apply-templates select="ORDER"/>
              </TABLE>
          </BODY></HTML>
      </xsl:template>

      <xsl:template match="ORDER">


         <TH>Order Number:</B></TH>
            <xsl:value-of select="ORDERNO"/></TD>
         <TH>Customer:</B></TH>
            <xsl:value-of select="CUSTNAME"/></TD>
            <TABLE>
                      <xsl:apply-templates
                         select="POLINES"/></TD>
            </TABLE>
        </TR>
      </xsl:template>
      <xsl:template match="POLINES">
        <TABLE border="1" frame="border"
             rules="all" cellpadding="2">
          <th>Part No.</th><th>Quantity</th>
              <xsl:apply-templates select="POLINE"/>
        </TABLE>
      </xsl:template>

      <xsl:template match="POLINE">


            <xsl:value-of select="PARTNO"/></TD>
            <xsl:value-of select="QUANTITY"/></TD>
         </TR>
      </xsl:template>

</xsl:stylesheet>
```

Figure 15.2: Lotus's LotusXSL is an XSL processor that converts XML to HTML (part 2 of 2).

```
<HTML>
<BODY>
<H1>Open Purchase Orders</H1>
<TABLE>

<TH>Order Number:</B></TH>      11</TD>
    <TH>Customer:</B></TH>      Exxon</TD>
  <TABLE>
```

Figure 15.3: HTML can be generated from XML documents, based on the presentation specified in an XSL, using either IBM or Microsoft converter utilities (part 1 of 2).

```
        <TABLE border="1" frame="border" rules="all"
cellpadding="2">
        <th>Part No.</th><th>Quantity</th>

        9832</TD>        7</TD></TR>

        3241</TD>        4</TD></TR>
        </TABLE></TD>
    </TABLE>
    </TR>

<TH>Order Number:</B></TH>      12</TD>
    <TH>Customer:</B></TH>      Disney</TD>
    <TABLE>

    <TABLE border="1" frame="border" rules="all"
cellpadding="2">
        <th>Part No.</th><th>Quantity</th>

            7391</TD>        2</TD></TR>
        </TABLE></TD>
        </TABLE>
    </TR>
</TABLE>
</BODY></HTML>
```

Figure 15.3: HTML can be generated from XML documents, based on the presentation specified in an XSL, using either IBM or Microsoft converter utilities (part 2 of 2).

Parsing with DOM and SAX

Another strategy for presenting XML is to parse the XML document in an application program so that the parsed information can be presented in a graphical user interface. Parsing technologies are tedious but, thankfully, there is a variety of parsing tools available for XML. These parsing tools come in two basic flavors: SAX and DOM. SAX stands for *simple API for XML* and DOM is an acronym for *document object model*.

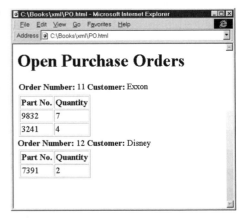

Figure 15.4: LotusXSL converts XML using an XSL file coded to IBM's implementation of XSL.

SAX works well for searching for specific elements of an XML document and DOM works best when processing all or most of the information contained in the XML document. There are many SAX and DOM parser utilities available, most notably from Microsoft, IBM, and Sun Microsystems (*www.sun.com*). In late 1999, however, both IBM and Sun turned over the source code for their respective XML parsers to the Apache Software Foundation (*www.apache.org*). The Apache Software Foundation subsequently began a project with the goal of providing a robust set of XML-related and XSL-related libraries and applications within an industry-wide, peer-based, open-source development process.

For a systems programmer or computer scientist, parsing an XML document, using either the SAX or DOM strategies, is straightforward. But for business programmers using SAX and DOM might not be so "straightforward." Typically, however, most industry-specific XML languages have an associated package of Java classes that provides an intuitive business-programming interface to that industry's XML documents.

If your company develops its own XML language or is using an XML that has no Java API, an alternative to using the SAX or DOM XML parsers is to use a Java applet called XMLDSO that is bundled with Microsoft Internet Explorer 4.0. The XMLDSO applet provides HTML access to XML data using a standard Microsoft's technique known as *data source object* (DSO). Figure 15.5 shows an HTML file that uses the XMLDSO Java applet to present the POXML document (Figure 15.1) in Internet Explorer as shown in Figure 15.6.

```
<HTML>
<BODY>Open Purchase Orders
<applet code=com.ms.xml.dso.XMLDSO.class
  width=100% height=25 id=xmldso>
  <PARAM NAME="url" VALUE="po.xml">
</applet>
<p>
<table id=table datasrc=#xmldso
              border=2 width=100%>
 <thead><th>Order</th><th>Customer</th></thead>
  <tr>
    <td valign=top>
    <div datafld=ORDERNO></div>
    </td>
```

Figure 15.5: Microsoft Internet Explorer 4.0 includes a Java applet that uses DSO technology to present HTML data (part 1 of 2).

```
<td valign=top><div datafld=CUSTNAME></div>
</td>
<td valign=top>
   <table datasrc=#xmldso datafld=POLINES
     width=100%><td valign=top>
   <thead><th>Line Items</th></thead>
     <tr>
        <td valign=top>
           <table border=2 width=100%
             datasrc=#xmldso
               datafld=POLINES.POLINE>
             <thead>
             <th>Part No.</th>
                  <th>Quantity</th>
             </thead>
               <tr>
                  <td valign=top>
                     <div datafld=PARTNO>
                     </div>
                  </td>
                  <td valign=top>
                     <div datafld=QUANTITY>
                     </div>
                  </td>
               </tr>
           </table>
        </td>
     </tr>
  </table>
 </td>
</tr>
</table>

</BODY>
</HTML>
```

Figure 15.5: Microsoft Internet Explorer 4.0 includes a Java applet that uses DSO technology to present HTML data (part 2 of 2).

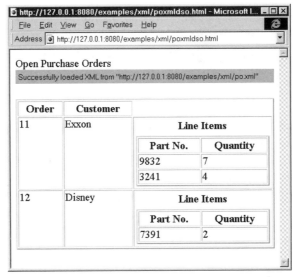

Figure 15.6: Microsoft's XMLDSO can be used to present XML documents in Internet Explorer 4.0.

Following the Rules with DTDs

For an XML document to be successfully parsed, it must be "well-formed." A well-formed XML document has tags that are properly nested and closed. While HTML documents also should be well formed, most Web browsers are tolerant of improperly nested tags or tags that are not properly closed. For an XML document to be successfully parsed, the document must be well formed. A well-formed XML document may be further classified as "valid" if the XML document meets the constraints specified in a document type declaration (DTD).

You can think of a DTD as a formal-constraints language for a specific XML language. An XML document doesn't require a DTD; the document simply needs to have tags that are properly closed and nested—which is to say, well formed. But whether or not the data within an XML is well formed, it may actually be worthless if it is not valid.

Consider, for instance, an order. An order is not valid without at least one line item, and a line item is not valid without a quantity or a part number. Relational databases ensure such constraints with features such as referential integrity and triggers. XML documents, however, don't have the benefit (nor the baggage) of database management systems to perform such validation. Nevertheless, recipients of XML documents need assurance that the information contained within an XML document is valid. That assurance can be provided through the use of a "validating" SAX or DOM parser.

All parsers report when an XML document is not well formed. In addition, validating parsers report when an XML document doesn't meet the constraints specified in the DTD associated with that document. Figure 15.7, for example, presents the DTD for the POXML for Figure 15.1. A DTD can either be embedded in an XML document or be completely external with a reference in various XML files. Usually, for modularity, DTDs are kept in separate documents and published as formal documents for the proper syntax of trade-specific XML languages.

```
<!DOCTYPE ORDERS [
<!ELEMENT ORDERS (ORDER)+>
<!ELEMENT ORDER (ORDERNO,CUSTNAME,DATE?,POLINES)>
<!ELEMENT POLINES (POLINE)+>
<!ELEMENT POLINE (PARTNO,QUANTITY,COST?)>
<!ELEMENT ORDERNO (#PCDATA)>
<!ELEMENT CUSTNAME (#PCDATA)>
<!ELEMENT DATE (#PCDATA)>
<!ELEMENT PARTNO (#PCDATA)>
<!ELEMENT QUANTITY (#PCDATA)>
<!ELEMENT COST (#PCDATA)>
]>
```

Figure 15.7: DTDs basically provide the constraints of an XML language.

Tightening the Rules with XML Schemas

Unlike XML, the syntax of DTDs hasn't been unanimously accepted. Critics complain that DTD's syntax varies too much from the XML that it describes. They further criticize that DTD's syntax varies depending on whether it's an internal DTD contained within the XML doc or an external DTD maintained in a separate file. Another criticism of DTD is that it has no support for data typing and it is non-extensible. DTDs, for example, don't allow you to define element content as anything other than another element or a string. The proposed solution to these problems is a schema language for XML that is, itself, written as an XML language. One such language, called, appropriately, XML Schema, was submitted for consideration by the W3C organization in mid-1999. Figure 15.8 shows a sample of XML Schema (courtesy of Microsoft) that is used to validate the information in an XML language called Customer.

While I'm sure that some form of a XML schema language will replace DTD, will the use of DTDs soon become obsolete? Probably not. DTDs will be around for some time because various industries groups already have developed some rather sophisticated industry-specific XML languages and a large volume of software has already been developed that is dependant on the complex DTDs of those XML languages. (To learn more about XML schemas, visit *www.w3.org/XML/Activity#schema-wg* and *www.w3.org/TR/xmlschema-1/*.)

```
<Schema xmlns="urn:schemas-microsoft-com:xml-data"
  xmlns:dt="urn:schemas-microsoft-com:datatypes">
  <AttributeType name='studentID' dt:type='string'
required='yes'/>
  <ElementType name='name' content='textOnly'/>
  <ElementType name='GPA' content='textOnly' dt:type='float'/>
  <ElementType name='student' content='mixed'>
    <attribute type='studentID'/>
    <element type='name'/>
    <element type='GPA'/>
  </ElementType>
  <ElementType name='class' content='eltOnly'>
    <element type='student'/>
  </ElementType>
</Schema>
```

Figure 15.8: XML Schemas provide XML constraints that are strongly typed and extensible.

Varied Uses

The applications for XML are innumerable. The three most obvious uses are as an improved HTML, as a universal database, and as a standard protocol for distributed applications. XML has already forced HTML to improve. On August 24, 1999, the Extensible Hypertext Markup Language, or XHTML 1.0, became a W3C Proposed Recommendation (*www.w3.org/TR/xhtml1*). W3C designed XHTML with two main goals: to be extensible and portable. This means that XHTML has no browser-specific tags.

When you want to use the strengths of a specific Web browser, you use an extension to the XHTML language and XML namespaces tell the browser which tags belong to which language. The XML namespaces prevents potential conflicts between identically named elements. Basically, you could say the XHTML broke up the HTML language into modules and applied all XML rules to HTML elements. Like XML, all XHTML elements must be nested and all tags require a corresponding end tag. Also, unlike HTML, which supports mixed case for its tags, all XHTML tags and attributes must be lowercase. Note that there are utilities available that convert HTML to XHTML.

Because XML cleanly describes its content, it seems a great strategy for distributing relational data. But SQL is already cross-platform as it is universally accepted. Sometimes, however, the database information needs to be staged to other platforms. In this scenario, because database management systems are so dissimilar, an XML-based database is a great solution. Thus XML is becoming known as the "universal database" of the Internet.

With the ubiquity of the Internet, there has been a great deal of effort developing distributed n-tier applications. Those n-tier applications must adhere to a standard distributed applications protocol. There is contention about which of the main distributed applications protocols is better: CORBA, COM, RMI, or EJB. While each of these protocols has their strengths, all of them share one common weakness—complexity.

It has been said that XML is the business programmer's revenge on systems programmers for developing a data distribution system that was too abstract and difficult to program. XML is a platform- and language-neutral mechanism for data encapsulation. It separates application logic from application data. Using XML rather than CORBA, COM, RMI, or EJB solves the Sun/Microsoft solution dilemma because XML becomes the mediator between computing systems and applications. Further, XML neatly handles large volumes of data, provides persistent management of text trees, and—because XML is text-based—it supports manual intervention. Further, the distribution of XML objects is not volatile, as are CORBA, COM, RMI, and EJB objects.

But the uses for XML don't stop with the three obvious uses of an improved HTML, a universal database, and a standard protocol for distributed applications. XML is like a new tool for your toolbox. You might not have immediate use for it but you'll be glad you have it when a need presents itself.

For example, IBM's AS/400 development team designed an XML that makes GUI development easier for AS/400 programmers. The AS/400 system programmers developed an XML language called Panel Definition Markup Language (PDML). The panels of a GUI application are described using PCML (thus decoupling the presentation from the business logic). Because of PCML's success, IBM subsequently submitted PCML to Sun for possible inclusion to Java's standard extensions.

Tools

Already, there is a wide variety of XML tools available on the market. For example, there are authoring tools that server as editors for writing XML documents. Xeena, from alphaWorks, is an XML editor that uses DTDs. Because many of these authoring tools are trade-specific, the complexity of developing XML tools for industry-specific groups is removed.

Another category of XML tools is *viewing tools*. Viewing tools (including browsers) use XSL to allow clients view of an XML document. Microsoft, an early adopter of XML and XSL, designed Internet Explorer 5.0 to allow XML to directly be displayed on when associated with an XSL file (that follows Microsoft's XSL standard). IBM's XML Viewer from alphaWorks is another XML viewing tool. Conversion tools that convert from HTML to XML or from RDB to XML are also available. Most of those tools use either SAX or DOM parsers to process XML documents into a form that legacy application programs are able to interpret.

Many relational and object-oriented database management systems also are being enhanced to provide persistent stores for XML documents. A new breed of Web servers—business-to-business servers—has evolved to take advantage of XML. These business-to-business servers enable application-to-application information exchange using XML. One example of a business-to-business server is Bluestone's XML-Server and another is WebMethods' B2B Server.

Another category of XML tools is content management systems that provide XML-based systems for document and content management. An example of an XML content management system is provided by WebSphere 3.0 Advanced Edition. WebSphere 3.0 includes added XML support that enables customers to parse, generate, validate, or modify XML and Extensible Style Language content.

Universal Data for the Internet

With so many different technologies available to develop e-business, it is refreshing that XML is one technology on which everybody agrees. XML has already been widely accepted by all computer manufacturers and developers of operating systems. While XML is completely platform and vendor neutral, almost all vendors support it.

The Internet already has a number of universal technologies: TCP/IP, HTML, and Java. TCP/IP is the universal connectivity protocol of the Internet. HTML is the universal presentation language for Web browsers. Java has become the universal application development language of the Internet because of its coupling of cross-platform and object-oriented capabilities. XML provides the single component that is missing from the partnership of TCP/IP, HTML, and Java—a universal data format. Therefore, XML provides the universal data interchange format for e-business applications.

For the official word on XML, read the XML specification at *www.w3.org/ TR/REC-xml.* For an XML tutorial, which takes approximately 45 minutes to complete, visit *www-4.ibm.com/software/developer/education/xmlintro/.*

God is in the details.

—Ludwig Mies van der Rohe,
New York Herald Tribune (June 28, 1959)

16

Unified Modeling Language

RANDY RUHLOW

If you've ever had the pleasure of adding an extension to your house, you know that building codes must be followed before you will be issued a permit for the construction. The local authorities will use your blueprints to verify that what you plan on doing conforms to all local, state, and national codes and that your plans are of sound design and meet the needs of the structure you are building.

Software systems are modeled for much the same reasons. You need to verify that you can build what needs to be built and that it meets system requirements. During the modeling process, barriers to the success of the system can be identified and addressed. And because the modeling process occurs before the construction phase, fatal barriers can be discovered before a large investment is made in the construction of the system.

Editor's Introduction: Ludwig Mies van der Rohe made his famous quote about architecture, but it applies every bit as well to software. If you are a developer, you might sometimes feel that "the devil is in the details," to use one of the more common variations. UML is a modeling language that lets everyone see and agree on the details before they bedevil your organization (sorry, couldn't resist). As software systems grow larger, less monolithic, more object oriented, and more distributed, it becomes more important to model the behavior of the software system before committing it to ones and zero's. No one should build a house without a blueprint. No one should develop software without a blueprint. UML provides that blueprint. Randy Ruhlow does an excellent job of explaining how UML is the tool for software blueprinting.

–KR

Growing up I labored through building model naval ships. They were models of the old wood sailing ships with numerous sails and mast lines. The plans for the model were divided into sections and subassemblies. Each section defined the assembly for a particular piece of the model. Sometimes the section or subassembly was added to the larger assembly right away. Other times you had to have a set of sections or subassemblies before adding them. It was a test of my patience and perseverance because I wanted the model to look like something as quickly as possible. The challenge was to have enough patience to follow each step of the plan without jumping steps. The lesson I learned was that, while each step was not complicated in itself, it added a piece to an overall complex model and was a necessary piece of the model's construction.

This illustrates another reason software systems are modeled. It allows you to uncomplicate an otherwise complicated system. Understanding a software system can be overwhelming if you're looking at the big picture without analyzing all the little pieces that make up the system. A complete order-management system, for example, is not a system whose interaction of processes is understood easily. You must understand everything: order entry, fulfillment, inventory, billing, and even marketing. Yet, if you were to look at only the order entry or the fulfillment process, you could gain a reasonable understanding of that process. Piece by piece, you could learn each process in the overall system and gain an understanding of the entire system after all the individual processes are learned.

Software modeling provides a means of dividing a system into manageable, understandable, logical components for the consumption of viewers. The viewer might be an architect, a designer, a developer, a consultant, or even a manager. Modeling provides an architectural blueprint of the system to be developed. It describes the pieces that need to be built and is used to document how the pieces fit together and interact within the system.

What Is UML?

Unified Modeling Language (UML) is the industry standard modeling language as adopted by the Object Management Group (OMG) in January of 1997. Since then, the OMG's Revision Task Force has revised the UML standard. The latest revision, 1.3,was released in the fall of 1998.[1]

The OMG is a not-for-profit international organization of over 800 companies. Its mission is to develop standardized object software. Because of this focus, UML is primarily intended for, but not limited to, object-oriented systems. For more information about the OMG, visit their Web page at *www.omg.org*.

UML is a graphical modeling language that defines various visual elements that, when used collectively, comprise many of the artifacts of a software system. The visual elements are in the form of things, relationships, and diagrams. System artifacts are elements such as requirements, architectures, designs, and source code. This is not an all-inclusive list because an artifact can be anything that is needed to define, implement, or deploy a system. Mainly though, UML is used to model system requirements through use cases, high- and low-level designs, physical component layouts, and deployment configurations.

Because these elements can't be stuck together without some kind of glue, UML also defines rules of how each of these elements is to be used in the modeling process. Together, the elements and rules provide the necessary constructs for a well-defined model.

The power of UML comes from the fact that it is a very broad language. It has the capability to document all the common artifacts of a software system. This is possible because UML uses diagrams as the main tool for expressing an artifact. If an artifact can be defined by a diagram or graph, UML is capable of documenting it. Because UML also allows the creation of new kinds of elements, other types of artifacts can be documented within a system.

Keep in mind that the primary objective of a model is to communicate what the system is all about. It was important to develop standards for communicating the information about a system so that efficiencies could be obtained from conception through implementation to deployment and maintenance of the system. If developers, for example, had to learn a different modeling language for each project they worked on, time would be spent learning the modeling-language knowledge needed for the specific project. This training time is costly and takes away productive time from the developer.

It also was important to develop a modeling standard that has the capability to encompass all artifacts of a software system or at least a standard that provides for extensions that allows additional system artifacts. If this were not the case, instead of having one common model defining a system, there would be several narrower models, each with its own learning curve. Before an entire system could be understood, each modeling language would have to be learned. This could lead to confusion because some models would overlap in concepts and elements and would be difficult for the developer to keep straight.

The Origins of UML

From the late 1980s to the mid-1990s, three members of the software community emerged as leaders in the object-oriented technologies. Grady Booch from Rational Software Corporation, Ivar Jacobson from Objectory, and James Rumbaugh from General Electric had developed independent but widely accepted object-oriented design and analysis methodologies. They also had developed modeling languages that supported the different methodologies.

Grady Booch's method provided an object-oriented design and analysis approach supported by a very thorough modeling tool. Ivar Jacobson was known for his Object Oriented Software Engineering (OOSE). His approach capitalized on use cases and was especially useful for driving the requirements and analysis phase of a solution. James Rumbaugh had developed the Object Modeling Technique (OMT). His method centered on static views of the object and was more data centric than the other methods. This approach captured data-intensive system requirements and built objects around those data requirements.

UML is based on a merger of the technologies developed by these three men. In 1994, Rumbaugh joined Grady Booch at Rational Software Corporation, and was followed by Jacobson in the fall of 1995. Later, the development of UML was aided by a consortium of companies willing to invest in the development of a standard.[2] As mentioned, OMG adopted UML as a standard in January of 1997. UML is now maintained by OMG, and it is up to OMG to keep the standard current. This is done through the Revision Task Force (RTF).

An Introduction to UML

The next section of this chapter covers the elements of UML in a brief but thorough manner. It is not intended to be an in-depth exploration of UML and does not cover all the complexities of UML. This is a basic introduction to the concepts of UML and its capabilities as a modeling language.

A good way to understand the concepts of UML is by example. I've drawn up a brief scenario whereby a company would like to automate its billing process. This example is fictional and in no way intends to reflect an actual business opportunity. The remainder of the chapter is based on references to this example.

The Imas Mall Company Example

The Imas Mall Company owns a mall and currently leases store space to one tenant. Each month, Imas Mall Company bills its tenant for rent. The current billing process is manual because there is only one store. However, Imas Mall Company is expanding the mall and will need an automated billing process. They would like the bill to contain the tenant information, the monthly rental rate, the monthly amount of revenue the store received, an additional fee based on this revenue, and a total amount that reflects the monthly rental rate and additional fee. Also, the bill displays a header containing the Imas Mall Company information and the due date of the bill. Figure 16.1 shows a sample of the bill Imas Mall Company has submitted as part of the requirements for the system.

```
                              Imas Mall Company
                              Box 15
                              LittleTown, Mn.   10101

 Due Date: 03/15/1999                      Total Amount Due:      $1882.50


 Main Street Retail Inc.                   Monthly Rent:          $1500.00
 Imas Mall, Store #1
 LittleTown, Mn  10101                     Revenue Fee:           $ 382.50

                                           Current Amount Due:    $1882.50

      Current Monthly Revenue

  Reported Monthly Revenue: $2550.00       Past Due Charges:      $   0.00

  Revenue Rate:              x .15

  Revenue Fee:            $382.50
```

Figure 16.1: Imas Mall Company sample bill displays a header containing the Imas Mall Company information and the due date of the bill.

The informal requirements and the example shown in Figure 16.1 provide enough information to easily identify some basic objects:

- **Company:** A parent class from which all other Company classes are derived.

- **ImasCompany:** A subclass of Company representing the Imas Mall Company.

- **Tenant:** A subclass of Company representing a tenant of the Imas Mall Company.

- **Bill:** A parent class from which all other bill classes are derived.

- **TenantBill:** A subclass of Bill, which defines the monthly bill sent to all Tenants.

- **BillDetail:** The itemized portion of the TenantBill. A TenantBill will contain a BillDetail.

- **BillTotal:** The totals and due date line of the TenantBill. A TenantBill will contain a BillTotal object.

- **RevenueFee:** A class that knows all about rental rates and percentages to charge on a monthly basis. This class also is contained in a TenantBill.

This chapter does not provide a complete solution. These objects were identified through initial observation to aid in the introduction of the various elements of UML. Normally, these basic objects would be identified through the process of defining use cases and sequence diagrams, which are elements of UML and which are discussed later in the chapter.

Elements of UML

The organization of this section is modeled after chapter 2 of *The Unified Modeling Language User Guide*.[3] It was a perfect match for use in this chapter on how to convey an introductory look at the elements of UML.

Elements of the UML model fall into three categories: things, relationships, and diagrams. Each category has a set of elements that represent abstractions used by the model to define various artifacts of the system to be modeled.[4]

Things

Things are fundamental, object-based elements of UML that are used by other elements of the UML model to capture the abstractions of the real-world system to be modeled. The things category can be broken down into four types: structural, behavioral, grouping, and annotation.

Structural Things

Structural things are the basic elements of UML used to create logical and physical elements of the model. With the exception of two UML elements, all structural things are the static or non-dynamic elements of UML. There are seven types of structural things.

- **Class:** A class defines what an object is by encapsulating the attributes and behaviors of the object. A class describes all objects in a system. From the example, a tenant can be considered an object with such attributes as Name, Address, and Revenue, and a behavior of paying rent. Therefore, the class Tenant would define all attributes and behaviors that would give semantic meaning to Tenant. A class is rendered graphically as a rectangle. The name, attributes, and behaviors all can be shown in the rectangle.

- **Interface:** An interface defines a specific set of operations that can be used by a class. It doesn't define any attributes or imply any specific means for implementing the operations. It is up to the class that uses the interface to implement the operations. Therefore, an interface really defines a set of behaviors allowing each class, which chooses to adopt the interface to provide implementations for the behaviors. An interface is graphically rendered as a circle with its name below it.

- **Use Case:** Use case defines a set of sequences of actions that will produce a specific result required of the system. Use cases map to system requirements. The actions to bill a tenant, a requirement of the Imas Company system, could be a use case that defines the billing process for Imas Company. Use cases help identify basic objects and their behaviors for the specific sequence of actions. A use case is rendered as an ellipse with solid lines. The name of the use case is inside the ellipse.

- **Collaboration:** Collaboration is a representation of the set of structural and behavioral elements that are used to realize a use case. If you define "Bill Tenant" as a use case for our example, then "Bill Management" will be defined as the collaboration. Collaborations are rendered as ellipses with dashed lines and the name of the collaboration is inside the ellipse.

- **Active Class:** Active class is a class that owns a path of execution or a thread; it also may be the initiator of control. An active class is rendered just as a class, except that its rectangular border has a heavier line.

- **Component:** Component is a class that defines physical objects representative of development or runtime elements. If you were to define a Java source file, Tenant.java, a component of the same name would represent this source file in this model. A component is rendered as a rectangle with two tabs on the left side of the rectangle.

- **Node:** A node is a class that represents some type of physical computer or processing device. A node is rendered as a three-dimensional cube, typically with a name.

Behavioral Things

Behavioral things are the structural elements of UML used to represent the dynamic nature of the model. The two types of behavioral things are interactions and state machines.

- **Interaction:** Messages are the mechanism that objects use to communicate with each other. Messages are realizations of methods of classes. Interactions represent a sequence of messages between objects. They define a series of events as described by the interaction between a set of objects in a scenario. A scenario is a specific set of sequences of actions typically associated with a use case. A message is rendered as a solid line with an arrow at one end.

- **State Machines:** At any one moment in time, an object can have only one condition or state. This means, for instance, that the value of an object's attribute at an instance of time can have only one value. To change the value of an attribute requires some action on the object. An event triggers the action and the object is considered in transition when changing from one state to another. A state machine captures interactions between objects and the transitions and states of the objects as they progress through the interactions. A state element represents states of objects. It can contain a transition that defines actions to be taken by the object when an event acts upon an object. A state element is rendered as a rectangle with rounded corners.

Grouping Things

UML currently provides the package element for the grouping of all other UML elements. A package element can contain one or more package elements. Packages are used to group semantically, logically, or physically related artifacts of a model. Packages are rendered as a tabbed rectangle with the tab at the upper-left position.

Annotation Things

UML currently provides the note element for the capture of comments and other dialog necessary to better define the model. A note is rendered as a rectangle with the upper right corner folded down. Figure 16.2 shows the different structural elements and how they are rendered.

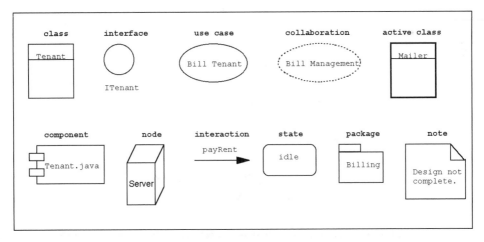

Figure 16.2: The structural elements of UML include the note element for the capture of comments and other dialog.

Relationships

Many elements of a model are dependent upon each other. Some dependencies are more tightly coupled than others, and some elements are derived from other elements. These statements reflect the fact that elements of a model have some sort of relationship with other elements of the model. UML provides visualization of these relationships through the use of four elements: the dependency, the association, the generalization, and the realization. Through these elements, you can begin to build a hierarchy or structure of elements that shape the artifacts with which to acquaint the consumers of the model.

- **Dependency:** A dependency relationship basically defines a "use" type of relationship where one element uses another element. In the example, the ImasCompany class uses the TenantBill class when it does its monthly billing process. This type of relationship is rendered as a dashed line with an arrow at one end. The line is directed from the "user" element to the "used" element.

- **Association:** Objects and classes are in an association type of relationship when there are strong common traits and or behaviors between the objects. Typically, one class will contain another class. This type of association is called *aggregation* or *containment*. It defines the "has a" relationship so well known in the object-oriented world. Our example has the TenantBill containing a BillDetail, BillTotal and RevenueFee class. Simple association is rendered as a solid line between the classes. A solid line with a diamond on one end denotes aggregation. The diamond is located next to the class that is doing the containing.

- **Generalization:** This relationship defines the parent/child dependency. Another way to define it would be as a super class and subclass where the super class is the parent and the subclass is the child. In this type of relationship, the parent provides general attributes and behavior that is common to all types of this class. The child will provide unique behavior that distinguishes itself from other types derived from the same parent. From the example, Company is a parent class that has common attributes of Name and Address and common behaviors of payBills and billCustomers. Tenant and ImasCompany both are children of Company but both have unique behaviors that distinguishes them from one another. A Tenant has an additional behavior of payingRent whereas ImasCompany has the distinct behavior of billTenant. Neither of these behaviors belongs in the parent class because not all Companies will require them. Yet, each child "is a" type of Company and does exhibit the behavior of all Company types; they need to payBills and billCustomers. This type of relationship is rendered as a solid line with a hollow arrow on one end. The arrow is directed toward the super class.

- **Realization:** A use case identifies what needs to be done based on system requirements. A *collaboration* defines the classes and interactions between the classes that are needed to achieve the results of the use case. The collaboration is said to realize the use case. Similarly, an interface describes a set of behaviors. Classes and components implement the behaviors described by interfaces. Therefore, classes and components realize interfaces. Realizations are rendered much like the generalization except that the line is dashed instead of solid. The hollow arrow is directed toward what is being realized.

Figure 16.3 illustrates the renderings of relationships.

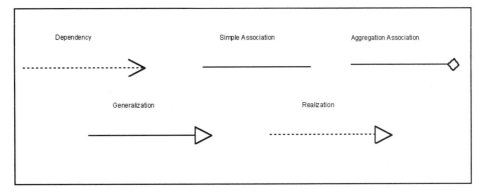

Figure 16.3: A diagram of renderings of relationships indicates that the elements of a model have a relationship with other elements of the model.

Diagrams

A *diagram* is the main message bearer of the model. Through the diagram, all concepts of the system are expressed. Things and relationships are used by the diagram and are a powerful part of the definition of the system. A model of a system consists of many diagrams where each diagram represents a perspective of the overall system. A perspective may be behavioral, conceptual, or physical in nature. This mechanism provides the capability to simplify the complexity of the model by subsetting larger, more complex abstractions into smaller, easier-to-understand units.

There are nine different diagrams in UML. Regarding the different diagrams, keep in mind that any particular type of diagram will be used many times to provide different views into the system. For instance, a model of a small system may contain three to five different class diagrams, each defining a particular static structure or view of the model. One view, in reference to the example, could be all classes involved in the Company hierarchy and another view might be defining all classes involved in the billing process. These smaller, less complicated views help the consumer understand the complete model. Figures 16-4 through 16.6 will help you understand what diagrams have to offer.

- **Class Diagram:** A *class diagram* defines a piece of the system at rest. A set of class diagrams defines the static structure of the system at rest. Class diagrams consist of a set of classes related by the necessity of each class portraying the diagram's specific view of the system. Each class diagram uses classes and relationships to provide this view of the system.

- **Object Diagram:** An *object diagram* is similar to a class diagram except it uses objects, which are realizations of classes. This infers that the object diagram not only provides a specific view of the system, but at a particular moment in time. Because objects are alive, they have state and the object diagram is identifying the state of the object at a given moment in time. Object diagrams use objects and *links*. Links are realizations of relationships.

- **Use Case Diagram:** *Use case diagrams* plot users of the system and the functions or cases the user requires of the system (hence the name, use case). This is where the requirements of the system are mapped to elements of a model. Use case diagrams use *actors* (not previously defined), and use case elements. Actors do not always have to be human, but are a representation of some producer, consumer, or activator of the system.

- **Sequence Diagram:** A *sequence diagram* describes the flow of interactions between classes from a time-oriented perspective. The sequence of interactions are developed to produce some desired result of the system and, typically, are very closely related to a use case in the sense that the sequence diagram will define the classes and sequence of interactions between the classes to fulfill the obligation of a use case. Sequence diagrams use class roles that are realizations of classes and can be considered objects, lifelines (which define the life span of an object), activations (which define the life span of a message), and messages (which provide the interactions between the classes).

- **Collaboration Diagram:** *Collaboration diagrams* also describe the flow of interactions between classes but do so from the class perspective rather than a time perspective. This is done to help visualize the classes and types of messages required of the classes to fulfill the requirements of a use case. Like the sequence diagram, the collaboration diagram is closely related to use cases. Like the sequence diagram, the collaboration diagram uses class roles. The other elements it uses are the relationship roles, which are realizations of relationships and messages.

- **State Chart Diagram:** *State chart diagrams* contain states and transitions and are used to model the dynamic aspects of a model. A state chart diagram captures the states of classes and the transitions between the different states of the classes in response to some external event or activity.

- **Activity Diagram:** *Activity diagrams* capture the states and transitions in response to internal activity or processing as opposed to any external influence. The diagram is divided into swim lanes or areas of responsibility and use action states (realizations of states), action flows (realizations of transitions), and object flows (which are objects used by the action states).

- **Component Diagram:** *Component diagrams* provide a physical look into the system by displaying the organization of and dependencies of the software components of a system. Physical components of a system may include source code, data files, libraries, etc. Component diagrams contain components and relationships between the components.

- **Deployment Diagram:** *Deployment diagrams* describe the physical computing resources of a system and which physical software components of the system will reside on those resources. Deployment diagrams contain nodes and components. The nodes identify computing resources and which components that reside on the nodes. Relationships on the diagram identify the connectivity between nodes.

This concludes the introduction to the major elements defined in UML. To gain a better understanding of what UML is and its capacity to effectively model a system, the following section is an exercise in modeling the Imas Mall Company example.

UML and Modeling

Figure 16.4 shows a use case diagram derived from input by Imas Mall Company customer administrators. From the diagram, you can see that, on a monthly basis, an Actor, defined as a Customer Administrator, updates monthly revenues for each tenant, creates and processes tenants' bills, and receives and processes payments from the tenants.

In a simple use case diagram such as the one shown in Figure 16.4, UML provides the capability to capture a small set of requirements of a larger system for architects and designers to analyze and design. Each use case in the diagram represents a process that is required by the Customer Administrator. This breakout of requirements is one process by which a large system can be dissected into more manageable and understandable units of work. From a use case diagram, individual use cases are explored and developed into sequence diagrams. Through sequence diagrams, you begin identifying classes and other artifacts you will need to create for the solution of the system.

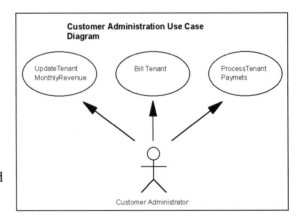

Figure 16.4: A sample use-case diagram derived from input by Imas Mall Company customer administrators can be dissected into more manageable and understandable units of work.

As shown in Figure 16.5, five class roles or objects have been identified for the BillTenant use case. The objects are identified at the top of the diagram by the rectangles with :class name in them. Therefore, this sequence diagram has identified the classes of UserInterface, TenantBill, BillDetail, RevenueFee, and BillTotal.

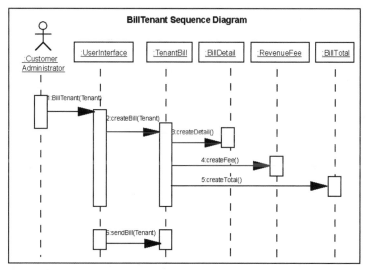

Figure 16.5: With the sequence diagram of classes, five class roles or objects have been identified for the BillTenant use case.

The sequence diagram also exhibits behaviors of objects and when those behaviors are to be expected from each object in the realization of the use case. Messages, which define an object's behavior, are identified by the arrow lines that go from one object's activation to another object's activation. Activations are the vertically inclined rectangles positioned on the lifeline of each object. An object's lifeline is the vertical dashed line extending from the bottom of the object. Notice the sequence number at the beginning of each message in the sequence diagram. This indicates a time perspective of when each object's message will be called.

With a sequence diagram in hand, designers can analyze the objects and messages already identified, provide their creative expertise to the process, and produce a class diagram or set of class diagrams that define the class structures required for the system. It is in the class diagram that details become rather specific. It is from the class diagram that coders will begin to code. Actually, many UML standard modeling tools provide code-generating capabilities from the developer-defined system model.

Figure 16.6 provides a class diagram that can be contrived from the BillTenant Sequence Diagram. With some object-oriented skills applied to the sequence diagram, a class structure is derived. Notice that two parent classes of Bill and Company have been incorporated into the design and that ImasCompany and Tenant are subclasses of Company, while TenantBill is a subclass of Bill. You can see that there is a "uses" dependency between Company and Bill. This dependency also exists between any subclass of the two parents.

A UML class element can be divided into three sections. The first section is the name of the class. The second section provides space for any attributes the class might have. The third section is where class methods may be presented. There is no requirement to display all attributes or methods. It is up to the designers to display the necessary attributes and elements that will give the best meaning for their model.

TenantBill derives itself from Bill and provides additional behavior of the sendBill(Tenant). TenantBill also contains the classes of BillTotal, RevenueFee, and BillDetail. This is denoted in the diagram by the aggregation association. Notice the arabic numeral 1 near each end of the aggregation association in the diagram. This tells the consumer that one TenantBill will contain only one BillTotal, one RevenueFee, and one BillDetail. This type of

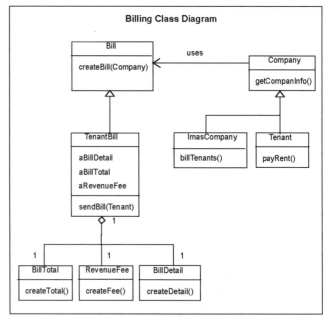

Figure 16.6: A class diagram can be contrived from the BillTenant Sequence diagram.

notation is known as *adornments*. There are many types of adornments defined in UML and they provide the model with more details about the specific elements involved.

And in the End

Modeling a system prior to any movement toward implementation is a very cost-effective use of your organization's time and energy. Modeling allows an analysis of the architecture prior to any large investment into the actual building of the system. It involves many different members across your organization and breeds familiarity to the project. It aids in identifying the skills required to produce the system and is a means for planning and budgeting for the project.

A system model breaks up the complexity of the project into manageable and understandable sections that individual groups or developers can grasp and implement. And if the language used to model the system is a standard, then training members of your organization in the use of the language is a one-time expense.

Many of these thoughts spurred the drive for developing a standard modeling language. Even before object-oriented design became the fashionable trend, structured or top-down development had flow charting as a standard means of conveying how the system and elements of the systems were structured and behaved. Object-oriented systems, however, did not fit into the formula for flow-charting. This started the new evolution of methodologies, methodologists, and methodology tools favored by Booch, Jacobson, and Rumbaugh. While Booch, Jacobson, and Rumbaugh each had factions of support, they—along with the rest of the software industry—realized the value of providing a standard modeling language.

The UML standard modeling language not only provides the software industry with a common means for systems communications, its strength also lies in its capability to aid in the analysis and design of the system. UML can be used to convey the simplest of programs to the most complex of systems and provides a framework for creating them.

References

[1]   Booch, Grady, Ivar Jacobson, and James Rumbaugh. 1999, pg. xx. *The Unified Modeling Language User Guide*. Reading, Massachusetts: Addison-Wesley.

[2]   Web site: *http://www.rational.com/uml/resources/documetentation/summary/summary5.jtmpl.*

[3]   Booch, Jacobson, and Rumbaugh, 17-26.

[4]   Alhir, Sinan Si. 1998.*UML in a Nutshell*. Sebastopol, CA: O'Reilly.

Spies are a most important element in war, because upon them depends an army's ability to move.

—Sun Tzu
The Art of War (Delacorte Press, 1983)

17

Web Security and Cryptography

RICH DIEDRICH

The World Wide Web has made it possible for companies to communicate with customers and potential customers around the world. It also has made it possible to automate customer service to levels to what would have been considered impossible tasks just a few years ago. However, this powerful communications technology has also made it possible for people around the world to try to break into computers and networks and to collect confidential information or change data without leaving their homes or dorm rooms. In addition, the World Wide Web also makes it possible for vandals without detailed technical skills to download tools (so-called "kiddie scripts") that allow them to scan Internet sites for any weaknesses and then exploit those weaknesses.

Another major difference between Web applications and internal applications is that Web

Editor's Introduction: Spies have been a part of warfare since the beginning of warfare, but spies were easier to detect when they had human form. Today, in the Web world, a spy can arrive with the utmost of secrecy and lie invisibly in wait to be activated by a faint signal from across the network. In some of the recent denial-of-service attacks widely reported by the news, the computers doing the actual attacking were infested with spies (parasitical programs) that seized control of machines on command. The owners of the computers used for the denial-of-service attacks had no knowledge of the spies. How can you prevent your Internet-accessible computers from being vulnerable to this or other kinds of security breaches? Read Rich Diedrich's chapter on security and put his recommendations into practice.

–KR

transactions flow through networks and computers that are not under the control of either party involved in the transaction. The transaction data can be intercepted (and possibly modified) while in transit. Because transaction data can include passwords, credit-card numbers, or other very sensitive and valuable information—and because programs can be written to automatically look through the data flowing through a network—this data must be protected while en route.

In addition to these types of attacks, security exposures and damage can result from programs downloaded from the Web and run on computers inside your network. Such programs can cause damage intentionally—because they were infected with a virus—or simply because they have an unintentional security hole that can be used by a malicious person.

Fortunately, there are techniques that can minimize these security exposures. Because cryptography plays a major role in modern computer and network security, an understanding of the capabilities of modern cryptography is important in order to understand the capabilities and limitations of these security techniques. There are three main aspects of Web security:

- Server security.
- Transaction security.
- Client security.

Server Security

The primary concern of most businesses connected to the Web is server security because of the complexities and risk of significant loss. Inadequate server security can result in:

- Exposure or loss of essential business data.
- Exposure or loss of sensitive customer data.
- Damage to company image through electronic vandalism.

Server security consists of protecting not only the Web server itself, but also all computers and networks connected (directly or indirectly) to the Web or the Web server.

Typical Network Configuration

Figure 17.1 shows a typical network configuration that bridges the Internet to an internal network.

The Internet is connected through a packet filtering router to the Web server, which is then connected to the firewall. The firewall filters packets between the Web server and the internal network and provides proxy services for the systems on the internal network. The network containing the Web server or servers is referred to as the DMZ.

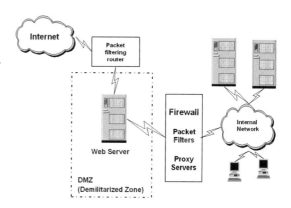

Access to Data

One of the first decisions to be made in designing a Web application is exactly what data must be served. Obviously, an application that

Figure 17.1: A typical network configuration bridges the Internet to an internal network.

provides static data that is not specific to any customer or set of customers is much easier to implement securely than one that provides sensitive personal data for specific customers. Many Web applications can be implemented on standalone systems that do not require continuous communication with production computers.

Some of the first questions that should be asked when designing a Web application are what data is required for the application and whether real-time access to production data is necessary. If real-time access is not required, and the application data can be served directly from the Web server without accessing production systems, a security problem with the Web server will not affect production systems.

If real-time access to production data is required, the application should be designed so that, even if the Web server is compromised, the amount of damage that can be done to production systems is minimized. This can be done by limiting communication between the Web server and production systems to a well-defined set of transactions. Direct access to production databases through a general-purpose interface such as SQL requires that database security be carefully designed, reviewed, and frequently audited in order to ensure that only the views required by the Web server are accessible from that server.

Layers

One of the most important techniques used in designing server security architecture is to use several layers of defense. Because mistakes will occur in Web server or network configuration, a layered architecture will minimize the amount of damage that can occur. The firewalls between externally accessible Web servers (and the Internet in general) should be configured to deny all communication except that which is required.

Firewalls

A *firewall* is a device that limits the TCP/IP traffic between two or more parts of a network and can hide information about one part of the network from another. A firewall uses techniques such as packet filtering and proxy servers to provide this function.

Packet filtering restricts the types of TCP/IP packets that are allowed to flow through the firewall. Packet-filtering restrictions can include what services are allowed through and in which direction connections are allowed. For example, a firewall might only allow incoming connections to a Web server on a specific machine, but may allow any outgoing connections.

Proxy servers prevent the addresses of internal machines from being exposed to networks on the other side of the firewall. This makes it much more difficult to attack the internal machines and it allows private Internet addresses to be used on the internal network. Proxy servers can be specific to an application (such as an HTTP proxy server) or they work at a lower level (like a SOCKS server) so that any application can use them. The application-specific proxy servers usually provide much better logging capabilities because they understand the application data.

Web Servers

One of the most important tasks in implementing a secure server environment is to ensure that the Web server is properly configured. While it is important to ensure that only the desired files are accessible through the server and that a directory listing is not displayable, it is vital that any programs or scripts used to dynamically serve data be designed and reviewed carefully. An error in one program can create a hole through which sensitive data could be exposed or files on the server could be changed.

It is particularly important to review any programs or scripts that are provided with the Web server and to enable only those required for the Web site. Any security holes in the standard programs are likely to be widely known by potential attackers.

Additional Information

Internet RFC (Request for Comments) 2196, entitled *Site Security Handbook*, contains more detailed information about "developing computer security policies and procedures for sites that have systems on the Internet."

Transaction Security

Transaction security is crucial for business that is conducted on the Web. Because Web transactions are transmitted through computers that are not under the control of either the customer or the vendor, any unencrypted data can be captured by anyone with access to any one of the intervening computers. Improper transaction security can result in:

- Exposure of sensitive business information.
- Exposure of sensitive customer information such as credit-card numbers.
- Modification of sensitive transaction data.

Transaction security is most commonly implemented with Secure Sockets Layer (SSL). SSL uses cryptography to provide server and client authentication along with transaction confidentiality and integrity. The most common configuration today uses a certificate to ensure that the server is authenticate and uses data encryption to ensure that the transaction data is not exposed during communication. However, SSL also can be used to authenticate clients or users.

This chapter's section on cryptography describes SSL and certificates in more detail.

When deciding whether cryptographic transaction security is required, one of the most important considerations is how valuable the information in a transaction could be to an attacker. Because encrypting transactions is computationally expensive, higher performance hardware could be required to maintain the desired performance characteristics.

Web Authentication

The HTTP standard provides for a password-based user authentication scheme. While this scheme can be used to limit specific users' access to part or all of the information on the Web server, it must be implemented carefully. The basic authentication scheme doesn't encrypt the user ID or password; information is sent with every transaction between the user and the Web server. Therefore, information can be obtained by anyone who can intercept the traffic unless SSL is used for every transaction between the user and the Web server.

Virtual Private Networks

Virtual private networks (VPN) provide a method for applications on specific networks to communicate over the Internet securely without having been written to the SSL interface directly. A VPN can be configured between two networks that are each connected to the Internet and all application traffic between those networks is automatically encrypted and decrypted. While this technology is useful for communication between specific networks, it is not usually applicable to general Web serving.

Client Security

Client security is important for anyone accessing servers on the Internet. Improper client security can result in:

- Exposure or loss of data on the client computer.
- Exposure or loss of data on other computers on a network with the client computer.

The essential part of client security is user education. While firewalls and proxy servers can protect a network from external attack, a user can inadvertently introduce malicious code or even open a security hole that exposes the entire network.

Cookies

A *cookie* is a small amount of information kept in a browser and sent in every transaction to a specific Web server or to any Web servers in specific domain within a specific time period. Cookies are set by Web servers in order to track sessions or to keep user preferences or information between sessions. While cookies can be used to track which sites or pages a user visits, they are not a serious security exposure for a computer or network.

Java

Java was designed to allow applets to be safely downloaded and run on client computers. Java applets run in a "sandbox" environment that does not allow access to the client file system or to devices attached to the client computer. In addition, the sandbox doesn't allow the applet to open a communication session with any computer other than the one from which it was served. While there have been mistakes found in some Java implementations, an applet running in the sandbox is relatively safe.

For some applications, the standard sandbox for Java applets is too restrictive. For example, an applet might display a complex table and allow the user to adjust the appearance of the data in the table. Because the sandbox doesn't allow the applet to access the user's printer, this table cannot be printed directly by the applet. In order to allow this type of functionality, applets can be electronically signed by the provider.

When a signed applet is received, the browser will display information about the signature and ask the user whether the additional functions requested by the applet should be permitted. In addition, the browser can be configured to automatically accept signed applets from specific sources.

Some requests, such as printer access, are relatively low risk. Other requests—such as read or (even worse) write access—to the client computer's file system are obviously high risk. One that is very high risk, but may not appear to be, is a request to open a socket connection to an address other than the one from which the applet was served. This request is very high risk because the applet could provide a channel for a malicious Web site to attack any computers on a network normally protected by a firewall.

ActiveX

ActiveX has a different security model than Java. While Java is designed to restrict the capabilities of an applet, an ActiveX component has full access to the computer on which it is running. Security is provided by having the components be digitally signed and by setting up the browser to only allow signed components to be run.

If a user allows an unsigned component to run, however, that component can access all file systems, communication capabilities, and devices to which that user has access. While the chance that a signed component is malicious is small (the originator can be found), there is a chance that the component author inadvertently could have created some security holes that could be exploited by another party.

Browser Plug-ins

Browser plug-ins have access to all of the file systems, communication capabilities, and devices to which the user has access. This means that only browser plug-ins from trusted sources should be installed. Because the plug-in will automatically handle files of the registered types when they are served to the browser, any security holes in a plug-in could be exploited by anyone who has discovered (or created) them.

Applications

The highest risk activity for a client is downloading and running applications. An application (even a Java application as opposed to a Java applet), has access to all parts of the file system, all the communication channels, and all the devices that the user running the application has. In addition, applications can be contaminated with viruses that can quickly spread within a site. Because malicious applications can be sent as attachments to e-mail and because e-mail can be forged, users should be warned not to run any applications they receive unless they know the originator and are expecting the application.

A malicious application that does something other than what it advertises is called a *Trojan horse*. In Greek mythology, a wooden horse built by the Greek army contained hidden soldiers. The Trojans brought the horse into their city because they thought that it was a gift. With computers, Trojan-horse applications can destroy a file system, find or move sensitive data to waiting servers, or even silently install themselves so that an attacker at another site can control the computer and all the devices (including microphones) attached to that computer.

Viruses

A *virus* is a piece of code that attaches itself to another program or file, and makes copies of itself when the program is run or the file is open. New program viruses continue to be developed and spread. The fastest-spreading and most pervasive viruses today are the macro viruses that are written in the macro language of a word-processing program and install themselves into any copy of the word-processing program that opens a document that contains the virus. There have been word-processing macros written that actively spread themselves by finding the e-mail program and address book on a computer and sending copies of the document containing the virus to the users listed in the address book. This type of infection is particularly hard to control, because, to the person receiving the document, it looks like someone they know sent it.

Additional Information

Internet RFC 2504, titled *Users' Security Handbook*, is a companion to the *Site Security Handbook*. It contains information that users need to help keep their systems and networks secure.

Cryptography

Cryptography is used to provide security in the inherently insecure environment of the Web. Cryptography can be used to provide transaction confidentiality and integrity and to authenticate users, systems, and programs. Modern cryptography uses a combination of symmetric key and public key algorithms along with secure hash algorithms for digital signatures. Signed certificates are used to authenticate systems and users.

SSL

Secure Sockets Layer is a technology that combines the techniques provided by modern cryptography into a protocol that can be integrated into applications in a standard way. When an SSL connection is opened, a standard handshake procedure is started. The two sides of the connection negotiate a public key algorithm, a symmetric key algorithm, and a secure-hash algorithm, and they exchange the required certificates.

Once the algorithms and certificates have been agreed upon, the handshake continues by using the public key algorithm to exchange a secret that is used to generate the session key that will be used by the symmetric key algorithm for the rest of the session. Technically, the session parameters could be renegotiated during the session, but renegotiation is rarely used. Figure 17.2 shows the SSL handshake.

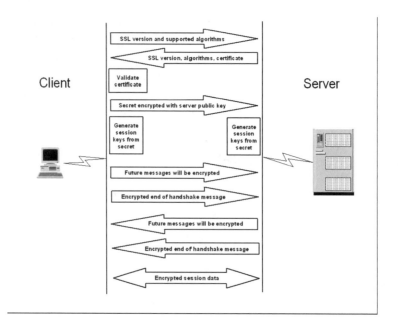

Figure 17.2: The SSL handshake is between client and server.

The algorithms that are currently in use by SSL are described in the following sections.

Symmetric Key Algorithms

Symmetric key-encryption algorithms use the same key for encoding and decoding a message. The properties of symmetric key algorithms include the following characteristics:

- They are usually much more efficient than public key algorithms.
- Both the sender and receiver must know the key.
- Anyone who knows the key can intercept and possibly modify the message.
- They are generally used for the exchange of the actual transaction data.

There are several symmetric key algorithms in common use:

- **DES (Data Encryption Standard):** DES has been a federal standard since 1976. While the 56-bit key length of DES was sufficient at that time, modern computers can search through keys quickly enough to make standard DES too weak for good security. However, the effective key length can be increased to 112 bits (which is beyond computer search capability) by using triple DES.

- **RC2 (Rivest Cipher 2):** RC2 is a block cipher designed by Ron Rivest and is owned by RSA Data Security, Inc. (RSADSI), and protected as a trade secret by RSADSI. It is designed to run more quickly than DES.

- **RC4 (Rivest Cipher 4):** RC4 is a stream cipher designed by Ron Rivest for RSADSI. While it was also protected as a trade secret, the source code has been posted to the Internet and is currently in wide use.

Public Key Algorithms

Public key encryption algorithms use a different key for decoding than is used for encoding, and it is not feasible to obtain one of the keys (the "private key") from the other (the "public key"). This property makes key distribution much easier because a user can distribute the public key to anyone while keeping the private key secret. Anyone can then encrypt a message with the public key, but only the user (who knows the private key) can decrypt the message.

Some public-key algorithms (including the most commonly used algorithm, RSA) also have the property that a message encoded with the private key can be decoded with the public key. This feature can be used to provide message integrity because only someone who knows the private key can create a message that can be correctly decoded with the public key.

Because public key algorithms are so computationally expensive, they are generally used to distribute the key for a symmetric-key algorithm, which is then used communicating the actual message. The public key algorithms also are used in digital signatures to ensure that the result of a secure-hash algorithm is not changed. The properties of public key algorithms include the following:

- They are computationally expensive.

- A message can be encrypted with a public key, but can only be decrypted with the private key.

- Some algorithms also include the property that a message encrypted with the private key can be decrypted with the public key.

- The algorithms are generally used for the exchange of the symmetric-key algorithm keys and for signing a message digest.

There is one public-key algorithm in common use:

- **RSA:** RSA (Rivest, Shamir, Adleman) is based on the difficulty of factoring a number that is the product of two large primes. While it is the de facto standard public key algorithm, it is patented in the United States.

Secure Hash Algorithms

Secure hash algorithms are used to convert an arbitrarily long message to a fixed-length message digest in such a way that it is not feasible to construct a second message that has the same digest. This digest can be encrypted with the private key of a public-key algorithm, like RSA, to form a digital signature. The two secure-hash algorithms in common use are:

- **MD5 (Message Digest 5):** MD5 is an improved version of MD4 developed by Ron Rivest. It produces a 128-bit message digest.

- **SHA (Secure Hash Algorithm):** SHA was developed by NIST, along with NSA, for use with the Digital Signature Standard. It produces a 160-bit message digest.

Certificates

Certificates are used for server authentication and can be used for client authentication. A server certificate contains the server's public key and domain name and is signed by a certificate authority. A client certificate contains the client's public key and is signed by that key and by a certificate authority.

Server Certificate

A server certificate contains the:

- Name of organization that owns the server public key.
- Server IP address.
- Server public key.
- Expiration date.
- Name of certificate authority.
- Unique serial number.
- Digital signature of certificate authority.

When a client receives the server certificate, it authenticates the certificate by:

1. Checking that the certificate has not expired.

2. Verifying the certificate authority is trusted.

3. Verifying the certificate authority's public key validates the signature.

4. Verifying that the domain name on the certificate matches the server's domain name.

Client Certificate

A client certificate contains the:

- Owner's name.
- Owner's public key.
- Expiration date.
- Name of certificate authority.
- Unique serial number.
- Digital signature of certificate authority.

If the server requires a client certificate, it is validated by:

1. Verifying that the user's public key validates the signature.

2. Checking that the certificate has not expired.

3. Verifying that the certificate authority is trusted.

4. Verifying that the certificate authority's public key validates the signature.

5. Optionally, verifying that the user name has a LDAP entry.

Certificate Authority

A certificate authority validates that a certificate accurately represents the entity it describes. The certificate authority can be a widely recognized, commercial authority, such as VeriSign, or it can be a private authority recognized by the entities involved in the transaction.

Additional Information

Applied Cryptography—Second Edition by Bruce Schneier contains detailed information about the algorithms and protocols currently in use. The Netscape Web site contains more detailed information about SSL and certificates.

References

Schneier, Bruce. 1999. *Applied Cryptography: Protocols, Algorithms, and Source Code in C—Second Edition.* New York: John Wiley & Sons.

Internet RFC 2196, *Site Security Handbook*.

Internet RFC 2504, *Users' Security Handbook.*

Web site: *http://www.netscape.com.*

Web site: *http://www.verisign.*

Any sufficiently advanced technology is indistinguishable from magic.

—Arthur C. Clarke

18

Pervasive Computing

JOSEPH BIGUS, PH.D.

Think back to your last business meeting. How many people in the room had notebook computers with them? How many checked their calendars or took notes on their Palm handheld devices? Any digital cell phones or pagers in the room? Chances are that there were quite a few such devices present. The age of pervasive computing is not coming; it's here. But what does that mean for

e-business? How will these personal devices impact e-commerce in the next decade? This chapter explores all of the major aspects of pervasive computing and how it will change electronic commerce and e-business in the coming years. Topics covered include:

- Basic elements of pervasive computing and what it means to users and businesses.

- The wide range of devices that are part of the pervasive-computing landscape.

> **Editor's Introduction:** Magic is just what pervasive computing can seem to be. A device that is no large than a calculator, in your hand or in your car, can access the large computer systems at your company and provide you with current—up to the second current—information about your business, no matter where you happen to be. There are many types of pervasive computing devices and they'll be put to uses as varied as human imagination. They will, mostly, use standard communication mechanisms, information-structuring and transport mechanisms, and information-presentation mechanisms. This is one of the most exciting areas in computing today. In this chapter, Dr. Joseph Bigus explains the technologies and the possibilities.
>
> –KR

- Some of the applications and services that will drive the use of pervasive-computing devices.

- The sometimes competing industry standards that will play a role in the growth of both devices and applications and services in this area.

- The impact pervasive computing will have on e-business and e-commerce.

I'll begin by stating the obvious. Things are changing so fast that any specifics detailed here would be out of date very quickly. Almost daily, announcements by startups and established companies, either individually or as consortia, describe new technical and business initiatives in pervasive computing. As always, the improvements in technology capabilities march on. So, my focus will be on the core issues and trends to give you some perspective on where things are today and where they might soon be going in the dynamic pervasive-computing arena.

Figure 18.1 shows the relationship of pervasive computing to network computing. In many ways, pervasive computing is a natural evolution of the networked computing e-business paradigm. The major difference is the impending explosion in the number and types of client devices. Their capability to connect to the network infrastructure through both high bandwidth wired and wireless connections using standardized content and flexible presentation formats will dramatically alter the foundations of e-commerce.

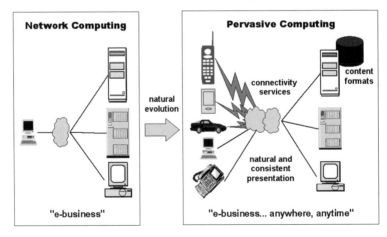

Figure 18.1: Progression from network computing to pervasive computing is a natural evolution.

Pervasive computing takes e-business into the realm of anywhere and anytime computing. Users will be able to take actions: respond to messages, search for information, and initiate personal and business transactions from small, easy-to-use, information appliances wherever and whenever they choose. The virtual "open for business" sign always will be on.

Introduction

If pervasive computing is going to have such a big impact on you and your business, exactly what defines *pervasive computing*? Figure 18.2 shows the major elements of pervasive computing. Client devices can be personal mobile devices that are handheld in automobiles or they can be part of information appliances used in the home. These devices will connect through network access providers such as America Online or cable and telecom providers. They will access applications and services provided by the network service providers. As shown in Figure 18.2, the cloud represents the network infrastructure connecting the world's homes and businesses.

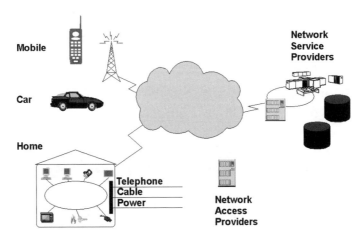

Figure 18.2: The elements of pervasive computing will connect through network access providers or cable and telecom providers.

Devices

This section describes the devices that are considered part of the pervasive-computing space. These include cell phones, pagers, palm-sized computers, and notebook computers. In the next few years, a vast array of new special-purpose devices is also expected to be introduced. Despite the widely varying types of pervasive-computing devices, they all share a core set of attributes: small form factor, network-enabled, and relatively low cost.

User Interfaces

Computer users have dealt with hard-to-use software for over 50 years. We've moved along from binary switches to paper tape to card punches and Teletype machines to the ubiquitous QWERTY keyboard with the mouse pointing device along for the ride. We've gone from green-screen text displays to 1280-by-1024 displays with high-quality graphics in 16 million colors. We've gone from terse, command-line interfaces to graphical user interfaces with three-dimensional icons and widgets. And while every new software release touts the new, user-friendly, easy-to-use interface, the need for voluminous help text has not gone away.

While this history is interesting, the lack of a truly easy-to-use interface has not hurt the growth of the computer industry. People keep buying PCs regardless of how easy or hard to use they are. However, we are now in the range of 300 million PC users and the penetration into homes is slowing greatly. Most PCs are now sold as replacements or second computers to avoid fights when the kids have school reports to do.

As we enter the pervasive computing era, the usability of these devices becomes a major issue. When people buy a cell phone or pager, they know intuitively how to use them. When someone buys a $500 multifunction personal digital assistant, they don't know how to use it. As computers evolve into true consumer electronic devices, their usability has to improve. A single help-desk call could swamp the profit margins on some of the new low-cost devices.

The majority of pervasive computing devices will not have QWERTY keyboards. Most will not have mouse-pointing devices. How will users interact with them? With a TV remote control? By talking to it? By writing on it with a digital pen? By mental telepathy or some other sort of biometrics input?

Speech

Speech recognition software has been a research topic for over 30 years. Speech recognition systems have been used in defense applications and in other work in very controlled environments. During the last few years, several successful products—ViaVoice from IBM, NaturallySpeaking from Dragon Systems, and Voice Xpress from Lernout & Hauspie—have emerged. These systems can understand continuous speech as well as spoken word commands and relay them to applications.

For example, you can surf the Web or edit text documents using voice commands. Dictation also has become a viable application for certain domains such as the medical field where the vocabulary is constrained or specialized.

Most children learn to talk by the time they are a year old and are uttering two- and three-word sentences when they are 18 months. Speech is a natural interface. No manuals are required. So easy a toddler can do it. The software technology has certainly evolved to work reasonably well. The computer-processing power is now more than enough in a 166MHz Pentium machine to recognize continuous speech.

So, will speech be the killer-input method for pervasive devices? It depends on the device and the application. Imagine being in a meeting with 50 people as they all dictate into their personal dictation machines. It's not a pretty thought. And simply sticking voice navigation on top of Windows menu-manipulation paradigms is not the answer. We need natural-language understanding that is still years away. But barking out voice commands to your PDA is definitely in your near future.

Pen

Pen input is very natural in many settings. Walk into a restaurant with a young child, and the first thing the host or hostess does is hand the child a coloring book with a set of crayons. You can draw. You can write. You can use a stylus to provide input to a PDA. If you've ever used a Palm computing device, you know how easy it is to learn the Graffiti alphabet and almost immediately get reasonably good input recognition. You can be in a meeting or conference room and easily whip out your Palm computer and scribble down a note to yourself or add a meeting to your calendar before you forget it. However, I wouldn't want to write a book using a digital pen or stylus. So like voice, pen input will have its place in future pervasive devices.

Other Input Techniques

You can type, you can talk, you can write. How about blink? Give a scowl and your computer will hurry up because it knows you are getting impatient. Biometrics, where the computer watches you through a camera or skin sensor, could be another way to tell a computer where you want to go today. Initial applications are expensive and have been limited to security features—such as fingerprint identification and retinal scanning at ATMs—but research is active in this area. Don't be surprised to someday be able to select a menu item by looking at it and blinking or thinking "click."

Content Representation

With personal computers and Web browsers, the content is either coming from Windows applications or from Web servers. The standard representation is in HTML, the hypertext markup language that has revolutionized information publishing on the World Wide Web. However, new pervasive devices will probably not have 800-by-600 color screens, and most will not "do Windows." How will we represent data or content and display it on these devices?

HTML

The hypertext markup language (HTML) is the king of Internet content. There are millions of pages of HTML content available on the Internet today. Who knows how many HTML pages are available many intranets? HTML is powerful and flexible. It makes it easy to author and get information out on the Web. However, HTML has some limitations. The data in an HTML page is tied to its format or layout on the screen. The HTML parsers that are used in Web browsers can display badly formed HTML documents. Also, there are many documents where there are mismatched begin-end tags and other such ugliness.

These limitations led to the development of the eXtensible Markup Language (XML). XML is a meta-language for information content and the corresponding eXtensible Style Language (XSL) is used to format the XML data for display.

XML

As detailed in chapter 15, XML is becoming the new standard in Web content. Designed from the beginning to solve the HTML limitations, XML use is growing. XML itself defines a way to define your own document types, including your own tags, through a document type definition (DTD). XML documents that use a common DTD are guaranteed to be interchangeable. Industry groups are working to define sets of DTDs for their particular domain requirements. For example, consumer electronic companies have banded together and developed a format for electronic supply-chain transactions called RosettaNet.

XML is fast becoming the common data format for all types of applications. Microsoft says that it will output Office documents and spreadsheet data in XML and is promoting its BizTalk framework for developing XML type documents for vertical industries. Database vendors, including IBM's DB2, will serve up relational data formatted using XML tags. XML also is being used to define graphics (using tags) as well as voice input data. The Voice Markup Language is an XML standard for representing voice-user interfaces. Other XML standards have been proposed for vector graphics and math-expression representations.

Audio and Video Content

While XML is fine for defining structured data, standards are needed for audio and video information. The MPEG3 or MP3 format has become famous as the standard format for encoding music. Hundreds of thousands of pervasive computing devices, such as the Diamond Rio players, have been sold for the sole purpose of downloading and playing back MP3 music files. This is a perfect example of a special-purpose device with an extremely easy-to-use interface that requires little or no help-desk support costs.

Cell Phones

The convergence of television with computers in the home is a familiar topic, but another place where convergence is occurring is in the blending of cell phones with computers and PDA functionality. Will it be more natural to turn PDAs into cell phones or turn cell phones into PDAs? Will the voice interface be the most natural way for users to interact with their PDAs or will pen input work best? Ease of use might be the deciding factor.

While cell phone use is growing in the United States, use has exploded in Europe for several reasons. One factor is the high cost of wired communications. Another reason is the standardization on the global system for mobile communications, known as GSM, technology. Over half the Finnish population owns GSM cell phones.

Mark Bregman, IBM's general manager for pervasive computing, says there are approximately 300 million PC users worldwide and almost 250 million cell phones, but the number of cell phones is growing at 70 million a year. In Europe for example, over 2 billion messages a month are sent via short-messaging services. In Finnish schools, cell phones are taken from the students when they go into exams so that the students won't send messages to each other during tests. Does that sound pervasive to you?

The Nokia 9000 phone is a GSM phone that can be used to make telephone calls throughout Europe. It also has a full keyboard and a screen, with a user interface similar to Windows, that can be used to do word processing and schedule appointments. A single button labeled "Internet" allows access to a Web browser through a wireless connection. So, when is a digital cell phone a Web browser? When it has a keyboard and a display screen and access to the Internet. In short, now!

Pagers

Numeric and text pagers have been available for many years. Talk about easy to use. You can put one in your pocket and go about your business. When someone wants to contact you, they dial a phone number and send you a numeric or text message, depending on the capabilities of your pager. The pager service sends the message to your pocket and the device beeps, chimes, or vibrates. You take it out, read the message off the display and decide whether to ignore it or call the person back. If you have a two-way pager, you input a reply using a small keyboard and send it to the person who contacted you.

Personal Digital Assistants and Palm Computers

Personal information managers and electronic personal organizers have been available for several years. However, they are mainly stand-alone devices, with tiny keyboards, and they are very difficult to synchronize with address books and calendars on PCs. However, the development of personal digital assistants like the Palm devices has totally changed things.

The Palm hand-held computers developed by 3Com hold almost 70 percent of the market for palm-sized devices. The major advantage of the Palm is that its user interface and pen-based input language, called Graffiti, were developed expressly for the small form factor of the devices. Unlike other pen-based computing efforts, such as the infamous Apple Newton, the Palm pen input language is easy to learn and provides accurate character recognition. A large, third-party market for software has developed around the Palm computers.

Handspring, a startup led by the creator of the Palm computer, Jeff Hawkins, has recently introduced several lower-cost devices (using the PalmOS) that feature a flexible hardware expansion slot that supports Springboard expansion modules. These modules come with auto-install software and can quickly turn these devices into a pager, a cell phone, a music player, or anything else people can dream up.

Microsoft's Windows CE, which is a subset of their Windows programming environment targeted at Palm-sized devices, has had a difficult time displacing Palm computers in the marketplace. Microsoft was betting that the large community of software developers familiar with the Windows APIs would work in its favor. However, the consensus seems to be that the PC GUI paradigm with windows does not translate well to the smaller form-factor devices. A Palm-sized computer is not a tiny PC.

The development of pen-based input and easy data synchronization has made Palm computing devices compelling to users. Many IT organizations are now dealing with a situation similar to the initial uptake of PCs into mainframe shops. They now own diverse devices—purchased by individuals or departments—that have to be managed and integrated with the basic IT services. This issue is becoming so large that management of PDAs in the IT infrastructure is becoming a major headache for CIOs. Gartner Group reports that the support costs for a PDA could exceed the initial purchase price by five to six times.

Notebook Computers

The evolution from luggable, portable computers to laptops and now notebooks has resulted in a steady stream of innovations in display technologies, user-friendly keyboards, and pointing devices such as the IBM TrackPoint. While notebooks always seemed to lag the price/performance factors available on desktop systems, they are now at the point where they can be mobile desktop replacements.

Notebooks easily can be networked (using PC Cards through V90 modems) or connected directly to a LAN (using Ethernet or Token Ring cards). Wireless connections also have been available for some time. Add the Bluetooth type of wireless capability and a mobile computer makes a wired connection seem superfluous. Why spend the money on wiring an office when a wireless LAN and Bluetooth campus offers more flexibility?

Before you plan your business strategy around the millions of pervasive devices that will be coming onto the market, SRI Consulting says that notebooks, not PDAs or cell phones, will dominate the wireless data market through 2003. The current installed base of 80 million portable computers is expected to grow to almost 250 million by 2003. SRI Consulting estimates that there will be 12.5 million PDAs with wireless Internet connectivity at that time.

TV Set-Top Boxes

Television is one of the most pervasive of the consumer electronic devices. The development of the videocassette recorder (VCR) added time-shifting options and enabled the establishment of the movie rental industry. The broadband access of cable TV, combined with computer networks, is forming an entirely new set of devices. Set-top boxes are essentially intelligent cable boxes. They run software that provides value-added services to users. WebTV, controlled by Microsoft, and several startups, including TiVo Inc. and ReplayTV, are developing true anytime-viewing capabilities.

TiVo and ReplayTV allow users to automatically record programs whenever they are broadcast. The devices allow users to pause, rewind, and do instant replays even on live broadcasts. Features include monitoring of your viewing preferences and anticipation of your future needs. How do they do this? Programming is cached in digital format in the set-top box. WebTV also allows users to surf the World Wide Web from a couch or easy chair. All of these services provide enhanced program directories, including searching listings by categories. Additionally, interactive game shows—where the studio audience as well as the home audience can play along—are a possibility. The electronic town hall is now a reality.

Direct service line connections enable users to surf the Web at a much higher speed than most users who access the Internet through dial-up lines at 28.8 or 56.3 Kbps data rates. Cable connections allow data to flow at rates approaching 256 Kbps. This enables entirely new classes of Web applications, including real-time streaming video.

How will set-top boxes impact e-business? Instead of millions of tech-savvy users accessing your service from their office or home PCs, set-top boxes will enable hundreds of millions of technical novices to request information or conduct transactions from their family rooms. It will be as easy as turning on the TV and finding the remote control.

Smart Cards

While just gaining acceptance in the United States, smart cards have had very good penetration in Europe. A smart card is a credit-card sized piece of plastic with a computer processor and memory circuits embedded into it. The memory circuits can store information about the user and the processor can perform simple transactions on the data. The advantage that smart cards have over magnetic-stripe cards is that the data is stored in an electronic memory chip and the on-card processor can encrypt the information. This helps prevent unauthorized reading and duplication of cards and their contents. Smart cards can be read by inserting them into special readers and newer noncontact cards even contain radio modems for wireless data transfer.

Screen Phones

Chances are that other special-purpose devices, like the Rio MP3 music player, will find success in the marketplace. One possibility is a screen phone that also supports simple e-mail. Users would not have to learn to use Windows or typical PC-style operations. They would push a button to send e-mail and easily scroll through a list to read incoming mail.

Automobile PCs

While some might question the usefulness, automobile makers have become involved in the pervasive-computing arena. The AutoPC, developed by Clarion, is typical of this class of device. Using wireless connections, it provides access to the Internet for e-mail, Web browsing, communications, digital maps, and guidance. Some auto devices feature global positioning system receivers that give your location down to a resolution of a few meters. For obvious reasons, speech input is the preferred approach for using these devices. Another more mundane, but useful, application of pervasive computing to motorists are the automatic tollbooths being used in several cities.

Electronic Book Readers

Handheld electronic book reader devices, such as the Rocket eBook, are now available. Such devices feature designs ergonomically suitable for reading textual content that is usually downloaded from the Internet. Consumer electronics companies are working hard to come up with superior displays designed especially for mimicking the look and feel of conventional paper books.

The advantages of an electronic book reader are that it can be reused thousands of times, it can hold multiple books (current capacities are around 1,500 pages), and it has a small form factor. While major book publishers see this as a large, potential market for their wares, these devices also could be used to display product documentation and help information. It's another example of the blurring of personal consumer devices and business devices. Imagine walking through a crowded exhibition area at a conference and simply beaming in—through an infrared port into your electronic book reader—the product information from the selected companies. This would cut down on costs to the business for printed sales materials as well as reduce the amount of paper you would have to lug home on the airplane.

Wearable Computers

Wearable computers have been demonstrated in a variety of formats. Most examples consist of a package the size of a deck of cards (strapped to your belt), a voice input, and some sort of projection-display unit. Research universities, such as the Massachusetts Institute of Technology media lab, have shown wearable computers embedded into clothing. Other devices that have been mainstays of science fiction, such as the wristwatch computer, are coming soon to a consumer electronics store near you.

Software for Pervasive Devices

In addition to embedded software for controlling the device user interface and communications, pervasive-computing devices will require various types of middleware. This is especially true if the devices are to be used in a disconnected mode. Several database vendors are offering mini relational databases. IBM's DB2 Everywhere is available for free on the Web. Local databases allow transactions to be stored in the pervasive device and then uploaded to the application service provider when network connectivity is restored.

Services

The existence of millions of pervasive computing devices will have a tremendous impact on the Internet service providers and application service providers as well as e-businesses. The technical challenges range from adapting content to the display capabilities of the device, to sensitivity to the amount of bandwidth available, to ensuring user authentication and information security.

Web Browsing

The capability to browse the Internet (or intranet) from a pervasive-computing device is the Holy Grail of pervasive computing. While broadband connections are just starting to roll out by way of cable providers and telephone companies, the data rates through wireless connections are typically going to be slower than those available from wired connections.

Browsing the Internet from low-data-rate wireless devices, such as PDAs, is not practical today. A Web page with embedded graphics or Java applets that loads in a reasonable amount of time over a 56 Kbps dial-up line will be unbelievably slow on a low-bandwidth wireless link. Add to this the small, 300-by-300-pixel LCD display and the Web surfing experience will not be the same.

To get around these limitations of connection speed and display resolution, there is one solution. Download less information. This can be done by providing multiple sources of information coded for each type of device. Another approach is to dynamically modify the source data before it is sent down the line (or through the air). Web clipping is the technique used by Palm computing. In their wireless access service provided with the Palm VII devices, site content is modified specifically for the Palm display capabilities.

Because of the cost of maintaining multiple versions of the information content, transcoding the data using intermediaries between the sender and receiver of data is becoming a popular technique. Intermediaries can take the source data and insert, delete, or otherwise transform the information content for the particular needs of the user and the display capabilities of the client device. It could be that the intermediary knows that the user is French speaker and likes to receive all news in French. The intermediary translates into French any English-language article before it is sent down to the pervasive device. Or maybe the user commonly switches between a notebook computer, a PDA, and a cell phone; each has very different display capabilities. The intermediary could query the client device and transcode the information for the specific device that the user is currently holding.

E-mail, Calendar, and Address Book

It has often been said that e-mail is the killer application for the Internet. Indeed, several major Internet portals have based their business model on providing free e-mail services to users. By drawing traffic to their site, they can make money by selling advertising. Microsoft bought the HotMail site and added it to the Microsoft Network for that reason.

After e-mail, helping busy people manage their calendars has become the next big Web application. Major portals are starting to offer free calendar management to go along with the free e-mail services. After e-mail and calendar support, basic address-book services will be the next service This is the last piece of the personal-information device functionality. If you have a user's address book, manage their schedules, and hold their e-mail communications, chances are you can keep them coming back to the site.

Information Searching

The oldest and most effective way to draw traffic on the Internet has been to help users find information on the World Wide Web. Yahoo, AltaVista, Lycos, and Excite all started with either comprehensive indexes of Web sites or powerful search engines. Over time, these sites have had to continually develop better search algorithms and more personalized features to provide value to their users. As Web content continues to grow exponentially, this type of service won't go out of style or outlive its usefulness.

Financial Services

One of the first industries to embrace pervasive computing has been the financial-service providers. The need for real-time information on the stock markets and late-breaking news that might impact share prices have driven the demand for wireless, anytime, anywhere access to information. Today, you can monitor and actively place stock trades from pervasive-computing devices such as two-way pagers, cell phones, and Palm computing devices.

According to Meridien Research, the projected customer base for wireless finance services users by 2003 is estimated to be 40 million users worldwide. The projections include 18 million in Europe, 12 million in Asia, and 8 million in North America. Wireless banking is already following this path. Initially, services will provide access to checking account balances and transaction logs.

Shopping and Electronic Marketplaces

Online purchasing is a growth market. Consumers have overcome initial concerns regarding security and are happily plunking down credit-card numbers and filling electronic shopping carts. Convenient retail shopping has become one of the largest draws of new users to the Internet.

Another growing phenomenon on the Web is the use of electronic auctions. Sites such as eBay have extremely high margins (70 percent) because they are not stocking products but simply acting as market makers for thousands of individuals who have things they want to sell and for thousands more looking for bargains. Whether you are a buyer or seller, having a pervasive-computing device with you to keep in touch as your auction progresses is an important consideration.

For business-to-business e-commerce, similar market makers for vertical industries also are becoming established. Whether the commodity is electricity, chemicals, or institutional paper supplies, businesses like the auction model as a way to unload excess inventory and turn it into cash and as a way to quickly pick up low-cost supplies. Pervasive computing is a synergistic trend.

Standards

There are several different areas for pervasive-computing standards. There are standards for communications formats such as TCP/IP and the Wireless Application Protocol (WAP). There are standards for information content such as HML, XML, and Wireless Markup Language (WML). There are standards for device interoperability such as Salutation, Jini, and Universal Plug and Play. Name an area of pervasive computing where companies think they can get a competitive advantage and you'll find one or more standards competing for acceptance in that area. This section describes several important standards efforts.

The Salutation protocol includes architecture for the interoperability of information appliances such as printers, scanners, and copiers. Salutation defines how these business devices can discover each other, find out each other's capabilities, and access each other's services and information.

The OpenCard Framework is a standard that provides for interoperable smart-card solutions across different hardware and software platforms. Using the OpenCard framework, application developers and service providers can build solutions that use smart cards for authenticated access and secure transactions in electronic commerce.

Symbian, a consortium of companies, has developed the EPOC real-time operating system for use in pervasive-computing devices such as cell phones. Symbian recently struck a deal with Palm Computing to add the Palm user interface on top of the EPOC operating system in Symbian wireless devices.

Wireless Application Protocol (WAP) is a standard communications protocol and application environment for delivering tailored content from Internet and intranets to pervasive devices.

There are over 100 members in the WAP Forum (an industry consortium). In July 1999, Version 1.1 of the WAP specification was placed in the public domain. WAP-compliant devices and services already are being offered.

The Bluetooth specification developed by the Bluetooth special interest group (SIG) provides a standard interconnection protocol for connecting low-cost wireless devices to each other and to local area networks. There are more than 1,000 companies in the Bluetooth SIG. Devices with Bluetooth support contain a radio-on-a-chip that can instantly recognize when other Bluetooth enabled devices are in close proximity (around 10 meters) and will automatically establish a wireless connection. The impact of this function on a pervasive device user is profound. Walk into a conference room and you can automatically exchange information with other Bluetooth devices in the room, an overhead display device, notebook computers, PDAs, printers, or the Internet.

To extract the most value out of a world with hundreds of millions of pervasive computing devices, it would be nice if they all worked seamlessly. Most users of pervasive computing devices will be technical novices; so they aren't going to be configuring device drivers for printers. Sun's Jini and Microsoft's Universal Plug and Play are the two major competitors in trying to define how all these devices work together. To win, each needs to ensure that their software becomes part of the network infrastructure and that the consumer electronic companies put the software support into their devices. This shapes up to be a Beta-versus-VHS-format type of battle. At this stage, there is no clear winner.

Home Networks

Potentially, there is a large market for home networks that blend PCs, the Internet, intelligent appliances, and services provided over the network. Potential customer include parents using e-mail, online shopping, and research, and children playing games, having online chat sessions, and working on school reports. As soon as a home gets a second PC, the need for networking becomes apparent. Why have two printers when one would do?

Several trends are enabling the home-networking trend. Broadband Internet connections, through cable or telephone lines using asymmetric digital subscriber lines (ADSL), and low-cost local area networks in the home enable home-information appliances to access the Web through a single link.

Both computing and communications costs are continually dropping. Consumers want information access, peripheral-sharing, entertainment (video on demand, multiuser games), communications (telephone and e-mail), and home-security features all integrated into one system.

Figure 18.3 shows the major elements of a home network. The main goal is to provide a single Internet access point for the home and all of the pervasive-computing devices in the home. The connection to the Internet might be through telephone, cable, or even electrical lines. Inside the home, the pervasive devices might communicate through wired or wireless connections using phone, cable, and electrical

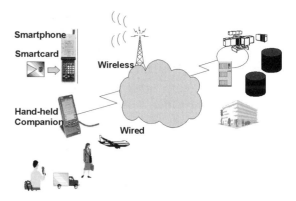

Figure 18.3: The main goal of a home network is to provide a single Internet access point for all of the pervasive-computing devices in the home.

lines to carry the signals. The services will include shared Internet service-provider access for multiple users in the home, an integrated firewall for security, voice communications (telephone) over the Internet, and shared peripherals to all users in the home.

A customer no longer will need to come in your store or sit at an Internet-connected PC to access your services. The Home Phone Networking Alliance (HomePNA) standard will allow computing devices connected through telephone lines to interact with home appliances connected through the power-line network.

Jini

Jini (pronounced genie) is a Sun Microsystems initiative for anytime networked computing. Based on the Java programming environment, Jini provides a protocol for all sorts of computing devices to automatically connect and interoperate on a network. This includes registering the device to the network, discovering the other devices and software services available to users of the device, and providing the latest software for accessing and using those devices or services.

Here's how Jini works. You plug the Jini device into a network connector. It broadcasts a message to a predetermined address where the Jini directory service resides. The directory service responds to the Jini device and the device sends additional code to register itself with the Jini networked system. Now, whenever any other

Jini device wants to talk to your Jini device, it asks the directory server, which sends it the Java code to access your device. Knowing nothing about the details of how your device works, it can ask it what services it provides and then use those services. Note that the "network" doesn't have to be a computer network, such as with Ethernet or Token Ring connections, it could be a phone line, cable, or power connector.

Universal Plug and Play

The Universal Plug and Play initiative led by Microsoft is an attempt to extend the successful PC plug-and-play standards to networked devices. It is Microsoft's answer to Sun's Jini. Microsoft has created an industry consortium, called the Universal Plug and Play Forum, to work to define and implement the Universal Plug and Play standards and to provide support for the Microsoft operating systems (Windows CE and Windows 2000).

Rather than being PC-centric, Universal Plug and Play adds a discovery mechanism—similar to that used in Jini—as such, so that devices can connect to a network, find other available devices, and then use them.

Universal Plug and Play is an Internet protocol (IP) that doesn't require each device to implement TCP/IP. Dynamic Host Configuration Protocol (DHCP) is the preferred mechanism for dynamically assigning IP addresses to devices when they connect to the network. The three major aspects to the Universal Plug and Play software are architecture, discovery, description, and usage. Discovery is enabled by the Simple Service Discovery Specification (SSDS). An Internet Engineering Task Force specification, SSDS features two modes of operation:

- On demand where clients can query for services.
- Availability of a service is announced when the device or service joins the network.

Universal Plug and Play is the basis for Microsoft's home-networking strategy, whereby home appliances, pervasive-computing devices, personal computers, and software services all communicate and interoperate seamlessly.

Business Impact and Outlook

How will pervasive computing impact your business? Perhaps the most direct way will be through the use of pervasive devices in the information technology operations inside your company. Figure 18.4 shows employees using a smart phone (or PDA) to connect to the corporate network through either wired or wireless links. This technology will provide access to enterprise applications and data whether the employee is in

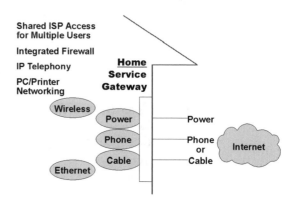

Figure 18.4: E-business and pervasive computing allows for wide access either through wired or wireless links.

the office or out on the road. The use of standards-based pervasive clients can lower application development and deployment costs while simultaneously improving the productivity of mobile employees.

The same forces that have transformed the computing industry over the past three decades will influence pervasive computing. Smaller form factors, faster and more powerful computer chips, and lower prices will almost surely be in the future. Will the value-added benefit and the real money to be made in pervasive computing be in the devices themselves, in the network and communications services, in the application services such as finance, or will it be in the suppliers of the computers in the cloud? Established companies and venture-capital-funded Internet startups are placing high-stakes bets right now.

Certain trends in the marketplace are unmistakable. First, today's desktop applications purchased in shrink wrap packages will likely be replaced by applications served up by Internet service providers or application service providers. Today's Internet service providers will move to value-added services such as application hosting and e-commerce services. Proprietary communication protocols will give way to international standards such as WAP. More pervasive devices will move to the cell-phone model and the new low-cost PC model of subsidized hardware costs in return for purchase of services.

According to information published by the IBM Pervasive Computing division, approximately 16 percent of Internet access is now by non-PC devices. By the year 2001, there will be almost 50 million non-PC devices. By 2002, approximately half of the Web-enabled devices will be pervasive devices other than personal computers.

Figure 18.5 shows a graphical representation of the pervasive computing space and its relation to the e-business infrastructure. At the bottom of the figure, enterprises and service providers connect information content and applications to millions of pervasive devices through both wired and wireless connections. At the top of Figure 18-5, the e-business infrastructure is shown ranging from solution providers, content providers, and information aggregators to Internet service providers that provide connectivity to pervasive-computing devices with innovative technologies embedded in them.

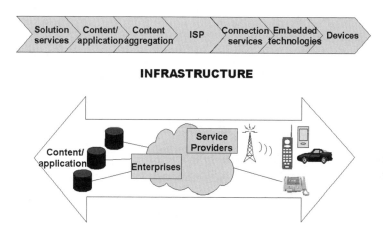

Figure 18.5: Pervasive computing and the e-business infrastructure present many opportunities.

From a business perspective, pervasive computing means opportunity across the whole supply chain. Consumer electronics companies can sell millions of electronic devices. Both wired and wireless communications companies can sell connectivity services and bandwidth to millions of consumers and businesses. Software developers can provide middleware to enable the network connections, basic services, and applications these devices will make possible. Service providers can sell everything from shopping to finance to insurance services through these devices. In many cases, the middleman is cut out. And what is the impact to the major computer manufacturers? They will be able to sell more large server systems, both for Web serving to handle the front-end transactions coming from all of these pervasive devices as well as large back-end application and data servers. Going from millions to a billion input devices will dramatically effect the entire computing industry (hardware, software, and services).

Summary

IBM's CEO Lou Gerstner talks about "a billion people interacting with a million e-businesses with a trillion intelligent devices interconnected." That single quote says a lot about the opportunities and challenges that pervasive computing will provide to the computing industry in the next few decades.

For individuals, pervasive computing brings the convenience of e-business to them using the device of their choice at the time and place of their choice. This enables new work styles and flexibility in their careers and convenience in their personal life.

So, what does pervasive computing mean for e-business? First, it provides an opportunity to reach new markets, as customers can reach your business from almost anywhere. Next, it allows you to keep in close touch with your customers, making sure they are satisfied with your products or services. Pervasive computing will allow you to grow the top line by increasing the number of potential customers buying your products or services. By shortening the supply chain between customers and your company (reducing middlemen), pervasive computing promises to reduce cycle times and costs. More potential customers combined with lower costs equals pervasive profit opportunities.

I must not fear. Fear is the mind-killer. Fear is the little-death that brings total obliteration. I will face my fear. I will permit it to pass over me and through me. And when it has gone past I will turn the inner eye to see its path. Where the fear has gone there will be nothing. Only I will remain.

—Frank Herbert
Litany against Fear, from the Bene Gesserit rite. *Dune*

19

Systems Management: Don't Get Caught without It!

NANCY ROPER AND INDER SINGH

Launching an e-business venture is exciting. It has high visibility within your organization. Energy levels run at an all-time high, and everybody—from the programmers right up to the CEO—wants to get involved. Launching an e-business changes the way your organization views your IT department and how your IT department views your organization. Your IT department becomes a strategic enabler rather than a cost center for the success of your business. Computers become your storefront. This is where you conduct business. This is where tremendous volumes of eager customers come to browse and then buy. Your company's reputation is no longer based only on a traditional store and the courteous people inside it. Now it's also based on your Web site and the computers and people who keep it running. Your company and your IT department need to be ready for cybersavvy customers.

Editor's Introduction: Systems management strikes fear into the heart of many a seasoned information technology professional and with good reason. Systems management is firmly in the category of thankless task if properly done, but can be a career-threatening activity if botched. Never was so much essential activity underappreciated by so many, to distort an old aphorism. After reading this chapter by Nancy Roper and Inder Singh, you'll have less reason to fear. Face your fear. Manage your systems. Nancy and Inder tell you how and why.

So, you've been preparing for your e-business launch for several months. The content looks great, your marketing department has generated tremendous "hype" in the marketplace, and you've thought of everything! Who needs to worry about systems management now? Tell that to some of the early adopters who unexpectedly found themselves in the headlines.

By now, I'm sure you've heard news about one company or another having their site go down or having their site become overloaded so visitors received a "site not available" message. While some say any publicity is good publicity, you'll question that if it's your site that's down, it's your company's reputation that is on the front page of the business section, and your competitor is open for business down the cyberstreet.

The attention span for consumers on the net is less than 40 seconds. If you can't keep visitors tuned to your site, say goodbye to those customers because two clicks of a mouse will take someone to a cybercompetitor located anywhere in the world. They'll bookmark that Web site instead of yours and the rest will be history. That's why it's essential that your e-business be available all the time. When you're on the Web, everything is just a click away. You want to make sure it's your site that people are coming to instead of leaving.

So, what are you going to do about this? The answer is systems management. Perhaps you aren't familiar with systems management. For now, think of it as a bit of magic that makes your organization run like clockwork and ensures that your e-business is always available when your customers need it. Among other things, systems management is essential for:

- A rapid and successful launch of your e-business.

- An e-business that is open and available for business when customers come clicking.

- A secure e-business that protects your customers' privacy and your company's assets.

- An e-business that fills customer requests quickly and efficiently and delights customers with outstanding customer service.

- A scalable e-business that can grow quickly to meet explosive customer demands.

- An e-business that presents a strong corporate reputation and brand image in a highly competitive global market.

Are you surprised to see that this chapter is at the end of the book? Don't be. Systems management usually does end up as an afterthought at the end of a Web launch or as part of a panic plan after difficulties are encountered with a Web site. If you want to open the doors of your computer system to the world and if your entire company is ready to greet that next customer that visits your Web site, then make sure you do not leave systems management as an afterthought!

By detailing the following topics, this chapter explains out why systems management is a crucial success factor in your e-business timeline:

- What is systems management and why is it important to an e-business?

- Assess yourself: How do you stack up today?

- What are the key areas of systems management that you must address to be a successful e-business?

- How do you get started with systems management for your e-business?

What Is Systems Management?

Many people find that they really don't understand the term *systems management*. Some people might think systems management is some sort of product or tool that they can buy, but it's actually a set of disciplines. It is a combination of an effectively managed organization and a series of processes that well-managed businesses follow to maintain a state of control and order.

A Tool, a Tool...My IT Shop for a Tool

Often a company's systems management environment will include tools to automate processes. Nevertheless, companies must avoid falling into a trap and thinking that a tool alone will make them successful. The underlying organization and processes first must be in place. Tools then allow the company to perform the processes more quickly or more thoroughly. Just slapping the tools into production over bad or non-existent processes will be of no help. The tools alone will just transport the company to a state of chaos more quickly.

"Vaporware! Give Me Something Concrete!"

At first glimpse, your reaction to the systems management disciplines might be that some academic was grasping at straws for an overdue research paper. You want a concrete tool that you can implement to do your systems management for you. However, time and again experience shows that companies with a strong systems-management process in place are happy with their computers. Through careful planning and orderly operations, companies can avoid the misadventures described in this chapter. Their systems are available when they need them. If a problem does arise, they notice it right away and address it quickly and efficiently with very little impact to their business.

On the other hand, companies that have neglected systems-management theories seem to be in constant turmoil. Their systems are down often and their personnel work long hours to fight fires, never becoming efficient, and never doing anything of strategic benefit to the business. Meanwhile, everyone—from the users right up through the ranks to senior management—is unhappy.

"Just the Big Guys, Right?"

A typical reaction to the term systems management description might be something like, "But that just applies to the big companies; not us, right?" *Au contraire!* Every company must consider systems management theories in light of current business requirements, and then implement each area to a greater or lesser extent (depending on specific needs).

Traditionally, big banks, with their high-security requirements and 24/7 commitments, typically have had very formal processes. They have had large staffs of highly skilled people to make sure that they were using technology to their advantage. Their systems were up all the time. In contrast, smaller companies, with simpler environments and lower availability requirements, often could be considered well managed with a much less rigorous approach.

However, e-business has turned this theory inside out. Now, even little companies are 100 percent dependent on their systems, and they need them to be up 24 hours a day, 7 days a week, 365 days a year to service their cybersavvy customers. Suddenly, small companies also need to be first class in their systems management, but they must achieve this without the benefit of a large, highly specialized staff.

"Will Systems Management Make My e-business More Competitive?"

The Internet has made it possible for small companies to compete against big companies locally and in the global marketplace. For every customer, there usually are many, many suppliers who are eager to win that customer's business. In order to be competitive, each e-business must differentiate itself and create unique value. Some early e-business adopters brainstormed what they believed to be the key factors that would differentiate their initiatives from their competitors. They came up with the following list:

- Customer service.
- Fulfillment speed.
- Ease of use.
- Site content.
- Reliability/security.
- Price.
- Brand recognition.

It's interesting that systems management sets the stage for achieving each of these differentiators. In order to provide excellence in customer service and order fulfillment, you must have a highly motivated, quality staff that has fingertip access to information. In order to have an easy-to-use site with high-quality content, you need your business strategy to be closely tied to your IT strategy. For a reliable site that is available when needed and protected by strong security, you need a well-run operation that has all the appropriate controls in place. To maintain low prices, you need an economical and efficient infrastructure. For brand recognition, you need to be world class in everything you do. The organizational areas and the operational processes that are dictated by strong systems-management disciplines strive to make these crucial success factors a reality.

What's Different
for an e-business vs. a Regular Business?

Many hotshot job applicants, fresh out of university, will tell you that this is all cool and new and that you need people like them to guide you around this brave new world. Stop and think for a minute. Isn't this something companies already have been doing for years? Don't hospitals need to function around the clock? How about the electrical and water utilities and the phone companies? Would you be impressed if you picked up your telephone and received a message telling you that it was temporarily unavailable due to the nightly backup? How's this so different from your e-business?

Well, that's the point. Most of this theory has been around for a long time. It's just suddenly become relevant to many more companies. However, the following points describe a few differences to keep in mind:

- In the past, because your users all worked for your company, you had some control over them. You could send them for training and have rules about the way they used your system. You could require them to report problems to your help desk and help to troubleshoot them. You could ask certain users to do their work at certain times or in certain ways to control the load on your system. You could reprimand them if they breached security, etc. However, in your e-business, many users are external and that means you don't have the same control over their activities. As a result, you have to be a little more creative in managing your environment.

- In the past, because you owned your entire IT environment, you could force certain IT groups to do the things you required. For example, you could tell your network group to drop what they were doing and fix your problem as a priority. Now, considerably more of your environment (the Internet, your service provider, and the user workstations) is outside your control. You might need to use different tactics to guide their priorities to match yours.

You shouldn't try to reinvent the wheel. The big guys have built a wealth of knowledge about how you keep a high-availability environment running flawlessly. You need to tap into that knowledge, handle the differences related to an e-business environment, and then implement the best ideas.

How Much Will It Cost?

Now, you might be thinking that systems management sounds okay but it could cost you a fortune. Well, don't panic. Those who have gone before you will say that they encountered an initial blip in both cost and workload while they were getting organized but, once they had their systems management in place, they actually saved money. Their environments started running smoothly. Things started getting done properly the first time. Because most of the time the system was running properly, support costs dropped dramatically. Morale was high and people were eager to work hard. Meanwhile, IT was supporting the business vision and thus generating increased profits.

So, keep reading and learn more details about systems management for your e-business and what you need to do to get on board. A year from now, you'll look back and be glad you made the effort.

Assess Yourself: How Do You Stack up Today?

The following sections describe three companies at different levels of sophistication in their systems management. Read about them and determine the level of your own company. Don't feel embarrassed if you think you might be in the "barely coping" category. Many, many companies today are struggling along at this level. By identifying the problem, you will be taking the first step on the path to a world-class operation.

Barely Coping: Companies that are barely coping have systems that are often unavailable for one reason or another. Because the staff spends so much time answering the telephone, with people calling in to report problems, they never really have time to fix any of the problems. Getting even the simplest task done takes forever because none of the infrastructure exists. In order to print out a page of diagnostics to send to support, you first have to fix the printer. In order to send a file between systems, you first have to set up telecommunications. Major system changes, such as software upgrades, are done with hardly any planning, and all chaos breaks loose thereafter.

Management is frustrated that the staff isn't accomplishing more and the staff is frustrated because management just doesn't seem to understand. Meanwhile, users are really dissatisfied. If you were a fly on the wall, you'd hear people blaming the computers or the software for all the problems and proclaiming that a different computer or different software is in order.

Meanwhile, no one is taking a useful leadership role to improve the situation. If someone is attempting to make changes, that person is likely throwing tools at the situation. Deep disappointment sets in when the tools don't help. Therefore, a decision is made that *more* tools are needed.

This company has significant trouble keeping internal clients happy eight hours a day, five days a week. Are they ready for the e-business demands of tens of thousands of external clients, all expecting 24/7 service? Definitely not.

Trying Hard: Some companies are trying hard to run an orderly shop. When users call in with problems, the staff can usually figure out what's wrong and get it fixed. However, the staff doesn't always go back and put pins in place to avoid the same problem in the future. A fair bit of infrastructure is in place. Reasonable planning and signoff takes place prior to major system changes such as upgrades, but the staff reinvents the wheel every time (and usually misses a spoke or two). Some strategic project work is happening, but not as much as the company would like. The IT department works at understanding the users' requirements, but it sometimes takes a long time to get the solutions implemented.

This type of company has got a good start, and is probably managing to keep their internal users reasonably happy during a regular business week. Are they ready for the demands of e-business, where the world is moving at lightning pace and users expect instantaneous service at any hour of the night or day? Not yet; but they can get there if they want to.

World Class: A world-class company is a leader in everything it does. The IT department sees itself as a major contributor to the business and is striving to be even better. Everything they do is tied to the corporate vision. Morale is great because it's fun to be part of a winning team. While the staff is completely effective, they are continuously looking for ways to be better still.

Problems are identified and corrected before the users are even aware of them, and the root cause is researched and fixed so that the same problem doesn't recur. When a user does call in, the help desk knows the proper questions to ask so they can resolve problems quickly and efficiently. Users actually call in to say "thank you" rather than to complain. Happy users are so much more tolerant when the occasional problem does arise.

The entire infrastructure that IT needs is already in place, and they are constantly evaluating changes that would make them more effective. All staff knows the environment, knows how all the pieces fit together, and knows where they can look for detailed documentation on any component. Because several staff members have detailed knowledge in each area, the organization isn't dependent on a single person.

Staff members know where every piece of equipment is located and what service contracts are associated with it so that repair personnel can be dispatched quickly when needed. Appropriate backups are run without fail and appropriate security is in place to ensure that corporate data is safe. Major system changes are planned carefully and communicated long in advance. Checklists from similar previous projects are used to ensure that nothing is missed. If something does go wrong during the change, the appropriate people with the proper skills are available to correct the problem quickly.

The IT department is involved in business planning right from the start to ensure that strategic projects are researched, planned, and implemented on time to support the business vision. User departments work in partnership with IT to make sure the IT budget is being spent in the most effective way.

This is a company that is running like clockwork. Are they ready for e-business? You bet. As soon as the company states e-business as a strategy, these folks will be busy doing the planning to ensure that it will be a success. Because of their orderly work environment, they will be able to do things rapidly. Getting things right the first time allows the company to react to market quickly for competitive advantages.

Where do you think your company fits on this scale? Did the world-class description sound familiar? If so, then pat yourself on the back. You are working for a very efficient and well-organized company. If not, then perhaps you are starting to understand why certain challenges present themselves. Read on to see what you can do to help your organization run more effectively.

What Are the Key Areas of Systems Management for a Successful e-business?

The veterans of systems management have built a wealth of expertise over the years as they have helped companies get their shops in order. They kindly have documented that knowledge in various models and listings for others to use as checklists and project plans to embark on the same journey. An example is IBM's IT Process Model (ITPM).

While some models have 100 or more processes and subprocesses, others just have a handful. The processes are named and categorized differently in each representation. However, if you look at the overall picture, you will find that each model includes very similar ideas. These principles will help you to run a more orderly and successful organization.

Although it would be nice to implement each and every one of the processes, you will find that even just implementing a handful of them will make a big difference in how smoothly your operation runs and how effectively your systems support your business. You should start by reviewing and categorizing the disciplines in light of your business challenges. Then implement the highest priority items. When those are underway, you can review, evaluate, and then implement some more. Eventually, you will decide that your shop is running well and you can direct your attention to other initiatives.

The characteristics of an e-business dictate a core set of disciplines that are crucial for success. These are the disciplines that help you to manage a demanding, fast-paced, high-growth environment that is accessible to people outside your organization. If you do nothing else in the systems-management arena, you must make certain that your e-business timeline includes a plan to put these disciplines in place. Outlined as follows, three elements are essential to e-business: organization, process, and tools:

- Organization:
  - ➤ Matching your IT strategy to your business strategy.
  - ➤ Creating an organization that supports computer systems efficiently and effectively.

- Processes:

  - Running your day-to-day operations in an orderly fashion.

  - Planning and tracking changes carefully so they don't cause problems in your environment.

  - Noticing and handling problems quickly and efficiently.

  - Making sure your systems have enough capacity to perform well.

  - Handling various system problems without interruption to your business.

  - Minimizing the danger of unauthorized access to your system.

- Tools:

  - Automating the processes so that they are less labor-intensive to run.

  - Providing enhanced functions compared with what could be accomplished manually.

Organization

The e-business world is highly demanding and is moving at a lightning pace. In order to embrace and excel in it, you must have a highly effective, nimble organization completely dedicated to your corporate vision, and that runs like clockwork in every respect. Sounds like a great place to work, doesn't it? Is this corporate culture already in place at your firm today? If not, don't worry. The systems management organizational disciplines will help you to get there.

This section will not turn you into a professional organizational consultant. It is simply intended to remind you that—in addition to the technical side of systems management that deals with the computer systems and the processes that keep them running smoothly— there also is a human side that deals with the staff and their leaders and management styles. It includes corporate visions, strategies, policies, culture, and people's roles, skills, and values. In e-business, two crucial areas of organizational behavior involve the:

- Alignment of business strategy with IT strategy.
- Development of an effective structure for your e-business organization.

Aligning Business and IT Strategies

In years past, there was often no alignment between the strategies of the IT department and the overall business. Because an IT department was considered a cost center, it was not included in the corporate planning. Oblivious to the overall direction of the business, IT would dabble in technologies that interested them, but that were not necessarily relevant to the actual business direction.

Meanwhile, the business might embark on a new strategy. Because IT wasn't aware of the initiative, they didn't design or build the required systems; so the business would have to go to external providers. Often, the structure of the IT department didn't reflect the needs of the company. For example, the IT group might have been structured to react as a troubleshooting group. Actually, what was needed was a forward-looking, technology-enabling group. In addition, the reporting structure was frequently out of date. Even though most of the applications and services they provided were for other departments, many IT groups reported to the finance department. If the IT department reports to a given group, is it really a corporate resource?

As companies have embarked on e-business, they have realized that IT is essential to corporate success and must be in perfect synchronization with corporate goals. As a result, senior leaders throughout the world are now placing a high priority on aligning the business and IT strategies at their companies. Rumblings from industry analysts even predict the extinction of the "IT Shop" as we know it today. Future organizations will have their business and IT folks working as a single unit to provide high-value solutions to meet corporate goals. The more ambitious the goals, the more important it is for these two groups to be working as one.

An Example of IT and Business Working as One

When companies embark on their Web journey, they might choose to start small and test the waters or they might dive right in and decide to become a true e-business. There are many factors involved in the decision: a simple entry into the marketplace is the least costly, can be done quickly, and carries the least risk. However, if you are looking for the dramatic financial rewards of an e-business, you eventually need to dive right in. The various levels of e-business presence and the degree of linkage required between IT and the business in order to be successful at each level makes it clear why companies are moving to have their business and IT behave as a single unit. Here is a summary of the various levels and the relationship between IT and the business at each:

- **Web Presence:** Think of Web presence as being a tourist in an economy-class seat. You want to see what all the fuss is about but you haven't completely bought into the idea of e-business. You might test the waters by putting some information— such as marketing brochures, company, and contact information—on the Web. For this level of e-business sophistication, the linkage between IT and the business does not need to be too tight.

- **Web Interacting:** Think of Web interacting as being a business passenger in an economy-class seat. You've already got a Web presence, but now you want to interact with your clients. Rather than just giving them information to browse, you'd like to help them find the information they need by letting them do some searches. You might even communicate with them by e-mail. And maybe once they find what they need from your Web site, they will call or e-mail you to find out how to buy the product. Now you're starting to need a stronger linkage with IT. You need search engines and e-mail tools to be available. Because more people are coming to your site, you may want it to be up for more hours each day.

- **Web Transacting:** Think of Web transacting as being a business passenger in a business-class seat. Now you're making money using the Web. You're providing customer care and fulfillment and you also have personalized your site so that your customers feel that the site was developed specifically for them. You might even be using a personal profile to better track and serve your customers. You have integrated some of your business processes so they now are adapted to your e-business. Suppliers, financial institutions, distributors, and partners all can be seamlessly linked into your processes and your site. This is getting pretty fancy, and you need your IT group to be working side-by-side with you to be successful.

- **Web Transforming:** Not only are the revenues coming in but you've captured market share in areas that you never dreamed possible. Customer loyalty is at an all-time high and new clients are clicking at your site. Your employees love working for your company and everybody is sharing in the profits. Your company is a well-oiled machine and nothing is happening by chance. Everybody knows his or her roles. Each customer visiting your site feels as though your whole organization—including your suppliers, distributors, partners and manufacturers—are all in place just to serve each customer personally. You're not flying business class anymore; you're on the space shuttle! There isn't a separate IT shop in your organization because it's part of the business fabric. Business and IT are so closely linked that you can't even see the seams (because there aren't any).

- Leveraged technology is ubiquitous throughout the organization. Nothing is created from scratch, and all intellectual capital and knowledge is reused constantly to optimize and refine roles and processes. Instead of adapting to the market, your company is leading the change in the market at rapid speed.

Building an Effective e-business Organization Structure

When you embark on an e-business project, you add a whole new dimension to your business. You must decide on the most effective way to organize your staff so that you can be nimble and effective in managing this new business. Will a new e-business department be formed? Will it be part of the same company or a new company all together? Will people from various departments move to this new e-business? Will people from marketing and customer service move to this new department or will the e-business be integrated into the existing departments? Who will lead the e-business department? Will it be somebody from IT? Or will it be somebody from the business side of your company?

As you can see, embarking on the e-business journey can have a profound affect on the structure of an organization. Either directly or indirectly, e-business could potentially touch every role and process within your organization. There are no easy answers to these questions and each company and organization is different. Upfront planning, preparation, and information will help you make better decisions.

Outsourcing, Selectively Sourcing, or In-House Operations?

Depending on the level of e-business sophistication that you are trying to reach, your level of your systems management skill, and the timeline you are on, you might find that it isn't possible for your organization to run your entire e-business operation in-house. Some activities and functions that you will need to consider include payroll, human resources, marketing, fulfillment, technical support, customer care, content management, application development, and finance. It might make sense to outsource some business segments to take advantage of deeper systems management skills elsewhere. It doesn't have to be an all-or-nothing decision. You might even opt to selectively source some of these functions or even activities within each function. Your strategy, business objectives, timeframe, budget, and skills will be factors that will help you decide on whether to keep your operations in-house, to outsource them, or to selectively source them.

How Do all the Groups Interrelate in an e-business?

It's important not to lose sight of the human factor of an e-business. While an e-business is a virtual effort, there is still a human element. People run an e-business and it is important to understand how they are organized and what their roles and responsibilities are in this new structure. Because there are various functions required for an e-business, understanding some of the functions an e-business performs will help you lay a foundation for an organizational structure for your e-business.

As an example, let's say a company named XYZ wants to launch a Web site to sell widgets over the Internet. The content of the Web site would need to be current and always maintained as products or prices change. Customers will browse, place orders, and then orders would need to be fulfilled from the warehouse or distribution center. If customers have questions or problems with the product or service, they will want to e-mail or talk to customer service.

With linkages to a bank, money would change hands. Therefore, the finance department would have to be involved. Marketing would help with promotion and building of affiliates and other channels to the Web site. IT systems, applications development, and operations would gather new requirements, implement new functionality, and ensure the smooth running of the Web site. The human resources department might need to get involved to interact with current staff and hire new staff as the e-business grows.

From the preceding example, you can see that there are many different groups that must be created, aligned, or integrated into your e-business organizational structure, including:

- Content management.
- Fulfillment.
- Customer service.
- Finance.
- Marketing.
- IT.
- Human resources.

Each of these functions needs to be closely linked with the others. They might report to the same organization or a different organization, but they need to communicate well. Some examples of the linkages and challenges that could arise are as follow:

- If the marketing department doesn't communicate with the fulfillment department, then a promotion for a product might not be a success, as order volumes won't be fulfilled quickly enough.

- If the IT department doesn't communicate with content management, then a change to an application might cause the wrong price or details of a product to be shown.

- If the fulfillment department doesn't communicate with customer service, then an inquiry for order status from a customer won't be communicated accurately.

Because each organization is different, it's difficult to recommend one particular organizational or reporting structure for all situations. Instead, the important concept is to ensure that the linkages between each function are strong and synchronized. Some companies have succeeded by having all functions reporting to one organization, while others have integrated various functions of an e-business across their organization. Your e-business strategies as well as the other organizational components are important considerations in how you structure your organization.

Processes

Have you ever noticed that the second time you do a certain task, you do it far better than the first time? By the second time, you already know all the steps that are required, you've already built the required knowledge, you know the people who can help you get the job done, and you've learned from any mistakes you made the first time around. The result is better quality work that's done in a more orderly fashion and finished quickly and efficiently. This follows the same principles as a football playbook, a dress rehearsal for a play, or the imagery techniques used by Olympic champions: practice makes perfect. By doing things over and over again, and arranging who does what and when, you can do things better and better.

The whole idea of processes is that you want to figure out the smartest way to do the task and then write it down. Arrange for everyone to do it that way every time for consistency. Orchestrate the hand-offs to make sure they are smooth. Enhance the process as better ideas come to light.

If you need to do a task that is completely new to you, try to find a similar project from which you can learn. If you are in an environment where every project is different, try to find similarities in the way you attack the project successfully, and repeat that process on each project.

In your e-business, the entire organization must work perfectly smoothly in order to provide exceptional service to all those eager customers and online suppliers. The way to do this is to implement processes wherever possible. That includes processes for your systems management.

As a small subset of the systems-management processes, some of the factors that are the most important in creating a successful e-business are listed as follows:

- Change management.
- Problem management.
- Business continuity.
- Performance and capacity planning.
- Security management.
- Day to day operations.

Change Management—
Making Changes without Causing Trouble

Have you ever noticed that when you run into difficulties with your computer and call for assistance, the first thing you are asked is: "What has changed since this last worked?" Well, there's good reason here. Things don't just "stop" working. Someone, somewhere (maybe even you) changed something without thinking through all the implications, and that's what stops your computer from working. Then you have to play Sherlock Holmes to find the problem and fix it. If it's just your home computer that suddenly isn't working, then maybe all you're going to miss is a few games of solitaire. However, if it's your business computer, then this could be a problem. If it's your e-business server that isn't working, you've got big trouble. Remember all those eager customers who are just a mouse click away from your competitors? Well, when your system goes down, they'll be clicking away from your site.

To avoid the risk presented by changes in your environment, you must implement orderly change-management procedures. With the rate of change in the e-business world, you need to be particularly strong in this area. It's said that a "Web year" is approximately three months. Your e-business will be undergoing the fastest rate of change you've ever seen. This includes not only the Web content, but also the underlying technologies that are changing rapidly as the Web world evolves. You will find that you must make dramatic changes on short timelines to keep your e-business successful, and you won't be able to do that without strong change-management procedures. What, you ask, are orderly change-management procedures? Well, they usually have the following components:

- **A Change-Management Process Everyone Recognizes:** There is a clearly defined process that is well communicated to all staff. Everyone knows that every change to the computer system or e-business environment must go through this process. No one tries to do a quick change without first getting it approved. This includes new hardware, new software, new applications, upgrades, changes to the configuration, and security parameters, and changes to the scheduling of system activities.

- **Change Request Forms to Help Research the Change:** When someone needs a change made, they fill out a "change request form." This form guides them through all the things they need to consider to make a successful change. For example, the form lists what is to be done and why, the target date for the change, other areas impacted, the level of risk and how it is to be contained, a back-out plan in case of problems, a list of people and skills that are to be involved to ensure success, and criteria for deciding that the back-out plan should be implemented.

- **Review and Approval Process to Brainstorm Potential Issues:** The affected parties and a central change committee review the request and brainstorm any concerns not yet addressed on the change-request form. If additional research is required, it is handled and then the change form authorization is signed.

- **Scheduling the Change:** The change is then scheduled and it is coordinated with other changes in the same timeframe. While avoiding too much change at once, related changes can be grouped in one timeframe. Staffing needs to be arranged both to perform the change and to be available in case of any repercussions. In preparation for the change, scheduling sometimes will have prerequisites such as the development of skills.

- **Logging and Communication of the Planned Change:** The scheduled changes should be logged and communicated with sufficient lead time to everyone who might be affected. The log of changes is an important troubleshooting tool. Anytime problems arise, staff will review the log to see what changes were made recently to determine if those changes might relate to the problem. The log sheet will provide the required detail and contact names to resolve problems quickly. Communication of the planned changes in a timely fashion is important. Internal users might need to adjust work schedules or implement manual procedures to cover during the change window. Also, external users and customers might need to be notified of the business impact.

- **Perform the Change:** At the scheduled time, the change is made and appropriate staff members are on standby in case of unforeseen problems.

- **Track Trends over Time:** The final status and any details of the change are to be documented and retained for the long term. These records can be reviewed for troubleshooting or when similar additional changes are required. For example, if the safety committee schedules an annual test of the computer room fire alarms, prior to the test you review the change form from the previous year. Your review shows that one of the safety tests requires shutting off power to the floor, and that has implications for the computer systems. You would then handle the situation accordingly. The change log also can be helpful in figuring out the degree of risk in a certain change. For example, you might notice that installing fixes is done frequently and is almost always successful. Therefore, a new request for fixes will not create undue concern.

As an example of good change management procedures, consider the seasonal time change that must be reflected on the system. An organization with good change-management procedures would have this event documented so that the staff could start planning for it several weeks in advance. Rather than dashing to the office on Saturday morning after reading in the newspaper that it is time-change day, the staff would review their change-management database to find out how the time change was handled in the past, and what issues arose. The staff would discuss anything new installed on the system since the last time change that might create issues. For example, attention would be given to applications that could run into difficulties during the hour that gets "re-lived."

The back-out plan might include a system save, immediately prior to the change, with a plan to restore the backup if necessary. In advance, it would be decided that authorization to revert to the back-out plan would be made by the director of IT on the advice of an operator who would be monitoring the system throughout the "re-lived" hour.

Once the details were worked out, the staff would fill out a new change-request form, explain the change, outline any concerns, and detail how the concerns were going to be addressed. The form would be reviewed and signed off at the next change-review meeting. The change would then be scheduled and logged in the change control book or database. E-business partners would be notified of the planned time for the change, and any impact it might have on their transactions with this firm. On the day of the change, the operator and any additional staff who were deemed to be required would perform the time-change procedures and monitor the system for the set length of time. Results would be logged on the change form and then it would be filed for future use.

Problem Management—Minimizing the Impact of Computer Problems

Have you ever been an e-business customer yourself? Perhaps you visited a Web site, but something on it wasn't working properly. Perhaps you clicked the "send order" button but nothing happened. You retried it a few times without any luck. What did you do next?

- **Go Elsewhere:** If you're like most people, you just did two clicks of your mouse and located another vendor for the same item. On the Internet, this is easy. You don't need to search through the telephone directory and then drive your car halfway across the city. Two clicks and you're there. Why would you waste your time calling in to tell them they have a problem?

- **E-mail the Webmaster:** If you're a little more community minded, perhaps you dug around on the Web site until you found a Webmaster user ID and sent a note. Did you wait around for a response? Probably not. You had a deal to do and there was no shortage of other vendors eagerly awaiting your hit on their Web site. And all too often, no one ever answers those e-mails to the Webmaster anyway.

- **Telephone Their Support Line**: Perhaps you're a very responsible citizen. You search around the Web site until you find a telephone number. Fortunately, it's a toll-free number, so you call. And fortunately, they pick up after only a few rings. However, the person who answers doesn't really know how to solve your problem. How long are you going to stay on the phone while they diddle around? Probably not long. You'll excuse yourself, then click-click your way to their competitor's site.

So, now let's look at this situation from the e-business side. What should you do to keep those customers glued to your Web site? Here are some ideas:

- **Avoid Problems:** The best solution is to avoid problems in the first place. We know that you are striving for 100 percent availability and we know that it's going to be hard to detect problems. You should do as much as you can to avoid problems altogether.

- **Make It Easy for Customers:** If there is a problem, encourage your customers to contact you. If they are kind enough to do so, treat them like gold.

- **Handle Problems Effectively:** When a problem is identified, wrestle it to the ground quickly and efficiently.

Now you ask, "How do I avoid problems in the first place?" Well, the systems-management disciplines recommend the following:

- **Change Management:** Changes often introduce problems into the environment. By implementing thorough change-management procedures, you can minimize problems from inadequately planned changes.

- **Corrective Service:** Set a regular schedule for applying fixes and other corrective service to your system. It's embarrassing (and unnecessary) to fail due to a problem that has already been fixed.

- **Newsgroups:** Join newsgroups and user groups and attend conferences to keep abreast of what's going on in the marketplace. Avoid pitfalls that others have already experienced. For example, newsgroups will often give you enough warning about a new virus so that you can protect your systems before it strikes.

"This is great stuff," you say. "Give me a list of what I can do to make it easy for my customers to report problems to me when they do occur." A combination of common sense and the systems-management disciplines provide some guidelines:

- **Encourage Customers to Call:** In a prominent place on your Web site, invite customers to contact your Help Desk if they have a problem. Treat your customers well when they call. Remember that plenty of research shows that your most loyal customers are the ones who had a problem once and were "delighted" by your response to it. Here's your chance to shine.

- **Toll-Free Phone:** Provide a toll-free telephone number so that potential long-distance charges to the customer aren't a limiting factor.

- **E-mail Address**: Provide an e-mail address for folks who only have one phone line or who prefer to write rather than call.

- **Help Desk**: Staff the help desk with friendly, highly skilled people who remember to thank customers profusely for calling or writing, and who know what questions to ask to troubleshoot problems quickly and efficiently.

When problems arise, how do you make sure they are handled quickly and efficiently? Again, the systems-management disciplines provide guidance. You would be surprised at the number of firms that are aware of problems in their environment, but never quite get around to fixing them. They just keep suffering the consequences over and over again.

Putting a process in place will make sure that every problem gets wrestled to the ground and that fixes are done efficiently.

- **Identify Your Problems:** In any organization, it's always nice if you notice problems and fix them before your users are even aware of issues. Set up procedures for your operators to watch for problems on the system and feed them into the problem-management process. Implement automated tools to help. Encourage your customers to call you with any problems that slip through your safety net.

- **Log Problems:** Log problems in some centrally accessible place so that others are aware you are working on them. Share ideas. If other calls come in regarding the same issues, the log can provide more clues regarding the cause of the problems. The logs also can be used to do trend analysis or to come back to a problem if it recurs to see what was done to handle it. The log will guide you in gathering the pertinent information about a problem.

- **Collect Data about Problems:** In order to solve a problem, you will need to capture and review data from inception. Relevant data might include error messages, information about what the user was doing when the problem happened, and system logs. A checklist will ensure that you don't miss things. Whenever possible, try to gather data at the time of the first failure. Waiting for a subsequent failure to gather data delays resolution.

- **Analyze Problems:** You must analyze the data captured and figure out how to fix the problem. If the problem will take a while to solve, perhaps you will come up with a work-around that will make the system useable while you do your research. A checklist is helpful in stepping you through the thought process. Because your customers are probably not willing to spend hours on the phone with you troubleshooting, you will need a test environment that mimics various user configurations (including hardware, software, analog lines, and a variety of Internet service providers). Having staff with the appropriate skill sets and having suitable relationships and support agreements in place with your partners and vendors will be a big help in getting a quick resolution.

- **Support Agreements:** While it's strange, you would be surprised at the number of businesses that are unwilling to pay for a support agreement. Instead, companies will pay their people to fiddle around for days trying to fix a problem on their own, all the while restricting the business due to the unavailability of the system.

- **Implementing Fixes**: Once you know what causes a problem, arrange a fix. Depending on the extent of the change, the fix might need to go through your regular change-management process. Remember that you might need to make the same change to all your systems (not just on the one where the problem has already occurred).

- **Track Trends**: Once a problem has been fixed, make sure you record all pertinent information so the call record can be used to handle similar problems in the future. There is no point in reinventing the wheel every time. Also, plan to do trend analysis on the calls to make your environment better still. You might notice an area where further education would be beneficial for your staff and users or discover that a piece of software is not robust enough for your needs.

With the preceding items in place, you will be much more effective at avoiding problems and solving problems. Thus, you will increase the availability of your e-business.

Business Continuity—
Staying in Business Even When the Computer Isn't Available

Now you have a beautiful Web site up and running. Customers love the caliber of the information contained there and how quickly and easily they can do their business transactions. You have good processes in place to manage the changes and any problems that arise. Corporate revenues are flying high. What should you worry about?

Think about that terrifying moment when your operator phones to tell you that there has been some sort of problem and your system can no longer be used. All your loyal customers can no longer access your e-business. In an instant, those wonderful revenue counters have suddenly dropped to zero. All those potential customers are clicking over to your competitors' Web sites. The clock is ticking and you need to take charge. What are you going to do?

If you've included business continuity in your systems-management plan, then the wheels already will be turning. Depending on how elaborate a scheme you have implemented, your customers might not even know there is a problem on the home front.

Here are some of the many reasons your e-business suddenly might be put into jeopardy:

- Some hardware on the system failed and must be replaced.

- A disk on the system has failed and the new disk must be reloaded.

- Some software or an application has a defect in it that has ruined your data.

- A virus may have invaded your system and put the programs and data into question.

- A hacker accessed the system and no one is sure what damage has been done.

- A power outage struck the neighborhood where your e-business is centered.

- A disaster such as a fire, flood, earthquake, tornado, or hurricane struck your main e-business site.

No matter what the problem, you have to get your e-business back online as quickly as possible. Perhaps you've seen the statistics about the percentage of regular businesses that never recover following a multiday system outage. Imagine what the statistics are for e-businesses that are 100 percent reliant on the systems.

To design your business continuity plan, you should start by recording answers to the following questions:

- How much money do you lose when your e-business isn't available?

- What are all the different kinds of problems that could cause an outage?

- What is the probability of each type of outage happening?

- What are the different ways to mitigate each type of outage, and how much does each cost?

Next, figure out how much money would be needed in order to address each potential problem. In assessing these items, remember that it's not just your main computer system that you could lose. You also could have a site loss whereby you would need to come up with alternate office space and equipment, an alternate telecommunications network for both voice and data, alternate staff, alternate services such as a mailroom, a courier service, and supplies, and alternate ways to fulfill orders, etc.

For an e-business, your typical continuity plan would include the following:

- **Uninterruptible Power Supply (UPS):** A UPS keeps your system running even during a power failure. Remember to consider the other devices—such as networking devices, telephone systems that require power, workstations for your staff, printers, and lights—that also will be needed after a power failure.

- **Save/Restore:** A carefully researched save/restore strategy ensures that you have solid backups of everything that you will need to recover your system after a problem. You need processes in place to check that these saves occur as scheduled, without fail, and that someone is confirming that each save is successful. Then, if you lose a disk or if the integrity of your system is put into question by a bad application, a virus, or a security breach, you can restore to the most recent image in which you have confidence.

- **Redundant Systems**: It's necessary to have some level of redundant systems and sites. At a minimum, most e-businesses choose to install a second system that can take over the workload if the main system fails. The added benefit is that with a well-thought-out plan, the secondary system also can be used on a day-to-day basis to allow system maintenance without any impact to the users. The production workload can be swapped to the secondary system while backups are run or software updates are applied. By doing the swaps on a frequent basis for maintenance, you can rest assured that the process is well tested and the staff is comfortable with the procedure if an unscheduled swap should ever be required. Depending on the risk factors for the specific company, it might also be wise to put the redundant systems in different locations. For example, companies in earthquake, tornado, and hurricane zones would likely put the redundant systems in different cities or at least on opposite sides of the same city.

In addition to a well-thought-out business continuity plan, the following two key success factors will help you ensure that you can cope with any potential outage:

- **Keep Your Plan Current:** Although your original business continuity plan might be a work of art, it needs to be reviewed and updated on a regular basis as the business grows, the requirements change, or new applications are added. Each time the plan changes, documentation must be updated and all players must be made aware of the new procedures.

- **Practice, Practice, Practice:** The plan must be practiced frequently to ensure that it will work without a hitch when it is needed. This includes testing the plan carefully to ensure that it is technically correct and will allow a successful recovery. It also includes the human factor. Make sure that everyone who has a role in the continuity plan is completely comfortable with assigned duties and that various situations, such as absence of a key player, can be taken in stride.

Documentation must be at your fingertips when needed (not destroyed in a fire or "saved" on a system that has failed). At least once each year, a full test should be performed. The test should be complete with travel to any secondary location and should include the swap of all users to their interim system and procedures.

Surprise tests should be implemented periodically. Verbal walkthroughs in a meeting room can be held to ensure the steps remain clear to everyone. Better still, if redundant systems are implemented, the swap procedures can be done even more frequently for maintenance, thus making them second nature when required for a disaster situation. You will almost certainly find surprises in your first few tests, but a careful cycle of testing, identifying issues, brainstorming, implementing solutions, and then re-testing will get you to the solution you need.

Remember that an e-business is completely reliant on its systems. Problems can and will happen. Be ready with a thorough business continuity plan.

Performance Tuning and Capacity Planning

Based on recent examples in the e-business marketplace, you can anticipate that your business will grow dramatically once you build an e-business presence. This is the whole reason you got involved, right? Don't get caught off guard by this rapid growth; plan for it and enjoy it!

All too often, people neglect to manage the environment's performance. Performance is ignored until a fairly significant performance problem suddenly blindsides people. By then, they need to act quickly. Because they don't have good data on which to base decisions, they guess. Sometimes the outcome isn't productive. They might do a rushed and costly system upgrade when a simple parameter adjustment would suffice. They might switch to a different technology—thinking that the current one isn't serving them—when actually the real problem is in a completely different area. Meanwhile, users have been disrupted, which would not have happened if they had tracked performance and handled the issue earlier.

As part of your e-business timeline, plan to manage your performance:

- **Set Goals:** Start by deciding what your performance goals are. Typically, this is based on the response time that the user sees. However, response time also might drive out some related indicators—such as how busy your processor is, how full your disk is, how much of the response time is spent in the network as opposed to the processor—that you want to track. If you don't know what values to set initially, don't worry; just choose some numbers for starters. Part of the process is to review and adjust the goals periodically. Eventually, you will know whether your initial numbers made sense or not.

- **Performance Monitoring/Reporting:** Don't leave yourself in the dark. Track how your system is performing and report on it so that everyone is abreast. If performance is good, then everyone will be happy. If performance is not good, then you will have information you can analyze to determine what is wrong. Without good performance data, it's easy to make decisions based on perception rather than hard fact. And sometimes perception isn't accurate.

- **Performance Tuning:** Get the most out of the system you have. While looking at your performance reports, you might see figures that don't meet goals you have set. Using the data you have collected, you can figure out what is causing the substandard performance, and then adjust parameters to make the situation better. Perhaps investing in bigger, better, and faster components for your environment is what you need, but often a simple parameter change is all that is required.

For example, suppose you notice that your users are not getting as good a response time as you would like. Perhaps your system is too slow. Maybe it's your network or perhaps your Internet service provider is responsible for the problem. You could spend thousands of dollars on upgrades and accomplish nothing if your processor is not the bottleneck. By noticing the performance issue early, you can do the necessary investigation before the problem becomes urgent. You also can make sure that you are solving the right problem. Maybe you've allocated all your system's memory to one set of applications, but the majority of your workload is actually in another area. All you really need do is to move the existing memory around and everyone will be happy. Or maybe you're getting contention at a certain time of day and all you need to do is move certain jobs to run at a different time (when your Internet users aren't as active).

- **Capacity Planning**: Plan for the future. Gradually, over time, your performance- tuning adjustments will no longer be enough to meet your performance goals. This good news reflects the fact that your business is growing. You should considering upgrades. By tracking your performance over time, you will be able to predict when the enhancements will be needed and you will know which components of your system are the current bottlenecks. You can then plan and budget for the upgrades accordingly. You don't want to do a rushed job once you realize that your customers can't get access to your Web site because your system is too small.

If you are planning on bringing new applications or business functions online, you can model the load—based on what you have learned from the performance data on your existing applications—they will place on your system. You can then include the corresponding upgrades as part of your project timeline. In other words, you can avoid an out-of-budget panic while your new cybercustomers are standing on your e-business doorstep, unable to get inside.

When you choose your e-business solution, think ahead about the performance management disciplines and your growth path. Good performance is almost always one of the key business requirements. Therefore, make sure you either choose or write an application that is designed for good performance. Benchmark it before you go into production to ensure there will be no surprises on launch day.

You are investing in e-business because you are anticipating tremendous growth. Choose a solution where the growth will be easy to manage. As you require more capacity, will you be able to add to the existing system with a simple upgrade or will you have to start all over again with a bigger system? Think of the cost and the amount of change-management planning required with swapping in a new system rather than just upgrading the old one. Will you have to add more and more systems? Consider how you would gather and analyze performance data from all those separate systems. Think about the duplication of having so many copies of the operating system running. And think about how unwieldy it could get managing all those systems operationally. A carefully implemented performance plan will help you ensure that your system can keep up with the dramatic growth of your e-business.

As an example of performance management, think about the dashboard lights on your car. Your fuel gauge is like well-managed performance. Your objective is to keep the gas tank above empty (goals).

The gas gauge lets you know how you're doing at any point in time (tracking). If you're running low on gas, you can vary your speed or turn off your air conditioning to try to get by with less fuel (tuning). Meanwhile, you can monitor the overall trend and predict approximately when you will need to refuel (capacity planning). The system is scalable because you can refill the fuel tank. You don't have to throw away the old gas, install a new fuel tank, or buy a completely new car when your first tank of gas runs out.

By comparison, your oil light represents poorly managed performance. You have no idea (from the dashboard, at least) whether your oil situation is good or bad until the oil light activates. By then, the problem is likely to be so serious that you must pull over and address the problem immediately. You can't drive to the next service station and handle the problem when it's more convenient. You can't just add oil. You're supposed find out why the light came on and probably replace the oil as well as the oil filter.

Security—Not Just the Firewalls, but the Processes, too!

Everyone assumes that security is essential to an e-business launch. They make sure that it has a high-priority spot on their e-business project plan. Early in the timeline, they consult with experts on fancy firewalls and encryption algorithms. They know that security is not only important to the safety of their system, but that the perception of security is important to their e-customers. To make sure that security won't be an issue, they implement elaborate e-business security technologies long before launch date.

But wait. Does an elaborate firewall alone make your e-business secure? Definitely not. If it isn't combined with effective security processes, the fanciest e-business security technology in the world might be useless.

- **Firewalls:** You can have a beautifully designed firewall. Nevertheless, it might be worthless to you if no one is monitoring for error messages or attacks on it, or if erroneous configuration changes have allowed traffic to bypass it.

- **Passwords:** Your security officer can devise a detailed password scheme, with authorities carefully assigned by user, to ensure that only the appropriate people get access to your system. Then again your scheme might be jeopardized if everyone in the office knows the security-officer password, or if employees write their passwords on Post-It notes stuck to monitors, or your Webmaster replaces lost passwords without verifying identity.

- **Secure Physical Environment:** You might think you have all the appropriate hardware and software security elements in place. But take it from a customer in Australia: that isn't enough. Someone broke into their office building and used a sledgehammer and a hose on their computer. Certainly, they wished that the computer had been locked behind iron doors in a far-off corner of their building.

What should you do about potential security problems? Well, in addition to the e-business security technology described in chapter 17, you also must implement solid security processes. Here is what those processes involve:

- **Security Policy:** Start with a security policy. Think about how important your computers and the data held on them are to the success of your e-business. If your data is deleted or damaged by a hacker or by a disgruntled employee, you might find yourself with no customer list, no warehouse inventory, or no accounts receivable records. In other words, you would have a disaster. If your data is divulged publicly, privacy laws might be broken, criminals might misuse credit-card numbers, or your competitors might solicit your customers. Once you understand the importance of security, review the following items and decide how information security will be implemented in your firm. Write down the policy. Have your senior management confirm their support for the policy and make it clear that all employees are expected to uphold it.

- **Security Organization:** Put a security organization in place to handle the security processes. This team will include the following:

  - Managers who are responsible for overall security.

  - Analysts and designers who regularly review the technologies and processes in place to ensure the desired level of protection.

  - Programmers who ensure new applications are developed with appropriate security.

➤ Operational staff who implement security day-to-day (the operators, the Webmaster, the security officer, etc).

➤ Legal and public relations staff who are prepared to get involved if problems do arise.

- **Asset Classification and Control:** Make a list of all the essential information assets in your organization. Include the computers in the computer room, the system printers, the network routers, the workstation hardware, the applications from each vendor, the Web files, and the development system files.

Assign an "owner" to each asset or group of assets. That person will determine all the security dangers associated with each asset and what the business impact would be if it was not available. The owner will then balance the risk against the cost and decide the security policy for that asset, including who is authorized to use it and any other rules about its use. For example, the owner of the Web site customer information file will determine that this file is essential to the business and also that private customer information must not be divulged. The owner will need to make a corporate decision on how the non-private data—such as demographics, billing information, and mailing lists—will be handled.

- **Personnel Security:** To reduce the risk of human error, theft, fraud, or misuse of facilities, personnel security should begin as new recruits are hired. Employment contracts should require employees to acknowledge that they understand the corporate security policy and realize that violation of its rules and procedures could be grounds for dismissal. Ongoing training should be provided to all employees so that they will be aware of potential security threats—such as viruses, disgruntled employees, and Web attacks—and the appropriate procedures to follow to intercept and stop such threats.

- **Physical and Environmental Security:** Based on the asset classification and control list created above, various assets should be kept in a secure area where they are physically protected from unauthorized access and environmental hazards. For example, Web servers and routers should be kept in an extra-secure area. Locate printers and tape drives in a secure area that is more accessible to operators. Tapes should be sent offsite, in locked boxes, and should require a password to be recalled.

- **Computer and Network Management:** This area includes all the day-to-day operational tasks that support security. Backups must be made so files can be recovered to a known state after a security attack. Firewall logs must be reviewed. Security-related patches must be applied promptly. Virus-prevention software must be run. Unauthorized access must be detected and contained, and incident-management procedures must be initiated as required.

- **System Access Control:** For internal users, basic system-access security should be implemented. Valid user IDs and passwords should be required to sign on. Once signed on, people should have access only to the applications they need to do their job. Rather than giving access to everyone and retracting authority from those who shouldn't have it, access should be given specifically to users who need it. This way, access will not be inadvertently given to new users by default. Asset owners should regularly review lists of authorized users to confirm that the users still have a business need to use the asset.

There should be a separation of duties so more than one staff member is aware of essential changes. Procedures should be in place to protect against disgruntled employees by removing system access immediately upon dismissal. For external users, appropriate passwords should be required prior to accessing private data or conducting business. Procedures should be in place to ensure password resets are only given to their rightful owners.

- **Systems Development and Maintenance:** Developers must consider security in the design of new applications and ensure that test plans include test cases for security. Security also should be considered with each configuration change to the system. All too often, a comprehensive security plan is devised when the e-business is first launched, but then subsequent application or configuration changes introduce exposures that sometimes go unnoticed. In other words, no one is looking at the overall security picture.

- **Incident Management**: Some of the early e-business adopters ran into difficulty with their Web sites. A Web incident can escalate quickly in terms of the extent of the damage and the breadth of the related publicity. Hence, you need a plan in place to detect a problem quickly, contain it, and deal with the aftermath.

To make such a plan, first brainstorm all the possible incidents that could occur. These might include unauthorized access to private data, propagation of a virus, or fraudulent use of credit-card numbers. Classify the incidents according to severity and the desired corporate response. Write detailed procedures and practice them with your staff. Your night operator instinctively must know how to identify hackers and contain potential the damage. The operator must know the corporate policy for handling the situation:

- Who to notify within the firm.

- How soon to call the police.

- Where to direct any media calls.

- Whether to disable the hacker immediately, to prevent damage, or leave the hacker on the system so that the police will have more evidence with which to prosecute.

- Whether to restart the Web site immediately, allowing customers to do business. Whether the Web site should be left down until the hacker's loophole can be located and fixed. If there is concern that the hacker created a high-authority profile, damaged a file, changed the authority on certain files, or disabled audit logging, sometimes the system will have to be reloaded.

In all cases, all parties involved should keep a timed log showing everything that was detected or was suspected to have occurred so that the events can be pieced together later.

- **Compliance and Certification:** Regular audits should be performed to ensure that the design, operation, and use-of-information systems comply with all relevant statutory, contractual, and corporate security requirements. For example, some countries have privacy laws that will affect the way you can use data supplied to you by Web visitors from that country. You might also find it beneficial to hire a third party to audit your Web site and provide you with a certification that you can display on your site indicating their seal of approval.

By putting security technology and security procedures in place, you can protect your e-business from unauthorized access.

Day-to-Day Operations—Executing the Plan

The process areas discussed thus far will help you handle exceptions to regular e-business operations: problems, changes, business recovery, capacity, and security. By comparison, the day-to-day operational processes will help you handle the regular work of e-business. Day-to-day operations include such things as:

- Running various jobs, backups, and data loads at the appointed times each day and ensuring that they are successful.

- Monitoring the system for problems.

- Printing and distributing reports either electronically or in hard copy.

- Ordering supplies such as forms and toner for the printers.

- Various housekeeping and system cleanup tasks.

The operational tasks will often feed into the exception processes. For example, an operator might notice a problem on the system and use it to initiate the problem-management disciplines.

Because 24/7, day-to-day tasks are the ones that keep your e-business running, there are great benefits to having routine tasks run smoothly and efficiently. That means setting firm processes, with well-orchestrated handoffs, and following them consistently so that everyone knows what is getting done when and how. It is very tempting to try to juggle the order of tasks each day or slide extra jobs in order to get ahead, but that means operators won't have a standard, repeatable process. Instead, they would be asked to make decisions on the fly, thus leaving room for error and confusion.

In addition to getting the regular work done, operators form the first line of defense against exceptions. If there is a system failure or if a hacker breaks in, the operator must take action to handle the situation or notify others who will handle it. Once again, procedures should be created and practiced to ensure that these situations are handled smoothly and effectively.

Tools

Suppose you've just purchased a suite of software tools that makes your operations room feel like mission control. There are big displays all around with a variety of colorful graphs and online monitors. Everyday fancy charts print out and you file them in a binder. But wait. Did anyone notice that the Web server has been at peak capacity at lunchtime every day for a month? Oh!

Over and over again fancy tools dazzle people. They purchase and implement the tools thinking this will give them "systems management." Nevertheless, for some reason, their environment seems just as chaotic afterwards. What's the reason? By now you should know the answer. The newest tools were implemented without first putting the underlying processes into place. In the preceding scenario, the new tool was gathering fabulous data, but no one was paying any attention to it. That Web server had probably been denying access to potential customers for 30 days, and no one had thought to research and fix the problem. What should have happened?

In a world-class company, a trouble report would have been opened automatically after the second or third performance spike. A highly skilled problem-management staff member would have been notified immediately, and would have investigated the situation within minutes. The problem manager would have searched various databases and then gathered the appropriate colleagues and vendors to troubleshoot the problem. If the problem couldn't be resolved immediately, the problem manager would have arranged for the operations staff to juggle workloads to free up capacity on that server so that customers wouldn't be turned away while the problem was researched further. Eventually, a resolution would be found and implemented through the change-management process. The findings would have been documented for future use.

This story plays itself out over and over again. People buy beautiful backup-management products that track tapes, write reports, and even read the Sunday paper, but no one ever stops to determine if the backup strategy that they are asking the product to automate is really sound. They buy high-powered job schedulers to kick off their jobs and track their run statistics, but they neglect to check the reports in the morning to ensure all the jobs ran successfully. They buy slick performance-management products that print dazzling color graphs week after week, but the operator simply files them in a binder without ever analyzing the trends. When the system fails, the tools take the blame. Most people don't realize that it was the human factor that went awry.

As long as tools are implemented in conjunction with comprehensive systems management procedures, you should realize that tools can be a tremendous help in running your environment well. Systems-management tools typically fall into three main categories:

- **Tools to Monitor the Environment:** These tools keep track of what is going on in your environment. They can often handle routine problems on their own. For more complex problems, they will notify a staff member by pager, e-mail, or cell phone. Some of the products even support alphanumeric and two-way pagers that let you read the message and respond even if you are on the freeway or at a picnic.

- **Tools to Automate Processes:** These tools help you take your existing tasks and do them faster or better. For example, job schedulers kick off your jobs automatically according to date/time or specific contingencies and track job-run statistics along the way. Backup management products track your tapes and make it easier for you to recover your system after a failure. Help-desk tools log your calls and send you an alarm if a call has been outstanding for longer than a specified timeframe. Call results can be recorded in a central knowledge database for future reference, and daily and weekly statistics for call volumes can be printed. Performance management tools gather data about current system performance, print graphs, and informational reports, and even provide historical data for modeling purposes. Additionally, there are many, many other types of tools in this area.

- **Tools to Track Statistics/Measurements and Generate Reports:** These tools can generate and print professional graphs and statistics that can be used to help make informed business decisions. For example, there are Web-statistics packages that show you the level of site activity throughout the month or throughout the day. They show you which pages are being hit most often and what response time the users are seeing. Other tools can even track response time, including your site and external trading partners and Internet service providers. These tools are helpful in ensuring that service-level agreements are being met.

The following is a list of some of the benefits offered by tools for systems management:

- **Work Faster:** For example, the system can gather performance data and print colorful reports in a flash. That sure beats transferring the data to a spreadsheet or tallying the stats on your calculator. Just remember that you need to look at the reports once they are printed.

- **Work More Thoroughly:** For example, many shops do an adequate job of tracking their backup tapes using an inventory book and adhesive stickers. However, a backup management tool can do the same thing and more. Such a tool can log the entire contents of the tape automatically while the tape is spinning, then print off a comprehensive (and legible!) adhesive label, and also print a customized recovery report that indicates the actual tape volumes used that day.

- **Work More Consistently:** For example, at one shop, the users were frustrated because some days the reports dribbled onto the Web server throughout the morning. On other days, all the reports arrived at once but much later in the day. It turned out that one operator liked to move the files to the Web server as each job finished. A different operator moved reports in bulk once all files were ready. If a job scheduler had been used for this process, the reports would have been run the same way day after day and users would have known when to look for their reports.

- **Handling Tedious Work:** Although it is possible to monitor console messages on screen, this is a tedious job and it is easy to lose focus and miss a message. By comparison, an automated monitoring tool will check each and every message against the criteria you have set up, and notify you of any messages that are a concern.

- **Avoiding Errors:** At one shop, the operator submitted the jobs manually each night. However, with so many parameters to enter, it was very easy to make a mistake, which had dire consequences in the application. When the company implemented a job scheduler, the parameters were then calculated by the system each day and all the job contingencies were automatically enforced.

- **Knowledge about the Process:** Did you ever have a key staff member leave your company and suddenly you realized that no one else knew how certain things ran? If key process elements had been recorded in an automated tool, then the tools would have kept the business running smoothly. Examples of key elements include backups stored in a backup-management product, monitoring criteria stored in a monitoring product, job sequences programmed into a job scheduler, and problem resolutions stored in the problem-management database. Anyone trained in the use of the tools could easily look up the data.

In order to implement systems-management tools successfully, you should:

- **First Put the Process in Place:** Do it manually for a while to make sure you understand it well.

- **Research and Implement Tools to Assist in the Process:** Once the process is running successfully, you can start considering tools. Spend the time up front to really understand your requirements and then choose high-quality tools from reliable vendors. Wherever possible, choose tools that are integrated with one another For example, the help-desk system should feed calls into problem-management systems and change-management systems.

- **Implement the Tools:** Remember that implementing tools is a project on its own. Be sure to allocate appropriate resource, allow time for education, and plan carefully for contingencies.

How to Get Started

Strong systems management is mandatory for a successful e-business. Now you must formulate a plan to get the project rolling. Here are some suggestions:

- **Where You Stand Today and Why:** Start by assessing your current status. Do you already have a world-class organization? If so, then the road ahead will be easy. You just need to revisit and tweak your procedures in light of the new e-business environment that you are launching. However, if you're in the "trying hard" or "barely coping" categories, you must figure out how you got stuck there. Did you just not realize that life couldn't be better? Is there someone or something that is preventing your progress? Whatever the roadblock is, you must identify and resolve the problem before you can move forward. Then take stock of the road that lies ahead. If you are in the less-sophisticated categories, you have a lot of ground to cover but also a lot of benefit to gain.

- **Treat Systems Management as a Project:** Your systems-management endeavor should be treated as a project, complete with a project manager, an executive sponsor, project planning, a kickoff, staff education, and milestones. Companies are very good at defining formal projects for regular application development, but for some reason they forget all this logic when they start talking about operational projects. Somehow, they think that the operations staff should be able to handle their regular job during the day and work wonders in their spare time, reengineering and improving processes. And they should be able to do this, even though they have no leadership, funding, education, test time, or rollout plan.

- **Remember the Human Factor:** Remember that you will probably be implementing significant changes in both culture and procedures. You must use all the regular approaches to address the related human factors. It will be important to communicate the project objectives and benefits, generate excitement and enthusiasm, listen to employee feedback, and support the folks who are reluctant to change.

- **Prioritize the Disciplines and Get Busy**: Start by defining your specific requirements for systems management in your e-business. For example, you will probably be looking to offer 24/24 availability, fast user-response time, and solid security. Choose one of the systems-management models. Select and establish priorities for the key disciplines that must be implemented prior to your e-business launch. Chances are that your choices are among the ones discussed in this chapter, but do a status check just to make sure. One by one, research each discipline to understand how you are handling it today, what the issues and challenges are, and what you need to do to reach the level of sophistication that your e-business will require. Brainstorm different alternatives that will help you reach your goals. Research each idea until you can select the best one. Then execute your plan while treating it as any other implementation. Complete the process with testing, change management, user training, a back-out plan, etc.

- **Maintain Recent Changes and Get Busy on the Next Ones:** As you finish implementing your highest priority systems-management disciplines, you can review and establish priorities for the remaining disciplines. Then get busy implementing the next tier. Meanwhile, you should review the processes that are already in place periodically to ensure they are still effective and continue to meet your business goals.

As you implement more and more disciplines, it will be easy to see the improvement in your organization. Take the time to look back periodically and appreciate all that you have accomplished.

Summary

Congratulations! You have now completed your whirlwind tour of systems management for e-business. In addition to your newfound general knowledge on this topic, we hope you will take away the following key points:

- **The New World of e-business Computing:** Launching an e-business will catapult you into the world of fast-paced, high-growth, high-availability computing, complete with demanding and often impatient customers. Suddenly, your computer and your help desk become your corporate image rather than your stores and your sales staff. Your corporate reputation and financial success are now dependent on keeping your system running flawlessly, 100 percent of the time, in spite of the demands for regular maintenance, unexpected failures, and users who are outside your control.

- **Systems Management Improves System Availability:** Meeting these new availability challenges is a tall order. To be successful, you must run an orderly shop. Strong systems-management procedures will make this possible.

- **Cost Savings:** There will be an initial blip in your workload and costs as you move to a well-managed environment. However, in the long term, you will save money by running a more effective and efficient operation. Morale will increase because business will be running so much more smoothly. Revenues will increase dramatically due to your new e-business market and the excellent customer service that you will be able to provide.

- **Key Systems Management Disciplines for e-business:** There are a variety of systems-management models that you can use to guide your project. Most include similar ideas that are just organized differently. For a successful e-business, implement the following disciplines at a bare minimum:

  - Organizational disciplines.
  - Change management.
  - Problem management.
  - Business continuity plans.
  - Performance management.
  - Security processes.
  - Day-to-day operations.

- **Automated Tools:** Once you have strong systems-management processes in place, you can consider implementing software tools. These tools will help you automate your processes, provide additional functions that wouldn't be feasible to provide manually, and provide detailed reports to help you make informed business decisions regarding your systems management. Don't fall into the trap of implementing the tools without the underlying procedures.

- **How to Get Started:** To get started, you should create a systems management project team, establish priorities for disciplines to be implemented, and implement the elements one by one. You should reassess your existing processes periodically and continuously consider implementing other disciplines that will provide benefit in your business environment.

Good luck to you as you embark on your systems-management journey. Remember, a year from now you'll look back and be glad you did it.

The authors wish to thank Alex Apouchtine, of IBM Victoria, and Mark McKelvey, of IBM Seattle, for the ideas and experiences they shared during the research phases of this chapter.

Appendix
About the CD-ROM

Using your copy of Windows NT Explorer or the equivalent, click on the icon, which represents this CD, after the CD has been loaded into the CD drive. You will see the folders and files contained in the root directory. This CD contains a very complete introduction in a root file named WELCOME.HTML. This file, in turn, links to files which describe each of the four products on the CD. These products are:

1. NetObjects TopPage Version 1 for Windows 95, Windows 98, and Windows NT, Trial Version. The hardware and software requirements are:

   - 166Mhz processor minimum
   - 16MB memory (32MB recommended)
   - Hard drive space will vary depending on sample data installed
   - Minimum configuration requires 30MB
   - Standard configuration 120MB
   - Maximum configuration 150MB
   - VGA graphics card (640X480 or better, 256 colors), XGA recommended
   - Microsoft Windows compatible double speed CD-ROM drive
   - Microsoft Windows compatible mouse
   - Microsoft Windows 98, Windows 95, or Windows NT 4.0.

To install this product:

1. Read all applicable ReadMe and License Agreement files in the TopPage folder.

2. Run the "x:\TopPage\Setup.exe" program (where "x" is the drive letter of this CD-ROM).

3. Follow the instructions in the InstallShield windows.

Later versions of TopPage are known as WebSphere Homepage Builder and are available as limited-time trial versions from:

http://www-4.ibm.com/software/webservers/hpbuilder/win/download.html

2. WebSphere Studio Entry Edition, Version 3.0.2 for Windows 95, Windows 98, Windows NT Version 4.0 with Service Pack 3, and Windows 2000. This is an evaluation version, with a limit of 750 classes. The hardware and software requirements are:

- Any Intel Pentium class PC running Microsoft Windows NT server, Version 4.0 with Service Pack 3, Windows 95 or Windows 98
- 180 MB of free disk space for installation
- CD-ROM drive
- 32 MB of memory
- VGA, or better video adapter, configured for at least 256 colors
- Microsoft Internet Explorer, Version 4.0 or higher.

To install this product:

1. Read all applicable ReadMe and License Agreement files in the Studio folder.

2. Run the "x:\Studio\Setup.exe" program (where "x" is the drive letter of this CD-ROM).

3. Follow the instructions in the InstallShield windows.

3. VisualAge for Java, Entry Edition, Version 3.0 for Windows 95, Windows 98, and Windows NT 4.0 with Service Pack 3 or Service Pack 4. The hardware and software requirements are:

   - Windows 95, Windows 98, or Windows NT 4.0 with Service Pack 3 or Service Pack 4.
   - TCP/IP installed and configured
   - Pentium processor or higher recommended
   - SVGA (800x600) display or higher
   - A mouse or pointing device
   - 48 MB RAM minimum (64 MB recommended)
   - Frames-capable Web browser such as Netscape Navigator 4.04 or higher, or Microsoft Internet Explorer 4.01 or higher
   - Java Development Kit (JDK) 1.1.7 for deploying all applications (included on this CD as part of WebSphere Application Server).

   To install this product:

   1. Read all applicable ReadMe and License Agreement files in the VISUALAGE folder.

   2. Run the "x:\VisualAge\setup.exe" program (where "x" is the drive letter of this CD-ROM).

   3. Follow the instructions in the InstallShield windows.

   4. Reboot after installing VisualAge for Java.

   Note: The install process for VisualAge for Java may update environment variables and reboot, in which case you may need to restart the setup.exe program.

4. WebSphere Application Server Standard Edition, Version 3.0 for Windows NT Server Version 4.0 with Service Pack (SP) 4. Part of the Application Server installation, if it is not already on your machine, is the optional installation of IBM Developer Kit for Windows, Java Technology Edition, Version 1.1.7. The hardware and software requirements are:

   - Pentium II or comparable processor or later
   - Support for a communications adapter

- 75 MB of free disk space for product installation; plus 20 MB for installing IBM HTTP Server; plus 150 MB for installing DB2 Universal Database
- 256 MB of memory (512 MB recommended)
- Display with 800x600 resolution (1024x768 recommended)
- CD-ROM drive
- Windows NT Server Version 4.0 with Service Pack (SP) 4
- IBM Java Development Kit 1.1.7 for Windows NT (the supported level is included in the product package)
- A Web browser that supports HTML 4 and Cascading Style Sheets (such as Netscape Navigator 4.07 or Microsoft Internet Explorer 4.01 or higher)
- One of the following Web servers:
    - IBM HTTP Server Version 1.3.6.2 (available with the WebSphere Application Server package)
    - Apache Server Version 1.3.6
    - DominoVersion 5.0
    - Lotus Domino Go Webserver Version 4.6.2.5 or 4.6.2.6
    - Microsoft Internet Information Server Version 4.0
    - Netscape Enterprise Server Version 3.51 or Version 3.6
- Instant DB Version 2.1.

To install this product:

1. Read all applicable ReadMe and License Agreement files in the APPSERVER folder. Your use of the software code and other materials contained herein is conditional upon your acceptance of and agreement to the license agreements. By installing or using the software code and other materials contained herein, you are indicating your acceptance of and agreement to these license agreements.

2. Install the IBM HTTP Server by running the "x:\AppServer\httpd\Setup.exe" program (where "x" is the drive letter of this CD-ROM).

3. Run the "x:\AppServer\Setup.exe" program.

4. Follow the instructions in the InstallShield windows.

5. When the window entitled "Select Java Development Kit" appears, check the list box for the IBM Developer Kit. If it is not there, click the "Install JDK 1.1.7" button.

6. When a password is requested, enter any set of characters, and then enter the same characters in the confirmation fields.

Please be aware that the products on this CD are released by IBM on an as-is basis, without support. Nonetheless, some level of help may be available from various IBM Web sites. These sites are:

TopPage: *http://www.jp.ibm.com/esbu/E/toppage/questions.html*

WebSphere Studio:
http://www-4.ibm.com/software/webservers/studio/support.html

WebSphere Application Server:
http://www-4.ibm.com/software/webservers/appserv/support.html

VisualAge for Java:
http://www-4.ibm.com/software/ad/vajava/support.htm

As well as the above products, the CD includes five tutorials. They are:

1. Building Applications with WebSphere Studio.

2. Publishing Studio Projects as Web Applications on WebSphere Application Server 3.

3. Publishing WebSphere Studio Projects in VisualAge for Java .

4. Apache Tomcat Servlet and JavaServer Pages Development with VisualAge for Java.

5. Developing Server-Side Web Applications with JavaServer Pages and VisualAge for Java.

Editor

Keith Rutledge

Keith Rutledge is the AS/400e business unit executive for Central Europe, Middle East and Africa. Previously, he managed the Web Integrator Initiative for AS/400e worldwide and was the IBM AS/400e WebSphere/Java marketing segment owner for the Americas. He works with IBM customers to select, develop, install, and implement industry-leading e-business killer apps. Keith has held numerous positions in IBM marketing and has worked as a printed circuit-board designer and as a technical writer for IBM.

Outside IBM, Keith was a software development manager for a regional AS/400e Business Partner firm. At that firm, he started and built a successful Microsoft custom software practice centered around AS/400e. He also was the MIS director for Baby Superstore, a specialty retail chain of 80 stores.

Keith is an active writer and speaker. He has published articles in *Midrange Computing*, *MAPICS the Magazine*, *AS/400 Technology SHOWCASE*, and *Selling AS/400 Solutions*. Keith is also the author of the book *The Business Case for Java*, published in 1999 by AS/400 Press. He speaks on e-business technology at industry trade conferences, at Java and AS/400e user groups, and at customer-oriented technology events.

Contributors

Jennifer Bigus

Jennifer Bigus has over 20 years of experience in the computer industry, ranging from teaching business data processing on mainframe computers, to programming embedded microprocessors, to providing e-business consulting services. She was a team leader for the first release of Java on the AS/400 System and has designed and developed many e-business applications using Java, JSP, and servlet technologies. She wrote the initial white paper on Java for the AS/400 System and has spoken on the topic at a number of conferences and user-group meetings. She is coauthor of the Redbook *Introduction to Enterprise JavaBeans for the AS/400 System*. She also is coauthor of the book *Constructing Intelligent Agents with Java*, published in 1997 by John Wiley & Sons. She has a master's degree in computer science from Lehigh University and a bachelor's degree in computer science from Winona State University. Jennifer currently works as a consultant, designing and developing Java and e-business applications.

Joseph Bigus

Joseph Bigus is a senior technical staff member at the IBM T.J. Watson Research Center. He was an architect of the IBM Neural Network Utility and Intelligent Miner for Data products while working in the IBM Rochester, Minnesota Programming Laboratory. He received his master's degree and his doctorate in computer science from Lehigh University, and a bachelor's degree in computer science from Villanova University. He has authored one book, *Data Mining with Neural Networks* (published in 1996 by McGraw-Hill) and coauthored another, *Constructing Intelligent Agents with Java* (published in 1997 by John Wiley & Sons). Dr. Bigus's current research interests include learning algorithms, intelligent agents, and multi-agent teams and their applications to e-commerce and pervasive computing.

Don Denoncourt

Don Denoncourt is a senior technical editor for *Midrange Computing* magazine. Don is the author of the book *Java Application Strategies for the AS/400*, published in 1999 by Midrange Computing, as well as dozens of articles on Java and Internet technology. He has taught over a thousand hours of Java seminars to AS/400 programmers in various cities across the country. Don developed several successful AS/400 products, including: ASNA's *Extermin8 for Windows*, a PC-based source-level debugger for RPG, COBOL, and CLP; ASNA's *Activ8 Pool Manager*, an AS/400 performance tuner; and ProData's *SQL/PRO*, a low-cost SQL tool with report-writing capabilities. Don can be reached at *ddenoncourt@midrangecomputing.com*.

Don is perhaps most known for coining the phrase: "I'm not sure, but give me your e-mail address and I'll get back with you."

Rich Diedrich

Rich Diedrich is a senior technical staff member working in the IBM AS/400 Custom Technology Center in Rochester, Minnesota. He designed and wrote the Web server software used for the original AS/400 Web site and was instrumental in the introduction of the first product level Web server on AS/400. He has worked at the IBM Rochester site since receiving his bachelor's degree in electrical and computer engineering from the University of Wisconsin and has six patents issued and several pending patents. Rich's current job consists of designing custom solutions to customer requests, particularly in bridging existing applications to the Web or to other heterogeneous environments.

Jelan Heidelberg

Jelan Heidelberg is the AS/400 worldwide technical marketing consultant for groupware and e-business. In this role, she is part of a team that has responsibility for marketing strategy, market development, and technical-marketing deliverables for Domino for AS/400 and for AS/400 e-business solutions. From 1990 to 1998, Jelan worked in the AS/400 product development laboratory in Rochester, Minnesota. During her tenure in Rochester, Jelan was responsible for AS/400 documentation in a variety of product areas: security, backup and recovery, CISC-to-RISC upgrades, and most recently Domino for AS/400. From 1976 to 1990, Jelan was an IBM systems engineer, supporting customers of all sizes and requirements.

Jelan is the editor of Lotus Domino for *AS/400: Bringing the Best Together for Business*, published in 1999 by AS/400 Press. While in Rochester, she authored *Tips and Tools for Securing Your AS/400, AS/400 Backup and Recovery Guide, AS/400 Road Map for Changing to PowerPC Technology* (co-author), *IBM SecureWay: AS/400 and the Internet*, and *Installing and Managing Domino for AS/400* (co-author). In addition, Jelan has authored numerous articles that have appeared in trade publications. She is a frequent speaker at customer conferences.

Nahid Jilovec

Nahid Jilovec is a partner at marchFIRST, an information technology consulting firm headquartered in Chicago. She has been in information systems consulting for over 18 years in a wide range of industries. Nahid founded marchFIRST's e-commerce practice and has nurtured and directed its growth and evolution. For the last 13 years, Nahid has focused her efforts on electronic commerce and e-business and has assisted numerous companies with strategic e-business planning and implementation efforts.

A recognized name in e-commerce, Nahid has published many articles and is an award-winning speaker on e-business topics. Nahid is the author of three books: *The A to Z of EDI, A Comprehensive Guide to Electronic Data Interchange* (published 1994 by CAS Education), *The A to Z of EDI and It's Role in E-Commerce—Second Edition* (published 1998 by 29th Street Press), and *E-Business: Thriving in the Electronic Marketplace* (published 2000 by 29th Street Press). For the last four years, Nahid has served as a columnist for various publications. Her latest column on e-business topics appears in *AS/400 Network*. She also is a technical editor for *AS/400 Network*.

Nahid is a graduate of Lehigh University, with a bachelor's degree in social relations and French and a master's degree in finance and management.

Verlyn Johnson

Dr. Verlyn Johnson joined IBM in 1979. His background includes building and maintaining financial and manufacturing applications, database design and administration, and building application development tools. Since 1993, he has been working on the IBM SanFrancisco project and products. Currently, he is the senior software engineer for IBM SanFrancisco components and is working with the SanFrancisco support team to help customers understand how to best use SanFrancisco. Another current role is to help foster relationships between customers and the development team to ensure that the developers understand customer requirements for future releases of the product.

Tom Konakowitz

Tom Konakowitz has more then 38 years in the computer industry, with knowledge and skills that encompass hardware, software, and communications. He spent two years at Control Data Corporation in the development of missile guidance systems. His 31 years at IBM included service, support, and training for mainframe hardware and operating systems; reengineering and automation of internal processes and procedures; development of APPC/APPN communication architecture; and design and development of AS/400. Tom also has extensive experience in market analysis and in the creation of long-term technical and system strategies focusing primarily on the midrange market. His final project as an IBM employee was the market analysis, requirements definition, and the development of the AS/400 Advanced Servers. After retiring from IBM, Tom has done consulting work on communication networks and technical strategies for a variety of companies. During the past three years, Tom has returned to IBM as a senior marketing consultant as a supplemental employee to work on SanFrancisco, the IBM Java-based component initiative.

Marian O'Shaughnessy

Marian O'Shaughnessy is an advisory programmer in the Custom Technology Center (CTC) group within the IBM AS/400 Rochester, Minnesota laboratory. Her more than 20 years of experience within the AS/400 Development Lab includes writing S/36 diagnostic engineering code and tools, engineering business manager, designer, and test team leader for the OfficeVision/400 product, IBM departmental manager, and product owner for numerous advanced-technology products. Most recently, Marian has been a consultant in the CTC area where her specialties include Internet design and development.

Chris Peters

Chris Peters is president of Evergreen Interactive Systems, a software development firm specializing in client/server applications and programmer education. Chris has 23 years' experience in the IBM midrange and PC platforms. Chris is the author of *The AS/400 TCP/IP Handbook* (published 1999 by Midrange Computing) *AS/400 Client/Server Programming with Visual Basic 5.0* (published 1998 by Midrange Computing), and *Peer Networking on the AS/400* (published 1997 by Midrange Computing). Also a nationally recognized seminar instructor, Chris can be reached at *Chris@EvergreenInteractive.com.*

John Quarantello

John Quarantello is the Worldwide AS/400e segment manager for e-business. His responsibilities include marketing support for emerging technologies, including Java, XML, and WebSphere. Involved with AS/400 since it was introduced in 1988, John has 25 years with IBM and he holds a bachelor's degree from Ithaca College.

Nancy Roper

Nancy Roper is a consulting IT specialist – AS/400 systems management, working in the AS/400 Technology Solutions Center at IBM Rochester, Minnesota. In 1989, she joined IBM after completing her bachelor's degree in mathematics and computer science from the University of Waterloo, in Waterloo, Canada. Nancy held positions as an AS/400 large account systems engineer, AS/400 technical marketing specialist, and AS/400 services specialist before joining the systems management team in Rochester. Since 1994, she has been a leader in the worldwide AS/400 systems management community, driving new product functions, creating and teaching courses, presenting at conferences, writing technical articles, and working on-site with customers around the world as they implement systems-management disciplines and tools.

Randy Ruhlow

Randy Ruhlow is an advisory software engineer for the IBM Enterprise Systems Group at IBM Rochester, Minnesota. Prior to obtaining a bachelor's degree in computer science at Winona State University, Randy served four years in the U.S. Navy. He is part of IBM Rochester's Custom Technology Center (CTC), which designs and develops customized applications for AS/400 Business Partners and customers. The mainstay of Randy's work for CTC is in the development of e-business, Web enablement, and existing application integration solutions on the AS/400. For over seven years, Randy has worked in object-oriented technologies, including efforts with Taligent, SOM/DSOM, VisualAge for C++ for AS/400, and Java. He is a firm believer in the benefits of application design efforts and object modeling.

Mark Schreiter

Mark Schreiter is currently a senior software engineer for Kingland Systems Corporation of Rochester, Minnesota. Kingland Systems specializes in software for the financial industry (one of the key servers used by Kingland Systems is the IBM AS/400). Prior to joining Kingland Systems, Mark worked at IBM in the Rochester, Minnesota Development Laboratory. He held numerous development positions in both the engineering and programming labs. His areas of expertise include telecommunications and wide-area networking. Mark has worked with several IBM customers in implementing MQSeries solutions on the AS/400 within their corporate environment.

Inder Singh

Inder Singh is a principal with the IT Consulting and Implementation Practice at IBM Canada, specializing in e-business operations effectiveness. Inder manages a practice of consultants, architects, IT specialists and project managers that support the e-business initiatives of midsized Canadian clients.

Robert S. Tipton

Bob Tipton, CCP, is a partner and technology thought leader for marchFIRST, a consulting firm helping companies succeed in the new economy through its network of offices throughout the world. Bob has more than 22 years of experience in the field of information technology, including roles as the CIO of a large distribution company, the owner of an IT consulting company, and years spent "in the trenches" developing and supporting IT systems.

Bob has been a technical editor for the past 15 years, and currently writes the "Untangling IT" column for *AS/400 Network* magazine. Over the years, Bob has written more than 200 articles—one of which, How Hacker Proof Is Your AS/400, won an Award of Achievement from the Society for Technical Communications. Additionally, copies of Bob's information technology-related white papers have been translated into 10 languages and have been distributed throughout the world. Bob is a past president of the Institute for Certification of Computing Professionals and is a professional member of the National Speakers Association.

Index

Note : Boldface numbers indicate illustrations; italic (t) indicates a table.

Note : Boldface numbers indicate illustrations; italic (t) indicates a table.

Note : Boldface numbers indicate illustrations; italic (t) indicates a table.